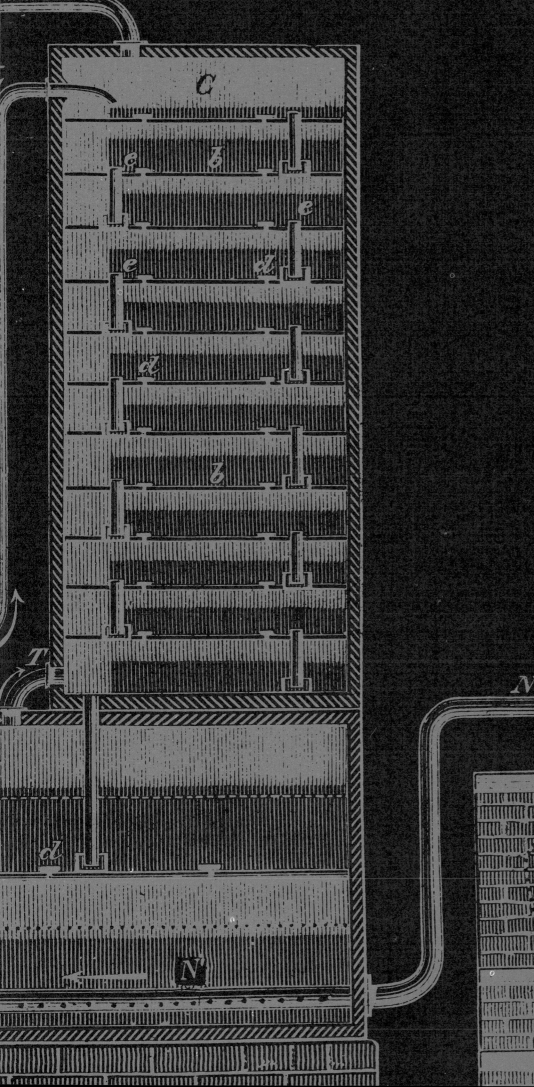

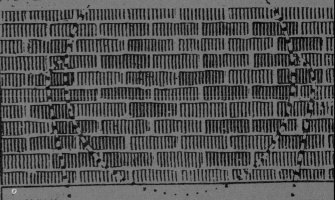

The World book of

Whiskey

by Brian Murphy

Published in U.S.A., 1979 by Rand McNally & Company,
Chicago, Ill.

© 1978 William Collins Sons & Company Limited

Printed and bound in Spain

SBN: 528–81096–0

Library of Congress Catalog Card No. 79–52630

The World book of
Whiskey

by Brian Murphy

Rand McNally & Company
Chicago · New York · San Francisco

CONTENTS

My grateful thanks are due to more people than I can possibly record but I would like to pay tribute to Mr Brian Spiller of D.C.L.; Mr Ron Brown of the Scotch Whisky Association; Mr Tim Morrison of Stanley P. Morrison Ltd; Mr Bill Gammie; Mr Bob McKinley and Mr Brian Curwen of John Walker and Sons Ltd; Mr Jim Gordon of Bunnahabhain; Mr Harry Cockburn of Bowmore; Mr Peter Straich and Mr Sandy Curll of Macallan; Mr Alastair Munro and Mr Colman of Glenkinchie; Mr McHardy of Bruichladdich; Mr J. H. Connon of Mortlach; Mr Hamish Scott of Ardbeg; Mr J. A. Duncan of Dalwhinnie; Mr Neil Gillies of Lagavulin; Mr S. McKay of Convalmore, Mr T. A. Stalker of Craigellachie; Mr R. Mitchell of Glendullan; Mr D. Nicol of Laphroaig; Mr Cooper, Mr Fletcher and Mr Hall of North British Distillers; Mr Sasaki and Mr Tsuda of Suntory; Mr Hakoshima of Asahi Shimbun; Mr Daruisz Gavronski of the Polish Embassy; Mr Viktor Kubekin of the Soviet Embassy; Mr Joe Chadwick of the Irish Embassy; Mr Campbell of Duncan, Gilbey and Matheson; Ms Wendy Curll of Dearden-Smith Communications; Mr John Cameron of Neilson, McCarthy and Partners, Sydney; Mr Herb Drinkwater, Scotsville, Arizona; Mr Jouke D. T. Eeemka of Bols; Mr Jorge E. Lonsdale of Destileria Boliviana, Mrs Parry Williams and to my secretary at the TUC, Mrs Shirley Unwin.

Finally, I would like to record my special thanks to Mrs Joan Levinson who oversaw the writing of this book at every stage and to my wife and family who have put up with two years of long absences, late nights and multi-flavoured breath.

Brian Murphy

INTRODUCTION

Like sex, whisky is a subject few people will admit to not knowing everything about. This may be because, by the same analogy, its enjoyment does not depend on knowing anything about it.

Today, however, despite its increasingly wicked price—why doesn't somebody bring out a blend called Chivas Plebeian?—whisky is spreading into more and more areas of our daily lives. As well as being the most popular of all the remedies that don't cure a cold, it has now made its way into chocolate bars and thick marmalades, with plans well advanced for introducing it into toothpaste, ice cream and scented cachous. Last March, one observer even noted that in the window of a noted whisky emporium in Glasgow the breathtaking display of malts and blends was surmounted by a banner. It read, "Remember Mother's Day".

The need for someone to write a definitive work on the subject has become so obvious that the only remaining doubt about the project might be "Why Brian Murphy?". It is in answer to that question that we are here to testify. The quality of Murphy is not strange. You have our personal assurance that, where whisky is concerned, he is not only a judge but an executioner. We ourselves, as mere innocent bar-standers, have watched him sample fourteen different bourbons blindfolded—and correctly identify every single one. (It was a feat of connoisseurship in no way diminished by the fact that he then went three days before realizing he still had the blindfold on.) As for his academic preparation for this book, our livers still cringe at the sheer quantity of snorts, spots, belts, shots, fingers and blasts he went round the world selflessly knocking back.

The results of that dedicated research now lie—as we so often found Brian himself—stretched out before us. Having sipped our way through it, we can report that—like the best whisky—it succeeds in evoking both desire and memory. Try it for sighs.

Frank Muir
Denis Norden

1 THE HISTORY OF WHISKY

The discovery of distillation

We do not know how far back into history the habit of drinking alcoholic liquids goes, or where the process of purposeful fermentation was first established. There are enough guesses. They range from primitive man drinking from pools full of rotting fruit to tasting rainwater which had accidentally filled and fermented in jars of store barley. But it is certain that the practice was well established before the invention of the written word. Some of the very earliest tomb paintings of Ancient Egypt show beer and wine in common use. The Old Testament, from the very earliest chapters of Genesis, is full of warnings about the dangers of strong drink. The Assyrians, the Hittites and even the Ancient Chinese cultivated vineyards and both the *Odyssey* and the *Iliad* are full of references to wine. Wine was an essential part of a Roman soldier's rations and, indeed, the Roman legions planted the first vineyards in England. Wine was one of the earliest articles of world commerce and the floor of the Mediterranean is littered with the wrecks of ships carrying amphorae of wine—Phoenician, Greek, Persian and Roman. Vineyards, along with flocks and herds, were an index of wealth and prosperity.

The discovery of distillation is equally hidden in the mists of history although we know that the principle was understood at a very early date. The simplest way of demonstrating it is to hold a cool surface over boiling water and watch the steam condense into water droplets that can be collected and drunk—a useful tip for emergencies. We know, for instance, that Ancient Greek sailors used to hang sponges over boiling sea water when fresh water supplies ran out, and there is no doubt that similar life-saving devices were in use in other parts of the world.

This primitive technology was improved by the use of bowls of cold water which collected the droplets on their outer surface. These droplets would then be funnelled away either into a bowl suspended beneath, or into a channel which led to a container outside. We know from early illustrations some of the ingenious tricks dreamed up by our forefathers.

The next technical advance was to convey the steam itself to a vessel outside the boiler where it could be condensed and

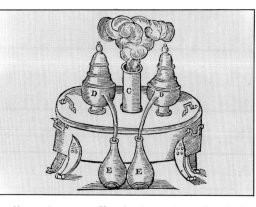

This illustration from *The Art of Distillation* by John French, published in 1667, shows two alembics and a water bath. It could never have worked in practice.

collected more effectively and easily. Subsequently the steam pipe itself was chilled, which is a short step from distillation as we know it today.

Primitive stills of various types are still in use in many parts of the world and anyone wanting to make illicit spirit cheaply and simply has a large selection of well-tried and effective models from which to choose.

We are on firm historical ground with the Arabs, who certainly discovered the art of distilling alcohol. Indeed, the word itself comes from the Arab word 'kohl', the powder that Arab beauties used—and still do—to darken their eyes. Ironically, Islam forbids its followers to drink alcohol in any form and it is only used in the preparation of scents and essences—the 'perfumes of Arabia'. But once Moorish alchemists brought their furnaces and alembics into Europe in the wake of their conquering armies, it did not take long for ingenious Europeans to use the process to produce liquids more interesting than perfume. By the 13th century the principles of distilling alcohol were known throughout the whole of Europe and medieval shippers under-

This late medieval (1508) alchemist would have been less interested in producing potable spirit than in his search for the universal solvent.

stood well the economies in freight charges that could be effected if they distilled their wine into a coarse form of brandy. These 'aquae forte'—strong waters—quickly became popular in their own right as a cheap and effective way of achieving the maximum possible intoxication in the shortest possible time. What it tasted like, thankfully we do not know, but it is recorded that a certain Richard Magnarell died of drinking too much 'aquae forte' at Christmas in 1405.

There is evidence that wine was being distilled in Italy as early as AD 1100, and 300 years later a highly sophisticated brandy trade was already established in France. But the more complex technology needed to produce alcohol from malt seems to have no known beginning, and its first mention in recorded history shows that it was well-developed long before men got around to writing about it.

The *Encyclopaedia Britannica* states categorically that oat and barley malt were distilled in Ireland in the 12th century, but gives no references. And although many authorities believe that the art of distilling was brought to Scotland from Ireland—there is some evidence that it spread eastwards from the west coast—nothing definite is known. The first and universally recognized mention of distilling from malt occurs in the Scottish Exchequer Rolls of 1494, which specify 'eight bolls—forty-eight bushels—of malt for Friar John Cor wherewith to make aquae vitae'. So we can be certain that malt spirit of a kind was being drunk in Scotland at about the time of the Wars of the Roses.

We have no way of knowing what these distilled malt liquors of long ago were like. The earliest illustrations of stills and alembics show that technical essentials had been grasped, but the liquor they produced must have been both weaker and coarser than modern palates could easily tolerate. And, of course, any thought of maturing or ageing the crude spirit would have been far from the mind or intention of medieval distillers. With the restricted diet and spartan living conditions of the time, alcoholic drinks must have been an immediate source of comfort and nourishment.

These early distillers used small and primitive versions of the modern pot still. They malted their grain or barley, dried, crushed, mashed and fermented it, and then heated the dilute alcoholic 'wash' in a copper vessel, from which the vaporized alcohol was conveyed along a pipe to the worm, immersed in cold water. The resulting drops of alcohol were then collected in a jar or other suitable container. Stills like this were still common in the Highlands of Scotland until the 19th century. In some parts every farm would have had its own. These stills had, by necessity, to be sturdy, simple and cheap and, although the whisky they produced would have been harsh and fiery by today's standards, it found great favour with the Highlanders for more than three centuries. In any event, they liked it well enough to call it 'usquebaugh', or 'water of life', the Gaelic word from which whisky is derived.

The history of whisky is naturally very closely linked to the history of Scotland, but it is also linked to the history of England and especially to the taxation as imposed by a distant parliament sitting in London. This 'foreign' interference with Scotland's great gift to the world has always been a sore point with the Scots.

Not surprisingly, the Scots parliament itself found whisky a useful source of revenue as early as 1644, but this tax was

The flue in this illustration of a still of 1500, was also used for refuelling. The essential condenser, or worm water bath, is missing.

abolished by Cromwell during the Commonwealth. It was reimposed in 1693 and in 1713 was increased by the British parliament. This, not unexpectedly, caused riots in Edinburgh and an immediate and inevitable increase in moonshining and illicit distilling. Oddly enough, this illicit whisky was very likely to have been of better quality than the legally distilled whisky. This was because the increased tax bore solely upon malt and so legal distillers would often succumb to the temptation to use cheaper corn rather than barley to avoid paying it. This obviously reduced the quality of their whisky. Moonshiners did not need to resort to such damaging economies.

As is always the case, the native population was firmly on the side of the illicit distillers, and the government and its agents found the greatest difficulty in discovering their secret stills. Moreover, the places where most of the moonshiners operated were the most difficult to get at—distant and trackless mountainsides and glens where the water was clear and the peat was plentiful—and the exciseman on his horse was visible from a long way off. But it was not only in the impenetrable Highlands that illicit whisky was made. In 1777 one dispirited government official estimated that there were 400 unlicensed stills in Edinburgh alone.

The life of a legal distiller was indeed a hard one. Commercial considerations compelled him to produce inferior spirit which was then cheerfully undercut by superior moonshine. By the end of the 18th century such quantities of illicit whisky were flooding across the border into England that the exasperated distillers finally persuaded the government to take action.

They were ill advised, for the government got it wrong yet again. They duly passed new laws which taxed legal Highland whisky more heavily than legal Lowland whisky, on the mistaken assumption that this would reduce the amount of Highland whisky actually produced. Its major, and surely unintended, effect was to turn the wrath of the legal Highland and Lowland distillers away from the government and towards each other. And while their mutual recriminations mounted, illicit whisky continued to pour from some 10,000 Scottish stills.

In spite of further spasmodic legislation the situation was not resolved until 1823, a year when no fewer than 14,000 illicit stills were discovered—and this was certainly only a small proportion of those actually operating. In that year commonsense finally appeared in the person of the Duke of Gordon whose extensive estates in Inverness-shire and Banffshire certainly produced a sizeable proportion of Scottish illicit whisky. He pointed out that there was no practicable way of stopping Scots

Although this primitive still was used in Ceylon for making arrack, it embodies the same principles as those used in Scotland and Ireland.

Oliver Cromwell who abolished the tax on whisky during his Commonwealth.

10

An 18th-century Chinese distiller pouring cooling water into the condenser or worm tub. The onion shape of the still can be seen quite distinctly.

from distilling and, this being the case, if you couldn't beat 'em, the sensible thing to do was to join 'em. If you legalized small-scale distilling, he said, and taxed it reasonably lightly, moonshiners would find it less troublesome and risky to operate legally and pay up than to distil in secret, in constant fear of informers and of the exciseman. He also promised that he and his fellow Scottish landowners would encourage their tenants to take out licences.

This proved decisive, for the Duke and his friends could encourage very powerfully if they put their minds to it and it would take a bold tenant to defy them. The new Whisky Act they sponsored taxed the spirit at 2 shillings and 3 pence (old currency) per proof gallon and imposed a £10 annual licence on stills of 40 gallons or more capacity. This did not, of course, stop illicit distilling overnight, but it made it much less attractive and profitable. In time it dwindled away until by the end of the 19th century the annual convictions

for illicit distilling could be counted on the fingers of one hand. Today, this time-honoured misdemeanor is extremely rare, although rumours still circulate about places where the adventurous drinker can get 'a dram of the real stuff'.

After the new Act became law, the production of whisky rapidly became concentrated in a few score of large-scale and efficient distilleries where local conditions —supplies of barley, running water and peat—were potentially suitable. The small private distiller soon found he could not compete, either in quantity or quality, with his larger rivals. This process of rationalization was also accelerated by the introduction of a new kind of still—the patent or continuous process still.

Looked at dispassionately, this voyage into new realms of whisky technology was all part of a whole ferment of experiment which produced the steam locomotive, new textile machinery and the paddle steamer. It was, in fact, a characteristic part of the Industrial Revolution.

Smugglers' tales

The battle waged between moonshiners and excisemen was a long and arduous one, with the advantages swinging first one way and then the other, the cunning and the daring of the smugglers being pitted against the organization and determination of the law. Yet in spite of numerous violent and bloody incidents, each side developed a curious respect for the other. Popular mythology, of course, always favours the flouter of authority and most of the stories that have come down to us favour the smuggler.

One tells of the exciseman who was convinced that an acquaintance of his was smuggling whisky past him but could not discover how. He accused the man of smuggling and the man freely admitted the crime and, moreover, offered him a challenge by saying that he would transport a barrel of whisky along a certain road on a certain day. On the appointed day the exciseman and his team carefully searched a succession of drays and carts loaded with hay, turnips, sheep and wool but could find nothing. Then came a funeral cortege but, just as this was passing, a cart loaded with oats made a sudden dash past the inspection point.

Convinced he had caught his prey, the officer chased after it, stopped it and went through it with a fine toothcomb. To his surprise there was nothing.

At the end of a long day he gave up. He knew no whisky had got through. He was angry at the deception practised on him and went to find the smuggler, whom he accused of breaking his word.

'I kept my word', said the smuggler. 'The whisky is in Inverness now. We brought the whisky along the north road between nine and five.'

'Have ye any witnesses?'

'Aye', said the other, 'ther's yersel. Man, ye took off yer hat to it.'

A similar story tells of a notorious smuggler who was also a pillar of his local kirk. On hearing that the excisemen were on their way to his house, he piled his whisky kegs into an empty room, put a coffin lid over them and covered the whole thing with a white cloth. He then assembled his servants and got them to kneel round the 'bier'. When the law arrived the mourners were wailing and, on hearing the whispered word 'smallpox', the excisemen took to their heels.

The women were often worse than the men. An over-enthusiastic officer once intercepted a signal that told him that illicit whisky was being made in a certain house. He went there, knocked on the door and, when it was opened, saw in the room all the equipment for distilling. He was overjoyed at his prize but neglected one small but vital fact. He was a small man and his prisoner was a large woman.

'Did anyone see you arrive?' she whispered confidentially.

'No', he answered.

'Then nobody will see you leave', was her answer.

He was never seen again.

It is an irony of history that one of the most notorious of the whisky smugglers and illicit distillers was one George Smith who was to become a model producer. Smith was the son of a farmer and a farmer himself, although he had originally trained as an architect. He was a tenant of the Duke of Gordon and his farm lay on a hillside overlooking Glenlivet.

In 1824 the Duke of Gordon persuaded him to take out the new licence to distil and thus to legalize his activities. He agreed and so became the first legal distiller under the new Whisky Act. This action did not endear him to his former acquaintances, as he graphically portrays. Writing about his experiences later he said, '. . . a Bill was passed in 1823 to include Scotland, sanctioning the legal distillation of whisky at a duty of 2 shillings and 3 pence per wine gallon of proof spirit with £10 annual

This illicit Scottish still would produce a dozen or so gallons or raw spirit for every charge. The precious worm is concealed inside the wooden tub.

In spite of continual raids and confiscation, illicit distillation continued for many years in the remoter parts of the Highlands.

the Seizure

licence for any still above 40 gallons; none under that size being allowed . . .

'A year or two before, the farce of an attempt had been made to inflict a £20 penalty where any quantity of whisky was found manufactured or in the process of manufacture. But there was no means of enforcing such a penalty for the smugglers laughed at attempts at seizure; and when the new Act was heard of, both in Glenlivet and the Highlands of Aberdeenshire, they ridiculed the idea that anyone would be found daring enough to commence legal distilling in their midst.

'The proprietors were very anxious to fulfil their pledge to the government and did everything they could to encourage the commencement of legal distilling; but the desperate character of the smugglers and the violence of their threats deterred everyone for some time. At length, in 1824, I, George Smith who was then a robust young fellow and not given to be easily "fleggit" [frightened] determined to chance it. I was already a tenant of the Duke and received every encouragement from His Grace and his factor, Mr Skinner.

'The lookout was an ugly one, though.

I was warned by my civil neighbours that they meant to burn the new distillery to the ground, and me in the heart of it. The laird of Aberlour presented me with a pair of hair-trigger pistols worth ten guineas and they were never out of my belt for years. I got together three or four stout fellows for servants, armed them with pistols, and let it be known everywhere that I would fight for my place to the last shot. I had a pretty good character as a man of my word and, through watching by turns every night, we contrived to save the distillery from the fate so freely predicted for it.

'But I often, both at kirk and market, had rough times of it among the Glen people, and if it had not been for the laird of Aberlour's pistols, I don't think I would be telling you this story now.'

In spite of George Smith's 'rough times', the legal distillery he pioneered prospered and within a few years he became the model of many others as men of commonsense saw the strength of his case. And today Smith's Glenlivet Distillery still produces some of the finest single malt whisky in the world.

Wild places with a plentiful supply of cold water and peat were ideal sites for illicit stills which could be dismantled and hidden within minutes.

The patent still arrives

During the latter years of the 18th century and the early years of the 19th century, a number of distillers and engineers were experimenting with alternative and more effective forms of distillation. They were concerned about the hit-and-miss character of pot still distillation and its variable end product. They were seeking a pure spirit, a standard spirit with none of the troublesome congeners—the interesting 'impurities' which gave malt whisky its power and pungency. Most of all they wanted a continuous process with none of the bother of cleaning and charging vats and stills every few days.

Most of these experiments used the principle of fractionating, a technique for separating out the various constituents of mixed liquids and well known in the laboratories of the time. But all kinds of odd devices were tried out. Gin distillers in London had some kind of continuous process still working in the 1820s, but it was a Scottish distiller called Robert Stein who made the breakthrough in 1827. In that year he took out a patent for a new kind of still and a further patent the following year. After an experimental trial in a Wandsworth distillery he installed the first practicable Stein still in his brother's distillery at Kirkliston near Edinburgh. A year later, his cousin, John Haig, installed a second in his own distillery at Cameron Bridge, Fife. The Stein still worked by injecting hot wash into a metal vessel which was then filled with superheated steam. This drove off the alcohol vapour from the wash and this vapour was then purified and condensed.

These stills were only moderately successful, although a number of them were built at various distilleries in Scotland over the following years. The one Stein installed at Cameron Bridge was still there a century later, though not in working order.

However, simultaneously with Stein's experiments, a fellow inventor was working on plans for a similar kind of still, but more refined and sophisticated in concept and promising far better results. His name was Aeneas Coffey, and he had for some time been Inspector General of the Excise in Ireland. Coffey was by training and instinct an engineer and inventor, and the concept of continuous distillation fascinated him. He worked out the design for his two-column still in Ireland and actually sold the idea to a distiller called Haig, a cousin of John Haig. However, nothing came of it. The Irish were suspicious of innovations and comfortable with the old and tested ways, so Coffey emigrated to Britain. He patented his own still in 1831 and distillers were not slow to see its superiority over the crude technology of the Stein still. It very quickly superseded this and a number were built over the next few years. These early Coffey stills had, for their time, the remarkable output of 200 gallons of pure spirit an hour. A normal modern Coffey still produces 1,500 gallons of whisky an hour.

The introduction of this revolutionary method of distilling did not have any immediate or dramatic effect. Indeed, because it was new it was quickly taken up by distillers with more enthusiasm than experience, and many subsequently went bankrupt. Certainly it was not seen as the fundamental threat to the traditional pot still whisky that it later became. Indeed, it was not until 1839 that the government got around to putting the Coffey stills

The Lowland malt distillery at Glenkinchie uses its old malting floor to house a fascinating museum of the history of malt whisky. The top picture shows a model of a still and worm tub. The lower picture is of a container used to measure malt. The roller was used to level the malt.

14

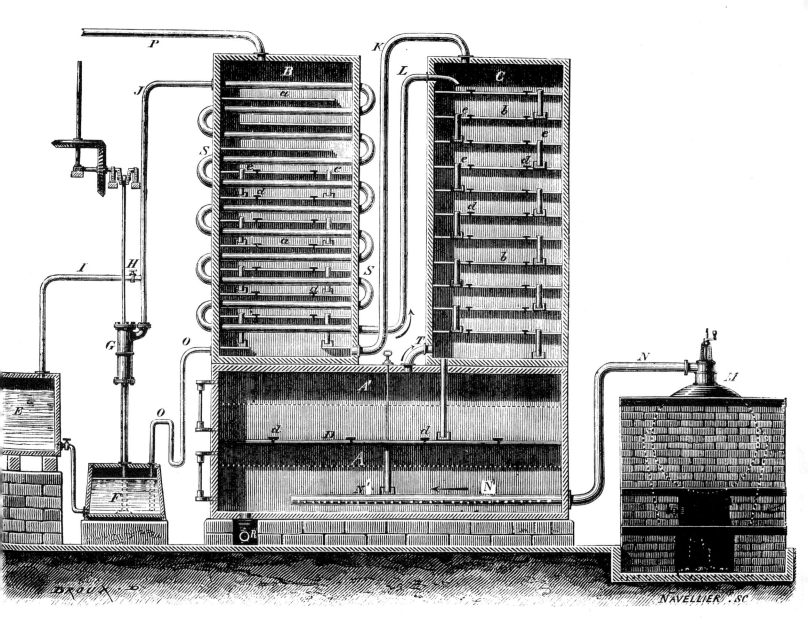

under the control of the excisemen, who now supposedly controlled all distilleries in Scotland.

At this time, nearly all the whisky produced, whether by pot or patent still, was consumed locally. It was not a popular drink south of the border and only a tiny amount was exported. At one time, nearly all the comparatively small amount of whisky that came into England was re-distilled into gin in London. Brandy was the popular spirit for English gentlemen and gin the artisans' solace. Whisky was considered a coarse drink, particularly suited to the damp and gloomy Scottish climate. Another difficulty was that previous legislation did not allow the importation into England of whisky in casks of less than 80 gallons, which was a prohibitive quantity for nearly all innkeepers. It was not, in fact, until 1860 that the Scots were allowed to bottle their own whisky for export to England.

The Lowland distillers were next hit by a particularly inept piece of legislation in 1848, which permitted English distillers to use almost any vegetable base for distillation, while restricting the Scots distillers strictly to cereals. They naturally felt very hard done by and looked around for means of mitigating this new and damaging law. A number of them decided that the very worst thing would be a cut-throat price war and that co-operation was preferable to competition. Accordingly, six of the biggest Lowland patent distillers formed a consortium in 1856 to control production and to divide up the market equitably. This agreement was renewed from time to time but, more important, a seed was sown which bore fruit in 1877 in one of the most significant events in the history of modern whisky . . . the formation of The Distillers Company Limited.

The formation of this whisky-producing conglomerate was one of the earliest examples of hard-headed economic rationalization, of which we can see the results today in the mighty multi-national companies which now dominate the world industrial scene.

This illustration of 1870 shows the workings of the Coffey or patent still. It demonstrates how little the principles of continuous distillation have changed over the last century. However, the output of such stills has increased quite dramatically: when they were introduced, their capacity was about 200 gallons of pure spirit every hour. Today the Coffey still is capable of producing 1,500 gallons in the same time.

The Distillers Company Limited

In spite of the less than satisfactory venture of the 1856 consortium, discussions about possible amalgamations continued to take place, approaches occasionally being made even to English and Irish distillers. But nothing came of any of these approaches until 1875 when a proposal was made which was to change the shape of the whisky trade forever. This was simply that 'the principal firms engaged in the grain distilling business should form themselves into one company under the Limited Liabilities Act'. After two years of discussion this proposal was put into effect and six Lowland grain distilleries amalgamated. They were:

D. MacFarlane & Co., Port Dundas Distillery, Glasgow.

John Bald & Co., Carsebridge Distillery, Alloa.

John Haig & Co., Cameronbridge Distillery, Fife.

McNab Bros. & Co., Glenochil Distillery, Menstrie.

Robert Mowbray, Cambus Distillery, Alloa.

Stewart & Co., Kirkliston Distillery, West Lothian.

The new company they formed on April 24, 1877, had a nominal capital of £2,000,000, split into 40,000 shares of £50 each. Of these, 12,000 were actually issued and taken up immediately by the six companies. The new firm was to be called The Distillers Company Limited and it was to change the history of Scotch

Coleburn distillery at Elgin. The elegant pagodas are now purely decorative as the distillery buys its malt ready-peated. Like many other Scottish malt distilleries, Coleburn is situated in a delightful setting. This is one of the attractions of drinking whisky—knowing that the spirit which one is enjoying is produced in beautiful countryside.

whisky. Indeed, within 50 years The Distillers Company Limited came to dominate the manufacture and distribution of Scotch whisky.

The early years were not without their difficulties. The partners in this new enterprise were powerful businessmen in their own right and used to getting their own way. It took some time to make them settle down and work together. But the company was rich and strong from the beginning and never less than extremely prosperous, principally because a policy of expansion and acquisition was followed from its foundation. And although it is not true to say that this policy was invariably successful—occasionally injudicious and uneconomic purchases were made—the mistakes were very few and greatly outweighed by the successes. The company grew swiftly and smoothly.

The partners saw quite clearly that the future was with blended whisky which had the double advantage of being more popular than malt whisky and a great deal cheaper too—a manufacturer's dream. They began to make offers for rival distilleries, both malt and grain, and refined their selling techniques in England where blended Scotch whisky was catching on extraordinarily quickly.

In 1880 they decided to go public to get the company quoted on the Scottish Stock Exchange and, consequently, reduced the capitalization by half to £1,000,000, divided into 100,000 shares of £10 each. The public were offered over 40,000 of these at a price of £13 10s. a share.

The investing public were not immediately interested and fewer than 10,000 shares were sold in the first few months. It took Distillers Company a good three years to establish itself on the Edinburgh and Glasgow Stock Exchanges but, once it was there, its success was swift and, within a year, the value of the shares had almost doubled.

Getting a quotation on the London Stock Exchange took even longer. There was considerable trouble over the first issue of shares and a great deal of legal and technical wrangling. The company first applied for a London quotation early in 1884 but this was not granted until the end of 1886.

Even this was not the end of its troubles. At the time of its London quotation a Glasgow newspaper launched a campaign of denigration, accusing the company of incompetence and implying that it would shortly collapse. On top of this the rival grain distillers, alarmed at the great and obvious strength of Distillers Company, formed their own consortium, the North British Distillery Company, to challenge its supremacy. This new company found it convenient to regulate its prices and conditions of sale in line with the original Distillers Company and so it never indulged in cut-throat competition. To that extent it did not represent a serious threat to the fortunes of D.C.L.

In 1878 the company had a stroke of good fortune it could hardly have realized at the time. It acquired the services of a 16-year-old clerk called William H. Ross. Not much is publicly recorded of his early life with D.C.L. but he must have been an industrious and far-seeing young man because eleven years later he was appointed Secretary and Accountant, a highly responsible and powerful post for a man still in his twenties. He was not long in putting this power and responsibility to impressive use and his influence is still strongly felt.

The Distillers Company Limited was not immediately successful when first quoted on the Scottish Stock Exchange. Three years later, however, those who had bought shares at the beginning had made a large profit on their investment.

Soon after he was established in his new position he began to push hard for expansion, not only in buying new malt and grain distilleries—which he certainly did—but by looking for new opportunities to sell whisky both in England and abroad. Special efforts were made in America and the British Empire, and blended Scotch whisky began to be seen all over the world.

In 1893 the Company started to build the first of its own malt whisky distilleries at Knockdhu in Banffshire. But by now the great whisky boom of the 1890s was in full spate and the history of the Distillers Company became so integrated with the history of the Scotch whisky business as a whole as to be difficult to disentangle.

The Distillers Company Limited makes a great deal more than whisky, of course. It is very big in gin and a number of other fields, often not directly connected with potable spirits. The list of its subsidiary companies is impressive: Ainslie & Heilbron (Distillers) Ltd; Baird Taylor Ltd; John Begg Ltd; Benmore Distilleries Ltd; John Bisset & Co. Ltd; James Buchanan & Co. Ltd; Bulloch Lade & Co. Ltd; John Crabbie & Co. Ltd; Cragganmore Distillery Co. Ltd; A. & A. Crawford Ltd; Daniel Crawford & Son Ltd; Dailuaine-Talisker Distilleries Ltd; Peter Dawson Ltd; John Dewar & Sons Ltd; Distillers Agency Ltd; Donald Fisher Ltd; John Gillon & Co. Ltd; John Haig & Co. Ltd; J. & W. Hardie Ltd; John & Robt. Harvey & Co. Ltd; John Hopkins & Co. Ltd; Low, Robertson & Co. Ltd; W. P. Lowrie & Co. Ltd; D. & J. McCallum Ltd; Macdonald, Greenlees Ltd; John McEwan & Co. Ltd; Macleay Duff (Distillers) Ltd; Mitchell Bros. Ltd; John Robertson & Son Ltd; Wm. Sanderson & Son Ltd; Scottish Malt Distillers Ltd; Slater Rodger & Co. Ltd; J. & G. Stewart Ltd; John Walker & Sons Ltd; James Watson & Co. Ltd; White Horse Distillers Ltd. As gin distillers, it owns Boord & Son Ltd; Booth's Distilleries Ltd and Tanqueray Gordon & Co. Ltd.

A full list of the distilleries it owns is equally impressive. There are five D.C.L. grain distilleries: Caledonian, Cambus, Cameronbridge, Carsebridge, Port Dundas. And 46 malt distilleries: Glenkinchie, *Rosebank*, St Magdalene, Caol Ila, *Lagavulin*, Port Ellen, Aberfeldy, *Aultmore*, Balmenach, Banff, Benrinnes, Benromach,

Brora, *Cardhu*, *Clynelish*, Coleburn, Convalmore, Cragganmore, Craigellachie, Dailuaine, Dallas Dhu, Dalwhinnie, Glen Albyn, *Glendullan*, *Glen Elgin*, Glenlochy, Glenlossie, Glen Mhor, Glentauchers,

Taking samples of malt whisky at the Mortlach distillery in Dufftown. These samples will not yet have been cut with distilled water to bring them to normal drinking strength.

Glenury Royal, Hillside, Imperial, *Knock-dhu*, *Linkwood*, Mannochmore, Millburn, *Mortlach*, North Port, *Oban*, *Ord*, Royal Brackla, *Lochnagar*, Speyburn, *Talisker*, Teaninich. The 15 in italics are bottled.

The company still maintains its practice of buying only British barley for its malt distilleries, although it stretches a point by buying Canadian barley for its grain distilleries throughout Britain.

The arrival of blending

Until well past the middle of the 19th century, there was no such thing as a blended whisky. If you wanted to drink whisky, you drank the product of a single distillery, grain or malt. And because of the limitations of the technology of the time, and factors such as the supply of water and the quality of the barley, the product of a single distillery could vary widely from year to year. If you bought a bottle of whisky, in fact, you could never be quite sure what you were getting.

This uncertainty began to concern H.M. Customs and Excise and, in 1853, they introduced regulations that allowed distillers to 'vat' their malts. In other words, to blend whiskies produced at the same distilleries but at different times. It was a well thought-out opportunity for distillers to standardize and improve the qualities of their whiskies. In 1860 they took the further step of allowing whiskies from different distilleries to be blended together, with exactly the same intention. But these measures were conceived purely in terms of vatting malt whiskies. The revolutionary thought of combining malt and grain whiskies was still to come.

Although we cannot be absolutely certain who made the breakthrough and when, we can make a reasoned guess. By the beginning of the 1850s the patent distillers were in a bad way and desperately looking for ways of selling their whisky. The trouble was that the Coffey process meant that very few congeners—the substances that give flavour and interest to malt whiskies—were carried over into the distillate. This meant that the grain whisky produced was a light, bland but comparatively characterless spirit. It had a certain appeal to those Scottish palates which found pot still whisky too powerful and pungent but it served a limited market and disproportionate taxation was actually depressing it.

Then, in 1853, a bright young distiller called Andrew Usher made a breakthrough. He saw that what had previously been considered the disadvantages of grain whisky—its blandness and lack of flavour—could actually be turned to advantage.

Andrew Usher, the eldest son of a distiller, was born in Edinburgh in 1826. He went into the family business but in his early years was as much concerned with blending and bottling wines as with whisky. But Usher was a shrewd and ingenious man and he recognized the fragility of the whisky market, racked by spasmodic over-production and arbitrary taxation.

He was the first to discover that the flat

In the 19th century bottling and packing were both done by hand. Today, whisky is bottled mechanically but, in a few places, the bottles are still packed into cardboard boxes by hand.

James Buchanan, one of the men who spearheaded the 'whisky invasion of England'.

and innocuous-tasting grain whisky could soften and smooth the harsher qualities of malt whisky, producing a light and pleasant blend which also had the enormous advantage of being cheaper than the expensive malts. He found the blends he produced were highly acceptable and he was encouraged to go on experimenting to improve them. When he was finally satisfied he decided to market his most popular blends under brand names.

Nevertheless, the knowledge of blends spread fairly slowly and, although Usher was technically helped by the Acts of 1853 and 1860, blended whisky remained a purely Scottish phenomenon. But in Scotland at least it began to do very well and by the mid-1860s the production of grain whisky had overtaken that of malt, a trend which was to continue over the years. This expansion was greatly helped by a sudden and accidental increase in the market and both distillers and blenders took quick advantage of this. The Franco-Prussian war was followed by greatly increased industrial activity in Europe, in which Scotland fully shared. Quite suddenly there were new demands on Scottish heavy industries and this was reflected in much bigger pay packets. Much of the surplus from these higher wage rates inevitably found its way into the public houses. This substantial new market gave the whisky producers a strong economic base from which to mount their next exercise—the whisky-marketing invasion of England.

Here, too, they were helped by circumstance. French vineyard owners, anxious to improve their native vine stocks, had begun to import American vines shortly after the middle of the 16th century. It was a catastrophic mistake. For along with the vines they also imported the phylloxera insect, a vine louse which attacks and destroys the roots and leaves of vines. American vines are resistant to the insect but French vines are not and their vulnerability was demonstrated in the most terrible of ways. By 1865, phylloxera was firmly established in French vineyards and it began to spread with increasing speed. In the 1880s it was the turn of the Grande Champagne region, the area where cognac is made. In the space of a few years, the vineyards of the entire district had been totally ruined and very little cognac was produced. This had an inevitable effect on the British market. If there was no brandy, what could you drink?

The Scottish whisky producers had the answer—and the invasion was spearheaded by some of the most brilliant and effective entrepreneurs and salesmen that Scotland has ever produced. Men such as James Buchanan, the Dewar Brothers and Alexander Walker established themselves in London, determined to replace brandy with whisky as the favourite English spirit. The extent of their success can be seen in every public house in the country.

Highland drinking parties were not always noted for their moderation. The punch being enjoyed in this Hogarth print would have contained a substantial amount of whisky. The lemon peel decorating the bowl is traditional adornment.

Barnard and his book

The growing importance of whisky as not just another picturesque Scottish craft but an important industry did not escape the attention of Alfred Barnard, a partner in the London publishing house that produced the drink trade journal *Harper's Weekly Gazette*—still, incidentally, going strong.

He was a bright, observant and industrious man and he resolved to visit every whisky distillery in the United Kingdom (which then still included the whole of Ireland). So he set off on his marathon journey, which could only be done by using all modes of transport—on foot, by carriage, train or steamer—and he finally accomplished the task of visiting 129 distilleries in Scotland, 28 in Ireland and four in England. His interest never flagged and he records in detail the capacities of mash tuns and stills, the state of the weather, the warmth of the hospitality and the beauty of the scenery with equal gusto.

It all came out in his massive masterpiece *The Whisky Distilleries of the United Kingdom*, published in 1887. Within the next eight years he published two more extensive works, *The Noted Breweries of Great Britain and Ireland* and *Orchards and Gardens Ancient and Modern*.

After this, Alfred Barnard fades from history. His book on whisky was republished in 1969 and still remains an invaluable and beautiful guide to anyone interested in the subject. His comments on the distilleries he visited are a whisky education in themselves. For example, using the Glenglassaugh Distillery at Portsoy as an example, Barnard discusses the siting of a distillery in these terms:

'We have noticed in our travels that all the Northern Distilleries are planted in the country, either on the sea-shore or by the mountain side, and seldom in towns and cities, and have asked the reason of the Distillers who generally reply: "We have plenty of water power and good water, so we select the banks of a quickly flowing stream. Then again, we use home grown barley and only peat of the finest quality for drying the malt. Also we believe that a good climate and pure air are indispensible in the production of a delicate spirit like Whisky." '

Barnard's book provides a fascinating view of the industry in the late 19th century

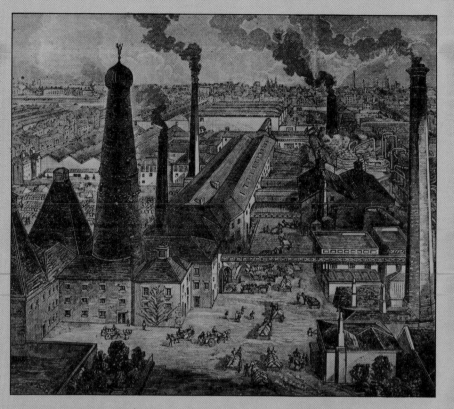

and is full of all sorts of intriguing stories and snippets of information. For example, he heard that rooks were regarded as lucky omens and had this to say about the Glendronach Distillery at Huntly:

'On driving up the avenue the first thing that attracted our attention was the charming house of Glendronach, next to the Distillery, itself enclosed in lofty trees, in the branches of which there is an extensive rookery. It is considered fortunate to have a colony of these birds over a Distillery, as they are said to bring good luck and, strange to say, there is no instance on record where this has not been the case.'

Then again he provides an unusual sidelight on the waste disposal problem: At Port Dundas in Glasgow he 'stepped into an open space of ground', in which there was a piggery accommodating over 400 pigs fed on the distillery refuse. Some of them, he noted, were highly-bred animals of great size and on entering one of the breeding sheds he was 'surprised to see the wall literally covered in prize cards'.

He also noted that at the Kirkliston Distillery in West Lothian the greater part of their refuse used to flow into the River Almond, 'but Mr Stewart, desirous to avoid polluting the stream, built two very large storage tanks into which it now pours'. There the burnt ale refuse was

At the time when Barnard was writing his book, there was no anti-pollution legislation in force. Whisky distillers were as guilty as other manufacturers of poisoning the atmosphere. Today, most of Britain has been designated 'smokeless' and scenes such as this one are, happily, quite rare.

22

An infant that failed to grow

allowed to settle and the liquid portion was then pumped into the sea at South Queensferry through a pipe which ran along the then North British Railway branch line into Queensferry, and for which permission was obtained by Act of Parliament. 'The solid matter', Barnard noted, 'is sold for feeding stock and is found to be very good for cattle and pigs.'

He was particularly impressed by the close friendships struck up by people working together in the industry. The managers usually had strongly paternalistic attitudes towards their workers.

Barnard wrote of Bunnahabhain Malt Distillery on Islay: 'Neat villas have been erected on the rising ground in the rear of the Distillery for the Excise Officers, and two large ranges of houses provide ample accommodation for the workmen. A Reading Room and Schoolroom have likewise, with praiseworthy liberality, been provided by the Company and in this latter the children of the workmen receive an elementary education.'

It was quite common, especially in the rural malt distilleries, for the jobs to run in families and maltman son would succeed maltman father—and grandfather.

There are stories of ideas that failed and that perennial search for an ageing process. Visiting the Yoker Distillery near Glasgow, which produced 600,000 gallons a year, Barnard wrote: 'The bonded warehouses are very extensive and eight in number. They are built of brick with slated roof and all are well ventilated . . . the no. 7 warehouse is not devoted to storage purposes although it is equally under the surveillance of the Excise. It . . . contains a patent "ageing apparatus" where new whisky is subjected to an immense pressure of heat. This process is said to have the power of destroying the aldehyde or fierceness of new whisky and converting it into a mature spirit of three to five years old. This patent is at present in its infancy . . .'

The infant never grew up. The distillery closed and the patent 'ageing process' disappeared with it. These accelerated maturing processes crop up again and again in the history of whisky. They are to the whisky trade what the gold brick is to the confidence trickster.

Many of Barnard's stories are too good to miss, including the story to cap all whisky stories which even has the ring of truth about it. It seems there was an aged woman who lived near the Hazelburn Distillery in Campbeltown.

'She was of a rather doubtful character', writes Barnard, 'and was charged before the sheriff with smuggling. The charge being held proven, it fell to his Lordship to pronounce sentence. When about to do so he thus addressed the culprit—"I daresay, my poor woman, it is not often you have been guilty of this fault." "Deed no, Sheriff", she replied, "I haena made a drap since youn wee keg I sent to yersel." '

Writing some 30 years after the introduction of blending and when the controversy about it was at its height, Barnard was shrewd enough to see that it would revolutionize the industry.

'Certainly', he commented, 'most palatable whiskies are being consumed by the public which, the blenders say, could not be sold at the money were it not for the cheapening and—they add—the improving qualities of old grain spirit. On the controversy between malt and grain we do not care to enter at greater length; still, all who have a knowledge of the various makes of whiskies will bear us out in affirming they are unsuitable for sale unblended. What is the best qualifier of their potent flavour and body we must leave to those who have to please the public to determine.'

The distillery at Kirkliston, a few miles outside Edinburgh, was just one of the many visited by Barnard. Everywhere he went on his tour, Barnard was impressed by the relationship between management and worker. Even now, industrial relations at the malt distilleries of Scotland are remarkably trouble-free.

23

The great whisky boom

It was the popularity of blended whisky and the highly successful efforts of Scotch whisky salesmen that resulted in a rapid expansion of the market in the early 1890s. By this time, too, the old distinction between malt distillers, grain distillers and blenders became increasingly unimportant on account of cross-ownership. The Scotch whisky business has always been—to say the least of it—clannish and most of the senior managers involved in it either knew each other or knew a great deal about each other. They all had a common interest in enlarging the market safely and sensibly and a degree of co-operation made sense.

Unfortunately, the attractiveness of this rapidly growing market went to the heads of some of its owners and even more so to the heads of the people on the outside who saw the chance of making a quick fortune and wanted to invest in it. Many new companies were floated and many new distilleries were built or planned. Those already in operation increased their output enormously, doubling or even trebling their production. It was, in every sense of the word, a boom.

Some companies did extremely well out of it. Two brothers, William and Arthur Gilbey, had started out as wine merchants in Oxford Street, London, in the 1850s, specializing in South African wines. But as their business developed they found that whisky was popular, at first Irish and then, increasingly, Scotch. They did so well that they were able to buy their own malt distillery in the late 1880s. They took full advantage of the boom, did not over-extend themselves and survived to become one of the largest and most successful companies in the trade.

Others were not so lucky. Booms are invariably ended by depressions and the whisky boom was no exception to this proven economic law. In this case the depression was triggered off by the spectacular collapse of one of the biggest and most prosperous-seeming companies of the time.

Robert and Walter Pattison had been wholesale grocers in Leith near Edinburgh and they involved themselves in the whisky-blending business in the early 1880s. Profits came quickly and easily and it soon made good business sense to turn the partnership into a limited liability company, Pattisons Limited. With the

John Dewar was the first to bottle his whisky and was one of the spearheads of the 'whisky invasion' of England.

Barrels are still made and prepared by hand, just as they were in the early years of this century.

money raised, the Pattison brothers embarked on a programme of frantic expansion. They were colourful figures in their own right and they spent a fortune on spectacular advertising. Nothing was too bizarre or too outrageous for them. At one point they trained hundreds of parrots to say 'Drink Pattisons' Whisky' and sent them off with their salesmen all over Scotland. Their personal lifestyle was equally flamboyant. They built themselves an enormous mansion in the most fashionable part of Leith and entertained in a princely manner.

Money was easy, the banks were willing to lend up to the hilt and everyone wanted to climb on the bandwaggon. Everyone, it seemed, except the hard-headed and cautious men who ran The Distillers Company Limited and had a shrewd idea of what was going on. More and more distilleries were built and a river of whisky flowed into the blending vats. Unfortunately, the demand for this quantity of whisky, in spite of sustained and heavy advertising, just did not exist. The grim signs of gross over-production soon appeared and word got around that Pattisons were in trouble. The final and catastrophic crash came in December,

1898, and confidence in the whisky market vanished overnight. The Pattison brothers were jailed for fraud and thousands of investors lost all they had. The fall of the house of Pattison brought many smaller companies down with it and the damage caused to the whisky business was still felt 20 years later.

The only people to do well out of all this were Distillers Company, who bought up Pattisons' new warehouses in Leith, built at a cost of £60,000, for the knockdown price of £25,000.

Writing of the Pattisons' collapse more than 20 years after, William Ross of Distillers Company said, 'Their extravagance in conducting business, including the somewhat palatial premises they erected, was the talk of the Trade, but so large were their transactions and so wide their ramifications that they infused into the Trade a reckless disregard of the most elementary rules of sound business. Encouraged by the ease with which financial assistance could be obtained from the Scottish banks of the day, investors and speculators of the worst kind were drawn into the vortex and vied with each other in their race for riches. The unhealthy demand thus created induced many malt

As late as 1907, when this picture was taken, whisky was being illicitly distilled in Scotland. The small stream supplied the cold water for the worm, hidden in the wooden barrel.

The SPIRIT of CHRISTMASTIDE.

PEACE, & PLENTY—OF PATTISONS'

A CHRISTMAS BOX OF GOOD CHEER.

Order through your Wine
and Spirit Merchant.

PATTISONS LTD., HIGHLAND DISTILLERS,
LEITH.   BALLINDALLOCH.   LONDON.
Head Offices: CONSTITUTION STREET, LEITH.

distilleries to double or treble their output, while the shares of new companies formed to acquire existing distilleries or to build new ones were eagerly subscribed for by a confident public. Such was the over production of Scotch whisky during that period that even until recent years the result was still felt . . . The boom which was then at its height completely collapsed, the banks withdrew their credit and many firms were obliged to ask protection from their creditors while others were hopelessly crippled in their future business.'

These wise words are a fitting epitaph to a most unhappy episode in the history of Scotch whisky.

The blow suffered by the whisky trade by the Pattison disaster and the subsequent collapse of the boom was followed by an even worse one in 1905. For many years the majority of malt distillers had been uneasy at the success of blended whisky, with its large content of grain whisky and the consequent decline in the share of the market held by single malts. Their delight was almost unconcealed at the events that took place in Islington, London, at this time.

In 1904, Islington Borough Council took proceedings against a number of local publicans for selling 'brandy' which was, in fact, a mixture of brandy and neutral spirit. It was a test case to see whether or not the drink sold was '. . . not of the nature, substance and quality of the article demanded by the purchaser', and thus unadulterated.

In November 1905 they did exactly the same thing to whisky. The publicans, of course, were selling blended whisky—a mixture of grain and malt whiskies—as they had done for many years. They were duly taken to court to see whether or not the whisky they sold was the genuine article. The magistrate ruled against them, which clearly meant that grain whisky was not, in fact, true whisky at all but an adulterant of malt.

The decision came as a terrible shock to the Distillers Company because, if this were so, it was effectively out of business. It immediately financed an appeal by the publicans, which was heard at the Quarter Sessions in May and June 1906. The bench sat seven times and the truth dawned that they were not going to reach agreement. This, in turn, meant that the original magistrate's decision stood. The grain distillers and blenders reacted strongly and promptly.

It was decided that Distillers Company Limited, by far the biggest and the most senior of the group, should approach the President of the Board of Trade and ask him to set up a Royal Commission to decide finally and definitively exactly what constituted whisky. Curiously enough, the President of the Board of Trade at the time was John Burns, a working class leader who had risen to the highest rank by his intelligence and integrity. A hater of strong, cheap drink himself, he was nevertheless a fair-minded man and he well understood the importance of his decision. In the end, he agreed that such a Commission was necessary and it was therefore set up in February 1908. The Chairman was Lord James of Hereford, a Liberal politician and lawyer; its members were six of the most distinguished and eminent scientists of the time.

The terms of reference were:

'1. Whether, in the general interests of the consumer, or in the interests of public health, or otherwise, it is desirable:

   (a) To place restrictions upon the materials or the processes which may be used in the manufacture or preparation in the United Kingdom of Scotch Whiskey [sic], Irish Whiskey, or any spirit to which the term whiskey may be applied as a trade description.

   (b) To require declarations to be made as to the materials, processes of manufacture or preparation and age of any such spirit.

   (c) To require a minimum period during which such spirit should be matured in bond; and

   (d) To extend any requirements of the kind mentioned in the two subdivisions preceding to any such spirit imported into the United Kingdom.

2. By what means, if it should be found desirable, that any such restriction, declarations or period should be prescribed, and uniform practice in this respect may be satisfactorily served; and to make the like enquiry and report as regards other kinds of possible spirits which are manufactured in or imported into the United Kingdom.'

These were the dry words of a civil servant, but they were words which could make or break the industry.

The Commission got to work with commendable speed and it quickly became apparent that, although they may have been distinguished scientists, they were amateurs in the matter of whisky. Some people objected to them on account of this and suggested that the Commission should have had at least one whisky professional on it. Yet others protested that although Irish and Scotch whisky were under investigation, the majority of the Commission were Englishmen. Be that as it may, the Commission took its work very seriously and questioned over a hundred witnesses.

The grain distillers went on to claim that their own whisky was better than malt because it contained no impurities. Therefore blended whisky was actually better for the drinker's health than straight malt whisky!

It is not recorded what effect this ingenious argument had upon the Commissioners. The malt distillers replied that their's was the only true Scotch whisky

Uam-Var Scotch whisky was one of the most popular of its day. It is no longer produced, but this splendid advertisement does show that there is no more effective way of advertising whisky than a straightforward picture of the bottle.

THE FAMOUS

UAM-VAR

SCOTCH   WHISKY

HIGHEST

INTERNATIONAL

AWARDS

THE

ARISTOCRATIC

DRINK

APPRECIATED FOR QUALITY.

because it had been made their way since time immemorial and that grain whisky was a 'neutral' spirit.

One unprejudiced witness, the Medical Officer for Health for Islington, pointed out that much that passed for whisky came from neither Scottish grain nor Scottish malt but was imported from the Continent and sold, with colouring and flavouring matter, to dishonest publicans at tenpence a gallon. The stomachs of the artisans of Islington were clearly at risk whatever the outcome of the enquiry.

One of the key questions was whether the purchaser who ordered a whisky, and was given a blend containing a majority of grain whisky, knew what he was getting. At the end, the Commission came to the conclusion that he probably did know and issued an interim report in June 1908, saying so. The relevant part reads:

'We have held twenty-two sittings and examined seventy-four witnesses. Certain of the Commission have visited distillers in Scotland and Ireland and have thereby gained much valuable information. Whilst the labours of the Commission are by no means terminated, we have arrived at certain conclusions, which we now humbly submit to your Majesty as follows:

1. That no restriction should be placed upon the processes of, or apparatus used in, the distillation of any spirit to which the term "whiskey" may be applied on a trade description.
2. That the term "whiskey", having been recognized in the past as applicable to a potable spirit manufactured from (1) and (2) malt and unmalted barley or other cereal, the application of the term "whiskey" should not be denied to the product manufactured from such materials.'

So grain whisky *was* true whisky, and the distillers had triumphed. The decision, in fact, confirmed that those whisky drinkers who preferred the lighter and blander blends—who were, after all, the majority—should not be denied their favourite drink.

The Commission's final report came out on July 28, 1909. After the important decision reached in the interim report, it did not arouse the same degree of interest. But it did do one vital thing. It defined Scotch whisky. It said:

'Our general conclusion therefore . . . is that "whiskey" is a spirit obtained by distillations from a mash of cereal grains saccharified [made into sugar] by the diastase of malt: that Scotch whiskey is whiskey, as above defined, distilled in Scotland . . .'

This definition stands in essence today, although it was modified by the Finance Act of 1969. The legal definition of whisky now reads:

'Spirits which have been distilled from a mash of cereals which have been:

  (i) saccharified by the diastase of malt contained therein with or without other natural diastases approved for the purpose by the Commissioners of Customs and Excise; and
 (ii) fermented by the action of yeast; and
(iii) distilled at less than 166·4 degrees proof in such a way that the distillate has an aroma and flavour derived from the materials used, and which have been matured in wooden casks in a warehouse for a period of at least three years.'

As far as the Scottish element in Scotch whisky is concerned, the Act goes on to say:

'The expression "Scotch whisky" shall mean whisky which has been distilled in Scotland.'

Nevertheless, in spite of the refinements introduced in the 1969 definition, it was the one taken 60 years earlier which really fixed the character of Scotch and remains the justification for the familiar bottles behind the bar today.

It was only after the Royal Commission had reported its findings in 1909 that companies such as Dewars could relax in the knowledge that their blended whiskies were quite legal.

28

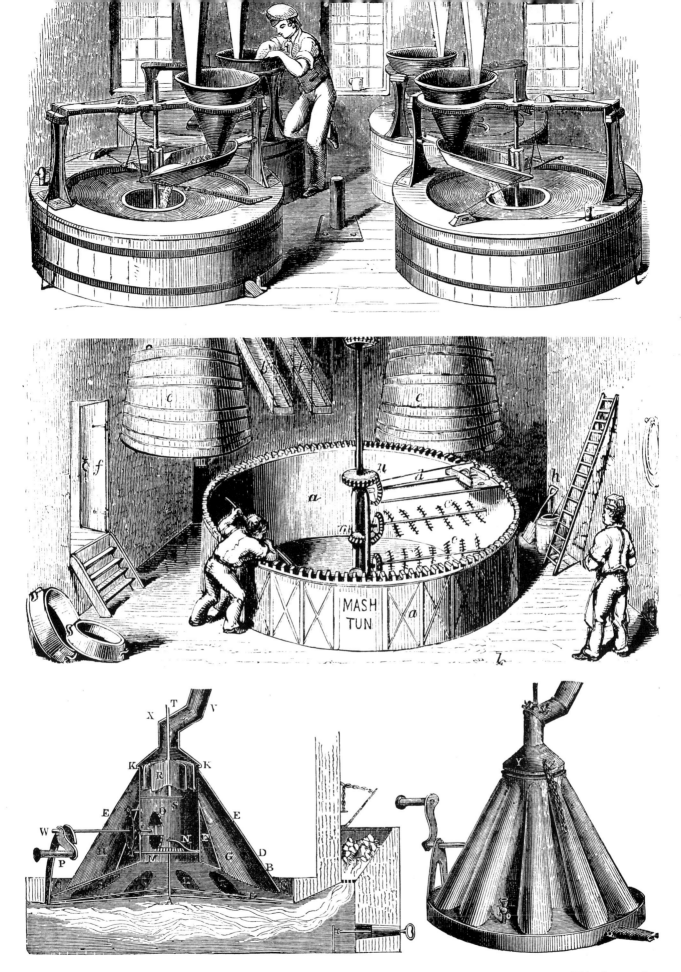

Top: These 19th-century grinding machines prepared the grist for the mash. Today one small modern machine can do the work of all four.

Centre: Modern mash tuns work on exactly the same principles as these: only the size has changed over the last two centuries.

Bottom: This diagram of an early Scottish still was designed to produce the maximum amount of spirit in the shortest possible time.

Twentieth century Scotch

Although Lloyd George's intention to close down distilleries made him an enemy of the whisky trade, his banning of impure spirits for use in the home trade did much to improve the overall quality of whisky in the United Kingdom.

The history of Scotch whisky in this century is complicated but it can be summed up very succinctly under four headings—taxation, amalgamation, exports and North America.

Taxation, its increase and its accelerated increase, has been a continual nightmare to the whisky producer. Successive chancellors of the exchequer have always seen the whisky business as a bottomless financial well and have brought bigger and bigger fiscal buckets to it more and more often.

Even allowing for the decrease in the value of money, the burden of taxation on whisky makes startling reading.

At the turn of the century it stood at 11 shillings a proof gallon. If the increases are tabulated, it is easy to see just how steep the increase in taxation has been since the beginning of this century.

The taxing question of taxation

Year	£ s d	Year	£ s d
1901	11s 0d	1964	£12 17s 6d
1909	14s 9d	1965	£14 12s 0d
1918	£1 10s 0d	1967	£16 1s 3d
1919	£2 10s 0d	1968 (Mar)	£17 2s 9d
1920	£3 12s 6d	1968 (Nov)	£18·85
1939	£4 2s 6d	1973	£15·45
1942	£6 17s 6d	1974	£17·01
1943	£7 17s 6d	1975	£22·09
1947	£9 10s 10d	1976	£24·63
1961	£11 11s 11d	1977	£27·09

Recognizing the effect of this grim and inexorable increase in taxation is essential to understanding the history of whisky. It is the constant background noise to everything else that is going on.

The early years of the century, immediately after the collapse of the boom, saw a gradual decrease in the number of distilleries from 161 at the height of the market in 1898 to 122 in 1910. The decline slowed down after that but the picture then became clouded by the advent of the First World War.

The Chancellor of the Exchequer on the outbreak of the 1914–18 war was Lloyd George. He had incurred the displeasure of the whisky trade by a swingeing increase in taxation in the budget of 1909 but now he had an even better idea. This was to close the whole industry down altogether, the reason being that he claimed to believe that the ready availability of cheap and immature whisky was poisoning the workers and making them unfit for war work. He was dissuaded from this draconian point of view by William Ross, among others, who told him of the absolute necessity of keeping the industry going, if only because of the needs of the military for industrial alcohol and of bakers for the yeast (an invaluable by-product of the patent still process). He was further persuaded that the answer was to prohibit the sale of raw spirit by introducing legislation which made maturing mandatory and this was duly done by the Immature Spirits (Restriction) Act of 1915. Ironically, this legislation did the reputation of Scotch within Britain much good by getting rid of the inferior, cheap and immature variety. (It is still in force today, but does not apply to the export of immature spirit.) It did, however, inevitably mean a sharp and immediate rise in the price of Scotch whisky.

It had the additional effect of ruining a number of blending companies because they could not survive financially through the time needed to mature the raw whiskies they were currently selling but which Lloyd George had banned. Their stocks of raw whisky were snapped up by Distillers Company, Buchanan-Dewar and Johnnie Walker—'the big three'. They also had another and accidental stroke of fortune. Lloyd George had agreed to the continuation of the distilling of grain spirit for

This whisky advertisement of 1902 is more remarkable for the oddity of its graphics than the clarity of its message.

industrial or military purposes but the actual amount of distilling allowed was severely limited. Malt whisky distilleries, of course, were not involved in producing an industrially useful spirit so the restrictions hit them particularly hard. Some were forced to close down and the rest were severely weakened. This made them particularly vulnerable to takeover bids, a situation of which Distillers was to take full advantage.

In 1925 Buchanan-Dewar, Johnnie Walker and D.C.L. came together to form one giant new company. Although Buchanan-Dewar was the largest of the three, it was decided that the new company would be called Distillers Company Limited. Two years later, White Horse came in. It will come as no surprise to learn that William Ross was active in all these moves. In 1937, William Sanderson (who owned Vat 69) merged. This inevitably increased Distillers' already considerable interest in the London gin business. It had acquired Gordons some years earlier and this new deal brought in Booths.

The Second World War brought another profound change to the whisky trade. Before the war home consumption took up the biggest single proportion of all whisky sold and, although total exports exceeded this amount, no single export market came anywhere near the quantity sold in the UK. By the end of the war this situation had changed and home consumption had become increasingly less important. By 1949, people in the United States were drinking more Scotch than in Great Britain and this disproportion has increased ever since; by the early 1970s the Americans were drinking nearly three times as much Scotch whisky as the British.

Typically, Winston Churchill had foreseen this and shortly before the end of the war he issued a famous minute to the then Minister of Food. It read: 'On no account reduce the barley for whisky. This takes years to mature and is an invaluable export and dollar producer. Having regard to all our other difficulties about exports it would be most improvident not to preserve this characteristic British element of ascendancy.'

This sensible advice was followed, although it inevitably led to whisky shortages at home, a situation exacerbated by the very high level of taxation. As far as the British—and more sadly the Scots among them—were concerned, whisky was now moving into the luxury class.

The flood of Scotch whisky from the warehouses of Scotland to the highball glasses of Manhattan and Los Angeles has also seen a reverse transatlantic trend which has increased considerably since the end of the war.

The Canadian distilling company of Hiram Walker had already established a connection in Scotland in the early 1930s when it bought an interest in a Scottish bonding company. In 1936 it acquired Ballantines—still its most popular brand —and the two malt distilleries of Glenburgie, near Elgin, and Milton Duff, a few miles to the east. In 1938 it built a grain distillery at Dumbarton so that its blending capacity could be fully exploited. It has since added a bottling and blending plant at the same site along with a massive

The worm tub of the Glenlivet distillery in 1896. This engraving gives a rough approximation of what the rest of the distillery looked like.

During the Second World War, Winston Churchill recognized the importance to British exports of all blended whiskies. He expressly said that barley should be reserved for it.

32

array of maturing warehouses. Uniquely, this great complex is guarded by a flock of geese, just like the Capitol in Ancient Rome—and no doubt very useful at Christmas!

In 1954, it took over the Glencadam malt distillery in Brechin, northeast of Dundee, and the Scapa malt distillery in the Orkneys. The next year it bought the famous Pulteney malt distillery at Wick in the far north of Scotland. In 1970, it bought Balblair malt distillery, north of Inverness.

Hiram Walker is a very decentralized company in its Scottish operations, rather like D.C.L. It does not market any Scotch whisky under the Hiram Walker label.

The second Canadian company to appear on the Scottish scene was Seagrams.

This company, controlled by a strange genius called Samuel Bronfman, bought an old company called Chivas Brothers in 1950 which almost immediately acquired the old Milton malt distillery, now renamed Strathilsa. Seven years later Seagrams built themselves a new malt distillery nearby, naming it Glen Keith-Glenlivet. Bronfman took a passionate interest in his Scotch whisky holdings and is said to have been instrumental in producing the rich, smooth blend 'Chivas Regal'. He died in 1971.

Other Canadian and American interests are also well represented in Scotland and, with Hiram Walker and Seagrams, it is estimated that they now control more than a third of the entire Scotch whisky business throughout the world.

One of the very best, and certainly one of the most expensive, of all blended Scotch whiskies, Chivas Regal. It was the brainchild of Samuel Bronfman who founded the mighty Seagram empire.

Whisky in literature

If the latter-day history of whisky has been dogged by such unpromising words as taxation and amalgamation, the literary references to whisky throughout the ages, although they are fairly sparse, have had a more joyous ring to them. Clearly the whisky of Queen Elizabeth I's day had qualities which have sadly deteriorated over the centuries if we are to rely on that source of historical knowledge from whom William Shakespeare gathered so much of his material. Writing in 1578 in his *Chronicles of England, Scotland and Ireland*, the great Holinshed says of 'uisge beatha':

'Beying moderatelie taken, it sloweth age, it strengtheneth youthe; it helpeth digestion; it cutteth fleume; it abandoneth melancholie; it relisheth the harte; it lighteneth the mynde; it quickeneth the spirites; it cureth the hydropsie; it healeth the strangury; it pounceth the stone; it repelleth grauel; it puffeth awaie ventosite; it kepyth and preserveth the head from whyrling—the eyes from dazelyng—the

The importance of cold clear water to Scotch whisky cannot be overemphasized; it is basic not only to the drink but to the industrial process.

34

Robert Burns, the bard of whisky, often wrote eloquently about his favourite drink. He was a fervent critic of excisemen, as shown in his poem 'The De'il's awa wi' the Exciseman', but he eventually became one himself.

tongue from lispyng—the mouth from snafflyng—the teethe from chatteryng—the throte from ratlyng—the weason from stieflyng—the stomach from wamblyng—the harte from swellyng—the bellie from wirtchyng—the guts from rumblyng—the hands from shiueryng—the sinowes from shrinkyng—the veynes from crumplyng—the bones from soakyng . . . truly it is a soueraigne liquor.'

Modern whisky advertisers should take note!

But in spite of this splendid encomium, the literature of whisky is, as we have said, curiously sparse—with, of course, the great and glowing exception of Burns. However, shortly before the flowering of his genius, two other 18th century writers described their acquaintance with Scotch whisky. In 1770, in *Humphrey Clinker*, Smollett wrote:

'Yesterday we were invited to the funeral of an old lady, the grandmother of a gentleman in this neighbourhood and found ourselves in the midst of fifty people, who were regaled with a sumptuous feast . . . the guests did such honour to the entertainment, that many of them could not stand when we were reminded of the business on which we had met . . .

'Then we returned to the castle, resumed the bottle and by midnight there was not a sober person in the family, the females

excepted. The squire and I were, with some difficulty, permitted to retire with the landlord in the evening; but our entertainer was a little chagrined at our retreat; and afterward seemed to think it a disparagement to his family, that not above an hundred gallons of whisky had been drunk upon such a solemn occasion.'

And elsewhere:

'The Highlanders regale themselves with whisky, a malt spirit, as strong as Geneva, which they swallow in great quantities, without any signs of inebriation; they are used to it from the cradle, and find it an excellent preservative against the winter cold, which must be extreme on the mountains. I am told that it is given with great success to infants, as a cordial . . .'

Three years later Dr Johnson and Boswell made their famous journey to Scotland and a meeting between Dr Johnson and whisky was inevitable. It must be remembered, incidentally, that Dr Johnson would never have encountered whisky in London. Thus it would have seemed a remote and savage potion, used only by the fierce and illiterate clansmen of the Highlands, quite recently crushed at Culloden.

Boswell records the occasion:

'We got at night to Inverary, where we found an excellent inn . . . We supped well; and after supper, Dr Johnson, whom I had not seen taste any fermented liquor during all our travels, called for a gill of whisky. "Come," said he, "let me know what it is that makes a Scotchman happy!"

18th-century drinkers would take their whisky straight from the still. Modern drinkers would find such spirit too rough and raw for their palates.

He drank it all but a drop, which I begged leave to pour into my glass, that I might say we had drunk whisky together.'

Dr Johnson remembered the incident:

'A man of the Hebrides . . . as soon as he appears in the morning swallows a glass of whisky; yet they are not a drunken race . . . but no man is so abstemious as to refuse the morning dram, which they call a *skalk*.

'The word *whisky* signifies water, and is applied by way of eminence to *strong water*, or distilled liquor. The spirit drunk in the North is drawn from barley. I never tasted it, except once at the Inn in Inverary, when I thought it preferable to any English malt brandy. It was strong, but not pungent, and was free from the empyreumatick taste or smell . . . Not long after the dram, may be expected breakfast . . .'

The tragedy of Culloden, which had taken place less than 30 years before Johnson's visit, was itself associated with whisky. A Scottish chaplain, preparing to give communion to the troops before the battle, discovered that he had neither host nor consecrated wine. He used oatcakes and whisky instead, sadly to no avail.

The whiskies that Smollett and Dr Johnson drank were locally brewed and distilled. Individual whiskies were quite unknown outside their own area. Curiously enough there is one famous exception to this, and the story goes back to the deposition of James II. Duncan Forbes of Culloden was a lawyer and politician and, in Scotland, had the rare distinction of being a Whig. He sided with the successful rebels who supplanted James with William and Mary, and he suffered for it. Robert Forsyth tells what happened in his book *The Beauties of Scotland* published in 1805:

'The small village of Fairntosh [or Ferintosh, in Ross-shire] only deserves notice on account of a singular privilege which its proprietor, Forbes of Culloden, long enjoyed. At the time of the Revolution, in 1688, Mr Forbes of Culloden was a zealous whig, in consequence of which his estates were laid waste, particularly the barony of Fairntosh, on which extensive distilleries belonging to him were destroyed. As a compensation, the Parliament of Scotland granted to him, in 1690, freedom from excise for these lands, on condition that he should make an annual payment of 400 merks Scots. The proprietors of this estate continued extremely loyal. The son of the grantee of this privilege, in 1715, raised in arms all the men upon his estate for the support of the Hanoverian succession; and the succeeding proprietor, in 1745, being then Lord President of the Court of Session, contributed greatly to prevent the extension of the rebellion, and prevailed with some of the most powerful chieftains to remain quiet. The privilege was, in 1786, resumed by government, and the sum of £20,000 was granted by way of

The whisky that Johnson and Boswell were offered during their tour of Scotland would probably have been produced in stills such as this.

A The Still	L A Pewter Crane
B The Worm tub	M A Pewter Valencia
C The Pump	N Hippocrates bag or Flannel
D Water tub	Sleeve
E A Press	O Poker Fire-shovel Cole rake
FFF Tubs to hold the goods	P A Box of Bungs
GGGG Canns of different size	Q The Worm within the Worm tub
H A Wood Funnel with a iron nosel	marked with prick'd lines
I A large Vessel to put the Faints	R A Piece of Wood to keep down
or after runnings	the Head of the Still to
K Tin pump	prevent flying of

A sad lament

compensation to the proprietor. Before that period Ferintosh whisky was much relished in Scotland. It had a strong flavour of the smoke of the peat with which the malt of which it was made was dried; but this was considered as one of the marks of its being genuine.'

Burns bewailed the loss of Ferintosh in his poem 'Scotch Drink':

'O Whisky! soul o' plays an' pranks!
Accept a Bardie's gratefu' thanks!
When wanting thee, what tuneless cranks
    Are my poor verses!
Thou comes—they rattle i' their ranks
    At ither's arses!

Thee, Ferintosh! O sadly lost!
Scotland lament frae coast to coast!
Now colic grips, an' barkin' hoast
    May kill us a'
For loyal Forbes' charter'd boast
    Is ta'en awa!

Thae curst horse-leeches o' th' Excise,
Wha mak the whisky stells their prize!
Haud up thy han', De'il! Ance, twice,
    thrice!
    There, seize the blinkers!
An' bake them up in brunstane pies
    For poor damn'd drinkers.'

(hoast = a cough; blinkers = spies)

Dr Johnson, here holding court, tasted whisky for the first time on his famous journey to Scotland. In the London of his day, gin was the popular drink of the streets while the rich preferred French brandy.

Despite these unkind words about excisemen, Burns was later to join their ranks. But as a poet he celebrated the delights of drink over and over again, as in 'The Holy Fair':

'Leeze me on drink! it gies us mair
Than either school or college;
It kindles wit, it waukens lear,
It pangs us fou o' knowledge.
Be't whisky gill, or pennywheep,
Or onie stronger potion,
It never fails, on drinkin' deep,
To kittle up our notion,
By night or day.'

(leeze me = I am grateful for; pennywheep = very weak beer; lear = learning; pangs = crams; kittle = tickle)

And again, in 'The Author's Earnest Cry and Prayer':

'Sages their solemn een may steek,
An' raise a philosophic reek,
An' physically causes seek,
In clime an' season;
But tell me whisky's name in Greek,
I'll tell the reason.

Scotland, my auld respected mither!
Tho' whiles ye moistify your leather,
Till where ye sit on craps o' heather,
Ye tine your dam
Freedom and whisky gang thegither
Tak aff your dram!'

(een = eyes; steek = close; moistify = to make moist; craps = crops; tine = lose; dam = water)

Although Burns is in a class of his own as a celebrant of the virtues of whisky, other Scots writers had their moments. Robert Ferguson, a poet who died in 1774, hymned his dram thus:

'And thou, great god of aqua vitae!
Wha sways the empire of this city—
When fou we're sometimes capernoity—
Be thou prepar'd
To hedge us frae that black banditti,
The City Guard.

O Muse! be kind, and dinna fash us
To flee awa beyont Parnassus,
Nor seek for Helicon to wash us,
That heath'nish spring!
Wi' Highland whisky scour our hawses,
And gar us sing.

(Capernoity = peevish; hawses = throat)

AULD LANG SYNE.—(BURNS.)

SHOULD auld ac-quaintance be for-got, and ne-ver brought to mind,
Should auld ac-quaintance be for-got, And days of Lang Syne.
For Auld Lang Syne, my dear, For Auld Lang
Syne ,We'll tak' a cup o' kind-ness Yet. For Auld Lang Syne.

We twa hae run about the braes,
And pu'd the gowans fine;
But we've wander'd many a weary
Since auld lang syne. (foot,
And there's a hand my trusty friend,
And gies a hand o' thine;

And toom the cup in friendship's
And auld lang syne. (growth,

And surely ye'll be your pint-stoup,
As sure as I'll be mine;
And we'll take a right guid willy-
For auld lang syne. (waught,

'A drop of Highland whisky O'

A little later Andrew Sherrif (1762–1800) was writing 'A cogie o yill':

'A cogie o yill
And a pickle aitmeal,
And a denty wee drappie o' whisky,
Was our forefathers' dose
For to sweel doun their brose,
And keep them aye cheery and frisky.
Then hey for the whisky and hey for the meal,
And hey for the cogie and hey for the yill!
Gin ye steer a' thegither they'll do unco weel,
To keep a chiel cheery and brisk aye.'

(cogie = drinking vessel; yill = ale)

William Aytoun (1813–65) celebrated in 'The Massacre of Macpherson' the growing reputation of Glenlivet:

'Phairson had a son
Who married Noah's daughter,
And nearly spoiled the flood
By trinking up ta watter,
Which he would haf done—
I, at least, pelieve it—
Had ta mixture peen
Only half Glenlivet!

But perhaps the most succinct saying about Scotch whisky is a proverb whose origins are lost in the mists of time. It merely says:

'There are two things a Scotsman likes naked, and one is malt whisky!'

However, the strong Scots tradition of praising their native dram was not restricted to men. Agnes Lyon, the wife of Dr Lyon, Minister of Glamis, who was born in 1762, some 200 years after Holinshed had extolled the medicinal virtues of whisky, wrote in 'Neil Gow's farewell to whisky':

'Alake, quo Neil, I'm frail an' auld,
And find my bluid grows unco cauld,
I think it maks me blythe and bauld,
A wee drop Highland whisky, O.
But a' the doctors do agree
That whisky's no the drink for me;
I'm fleyed they'll gar me tyne my glee,
Should they part me and whisky, O.'

Opposite above: The health of Scottish brides was normally drunk in good Scotch whisky—a custom that still persists in many parts of Scotland today.

Opposite below: Burns' 'Cup o' Kindness' would have been a dram of good malt whisky as this old songsheet suggests.

Dowie's Tavern in Edinburgh was one of Burns' favourite haunts during his visits to the Scottish capital. After his untimely death, the publican was quick to cash in on the poet's spreading popularity.

2 MALT WHISKY

There are at the present time, 115 malt distilleries in Scotland. This figure can fluctuate as old distilleries close down or new ones open. No two of them make their whisky in exactly the same way and they vary enormously in size and productivity. Ardbeg, for instance, has only two stills while Glenfiddich has more than two dozen. Some distillers insist on natural wood for their fermenting vats while others prefer modern stainless steel. A few cling to the old-fashioned worm tubs, others opt for technologically advanced condensers.

Yet the actual method of producing malt whisky remains almost identical and each individual step in the process can be instantly identified at every distillery. So this account, while applying to no distillery in particular and containing none of the idiosyncratic little variations which make Scottish malt whisky such a fascinating drink, is entirely typical of all of them. And as all processes have to have a beginning, there is no question that the beginning of malt whisky is barley.

Barley is the root and only begetter of malt whisky. Its sturdy resistance to wind and weather and its ability to survive the seasonal rigours of the Scottish climate made it the obvious basic material for a national drink, just as maize was the natural material for the Bourbon of the American South. However, not only Scottish barley is used to make whisky today. This is not only because superior barleys have been developed in other countries, but because some Scottish barleys themselves have deteriorated over the last century.

The use of artificial fertilizers has encouraged barleys which are high in nitrogen at the expense of starch, quickly and easily grown, and ideal for many purposes—but not for making whisky. So today distillers can go very far afield indeed for their barley—to Canada, Australia, South Africa and even India. Some East Anglian barley is also used, but this is tending to suffer from the same disadvantages as Scottish barley and only the economies of transport make it worthwhile. The barleys of hot and distant lands have an extra advantage in that they are dry and store exceptionally well, a highly important consideration for distillers. Here again the dominance of economics

in making whisky shows itself. It can sometimes be to the advantage of the distiller to use a less than ideal local barley with negligible transport costs rather than a superior foreign barley with heavy transport charges. He will get less potable spirit per gallon of wash but this disadvantage might be more than compensated for by the smaller amount he has paid to produce it. The quality of the final whisky need not necessarily be affected by economies of this nature. This is another example of the mesh of decisions that a distiller must constantly take. It is not only his ability to make good whisky that is in question, but his ability to make good whisky at an economical cost. It is commendable that Scottish Malt Distillers, the D.C.L. subsidiary that contains all its malt distilleries, uses only British barley.

What characteristics does the distiller look for in the barley he buys? First, it must be fully ripe. If it is the slightest bit unripe it will store badly—and mouldy barley is a distiller's nightmare. Next, it must contain the necessary proportions of starch and protein—starch for the production of maltose and protein for successful germination.

Today a distiller has sophisticated laboratory techniques at his command to help him determine these proportions, but a good eye and a few decades of experience will stand him in good stead. The barley must be dry, too. Barley has a natural

The distillery at Hillside in Angus (on the right) is quite dwarfed by the neighbouring malting plant.

Opposite: Barley for malting must be fully ripe and dry and have a low nitrogen content.

The barley starting to germinate (left). Germination produces heat which must be carefully controlled for successful malting. After malting (right) the barley looks much the same as it did before.

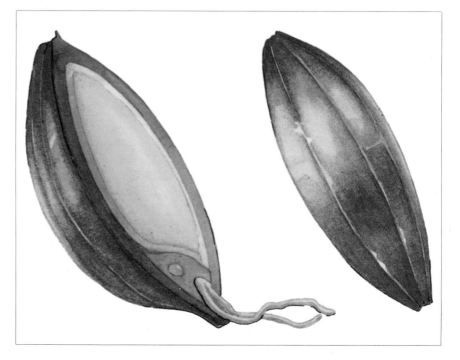

moisture content but if this is above the distiller's acceptable limit he will have to dry it until enough excess moisture is driven off. Nearly all distillers allow their barley to 'rest' a few weeks before using it. This, allied to any necessary drying, aids the natural period of dormancy that barley, like any ripe cereal, would go through in nature between harvesting and germination.

Finally, the barley must be clean and uncontaminated. Any significant amount of foreign material is not only lost weight but might actively interfere with the processes of malting.

Individual judgement on the part of the distiller in these matters is still important but, nevertheless, the trend is away from this and towards the expertise of the professional large-scale maltster. The traditional processes of malting are still occasionally used, especially in the smaller distilleries but to the larger distilleries it makes both economic and technical sense to bulk-buy their barley ready malted and so to cut out a major area of effort and potential trouble. The large-scale maltster also has the resources to maintain standards of consistency quite outside the capacity of the individual distiller to whom this is by no means the main area of concern. It seems likely that, in the future, even those few distillers who still take the time and trouble to malt their own barley will not be able to escape from the harsh realities of economics.

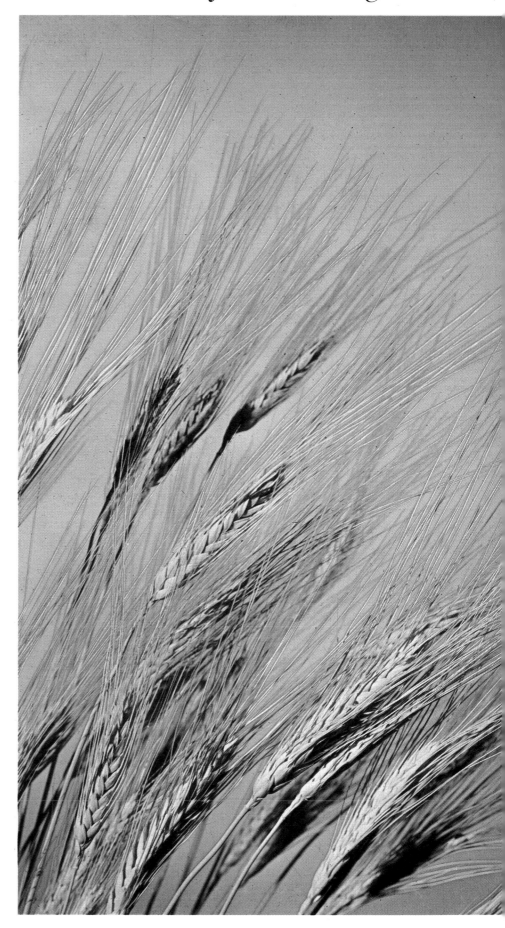

Water

The most mysterious—and even mystical —ingredient of malt whisky is the water that is intimately involved in every stage of making it. This water determines the geographical location of the distillery because the qualities the distiller demands from his water supply are highly specific. This has resulted in the happy circumstance that most malt whisky distilleries are found in places of superb natural beauty, in small towns, on mountainsides and by rushing burns. Knowing where it comes from is one of the charms of drinking single malt whisky.

The first requirement is for water in large quantities. It is not the amount of water needed for steeping or mashing that is important, although this is by no means negligible. It is the cooling process that uses large volumes of water. The worm tubs or condensers in a big distillery can swallow surprising quantities. The other factor here is the need for the distiller, for ecological reasons, to have a great deal more water than he can possibly use. If the water passing through a big distillery is discharged downstream warmed enough to raise the temperature of that stream, it could have unpredictable and even irreversible effects on plant and animal life. So the distiller needs a flow large enough to absorb, without any noticeable results, all the warmed water discharged.

A steady and continuous flow is also essential. Rivers which freeze in the winter and run dry in the summer are useless to the distiller. So distilleries generally site themselves by fast flowing and sizeable streams. A glance at a map of Speyside showing where distilleries are situated makes this point graphically.

Crystal clear water is vital, too, Cloudy or turbid water might damage the pumps even if it did not affect the steeping or mashing and the taste of the finished whisky. And no distiller could have any confidence in anything less than perfectly clear water since any hint of cloudiness might conceal much more dangerous and damaging defects.

The water used in making malt whisky must also be pure. This does not mean to say that it has to be free of any dissolved minerals but it does mean that it must not contain any substances which would adversely affect the flavour of the steeped barley, the mash, the wort, the wash and the final distilled whisky. The prospect, for instance, of a hint of contaminating oil getting through would be unthinkable.

Softness is very important. Quite apart from the fact that hard water—water full of dissolved lime—would soon fur up his pipes, the distiller also knows that it would affect the quality of the malt and the wort. Luckily the water is almost exclusively soft in Scotland.

The distiller also needs his water to be as cold as possible. Really cold water helps enormously in the cooling process and one of the luckiest distillers in Scotland is the man on Speyside whose stream flows down a mountainside on which the sun never shines. Again, most streams in Scotland are chilly, even in high summer, but a few degrees of permanent extra coldness can give a distiller an advantage which pays off handsomely in both the quality and quantity of whisky produced. Refrigeration is, of course, an alternative but an overhead the distiller would rather go without.

Finally, the stream should flow through peat and carry with it some of the qualities of peat—its acidity, its taste, its colour. The reasons for this are hard to describe but many distillers are passionately convinced that they are absolutely essential. There are even two schools of thought as to which kind of peated water produces the finest whisky—water that has come 'off granite through peat' or 'off peat through granite'. In an odd kind of way it does make sense. If peat is essential to the flavour of the finished whisky there is a kind of folk logic which demands that the water from which the whisky is distilled should be peated, too.

Some authorities claim that the acid in peat-borne water dissolves out substances other than maltose from the malt mash and that these dissolved substances give malt whisky its special characteristics. This assertion, like so many other assertions about malt whisky, is impossible to disprove. It is equally impossible to prove. What is certain is that if anyone who has any say in the matter believes that peaty water is essential for the making of malt whisky, then that is the way that malt whisky will be made. And, considering the magnificent results that peaty water gives, it would be a bold man who tried to make it any other way.

The distiller must use water that is cold, clear and pure. It is an advantage to him if the water also flows through granite.

Below: Rivers which flow through the lee of mountains and are thus shaded from sunlight for most of the day are especially valued for their extra chill.

Below right: This burn, flowing through the Carvel Hills, supplies the Mortlach distillery with water.

Peat

'Vegetable matter decomposed by water and partly carbonized by chemical change, often forming bogs or mosses of large extent whence it is dug or cut out and made into peats...a cant name for whisky distilled over a peat-fire and so flavoured with peat-smoke. Also, loosely, Highland whisky generally.' O.E.D.

Peat is the soul of Scotch whisky since it is the fragrant smoke of burning peat that gives Scotch its inimitable flavour, its 'nose', its otherworld pungency. Indeed, the siting of all early malt distilleries was altogether conditioned by the nearness of a peat bog. Even today, when transport is comparatively easy and distillers can choose where they obtain their peat from, a surprising number of distilleries are still within wheelbarrow distance of local peat. Yet where peat actually exists, it exists in enormous quantities—millions and millions of tons. So even if the production of malt whisky were to be multiplied many times over—a most unlikely event—your grandchildren's grandchildren and their grandchildren's grandchildren would still be able to enjoy their dram.

Peat only develops in climates with a consistently heavy rainfall, and the sheer size and thickness of Scottish peat bogs tell geologists a great deal about the climate of Scotland in the past. Briefly, it has rained an awful lot in Scotland for an awfully long time.

Technically speaking, peat is a compacted mass of dead vegetation which has not been allowed to decay into its constituent organic compounds as in the case of normal humus. This is because the bacteria and fungi necessary for successful decomposition cannot exist in the oxygen-starved and highly acidic water which soaks the landscape. Peat is thus an invaluable record of plant life in the distant past and fragments of plants in the peat many tens of thousands of years old can easily be identified by experts.

Over many thousands of years the slow accumulation of new plant debris gradually compresses the lower layers until they become a tightly packed soggy mass. Incidentally, given time and pressure, this mass is transformed successively into lignite and then coal. Over eons, some Scottish peat bogs have built up into deposits more than 50 feet thick, although

Much of the peat used in distilling is cut by hand. It is a highly skilled and back-breaking job.

Opposite above: Dried peat being stacked at the Speyside Imperial distillery.

Opposite centre: Mechanical peat cutters can do the work of many men but can only operate under ideal conditions.

Opposite below: Islay, with its huge peat fields, is ideal for mechanical peat cutting.

a thickness of some 10–20 feet is more common.

Peat varies in consistency depending on the kind of dead plant from which it is formed. Forest peat is almost entirely leaf, branch and trunk debris. Marsh peat is largely rushes, reeds and mosses. It is this latter kind of peat with, in some places, the useful addition of heather, that flavours most of the malts of Scotland. But even within bog peat there are wide variations. Some peats are light brown in colour and dry out to a tangled and loosely packed mass of vegetation. Others are almost black and dry out to a hard, dense brick. Both burn with their own characteristic type of smoke, both offer different fragrances to the finished whisky.

Peat for malting is still dug out of its bogs with specially-shaped spades in rectangular turves about two feet long. This is back-breaking work because raw peat is extremely heavy, with a dense clay-like consistency. Peat cutters soon learn the physical skills to make the job as easy as possible, but it remains a brutally demanding occupation. When first dug the peat is 90 percent water by weight, so it has to be carefully stacked in order to dry out as quickly as possible. This drying process usually takes about a year. By this time each turf has shrunk to the size of a large brick and can be handled easily. It is now clean to the touch, crumbles easily and is pleasantly aromatic. And once it has lost its own natural water it is impervious to moisture, a sure sign that it is ready.

Peat burns very slowly and produces a great deal of thick and pungent smoke. Some types of peat produce more smoke than others. Roughly speaking, the darker the peat the more slowly it burns and the thicker its smoke. This, again, is reflected in the character of the mature malt whisky.

Until comparatively recently, all distilleries cut their own peat but in recent years more and more distillers are buying their peat centrally. This makes sense but it is hard not to regret the relegation of the traditional peating spade to the museum.

Malting

The days are long since past when the distiller could look down from his bedroom window over the waving fields of barley which would later be scythed, stooked and winnowed, with the golden grains being brought to the distillery in rumbling horse-drawn carts. Then his brawny maltmen would shovel it into baskets to be hoisted by hand to the barley store where it would be laboriously heaped until it was needed for malting.

Today, the barley the distiller selects may have come from as far away as India or Australia and it arrives at the distillery in huge and impersonal grain tankers to be mechanically pumped and conveyed to his barley hoppers in the upper regions of the barley store. Any local fields of waving barley are likely to be used as cattle fodder because—alas for romance and history—distillers today find that not all Scottish barley is rich enough in starch and protein for their purposes. They need a barley that has ripened during a long, hot summer and is bursting with starch and without too much nitrogen. To obtain barley like this, they will go anywhere in the world, as long as the price is not astronomical.

Since distillation of malt whisky is a batch process, the distiller has to hold the balance between storing enough to ensure adequate supplies for future distilling without collecting so much that it might deteriorate in store. He also has to ensure that his barley is protected against infestation and damp and he will sometimes have his own methods of further drying barley that he considers not quite dry enough to store satisfactorily. (The ubiquitous distillery cat makes sure that other potential enemies are kept at bay.) He will then let the barley 'rest' for a few weeks. No distiller likes to use barley straight from the supplier.

When the time comes for the distiller to start a new batch of malt whisky, the first thing he does is to release from his hoppers the right amount of barley. This can vary from a few tons at a small distillery to some dozens of tons at a really big one. This then passes through a dressing machine to screen off dust or other contaminating debris. The barley is now conveyed either mechanically or by gravity to large vats of local water called 'steeps'. There it remains until it has soaked up the required amount of water for successful

Left: At the modern malting plant at Port Ellen on the Isle of Islay the finished barley is transferred to storage hoppers both mechanically and by hand.

Two processes take place on the malting floor. In the foreground the barley is being aerated by pulling forks through it. In the background it is being spread by 'skips' or special shovels.

germination, usually between 40 and 50 percent by weight. This steeping process can take from two to three days depending on the season, the weather and the type of barley. Today, the final moisture content would almost certainly be measured by special equipment in the distillery laboratory but some maltmen still reckon to be able to judge the proper degree by biting a barley grain or squeezing it between their fingers. In the past, of course, this would have been the only way.

When the barley is ready, the steeps are drained and the wet and heavy mass of barley turned out onto a large floor, concrete, stone or tiled, often thousands of square feet in area. Here, on a convenient part of the floor, it is stacked in a heap about two feet thick by the maltmen using big wooden shovels called 'skips'.

Germination soon begins and each individual barley grain produces a tiny rootlet. The process of growth automatically produces heat and it is very important to the success of distillation that this heat is carefully controlled. Every day, therefore, and sometimes twice a day if the weather demands it, the whole mass of germinating barley is turned over and exposed to the cooling air. The maltmen do this by plunging their skips into the deep layer of barley and throwing the heavy shovelfuls to one side. This is not work for weaklings.

A great deal of malting is done mechanically. Here, at the D.C.L. plant at Burghead, huge drums malt the barley quickly and efficiently.

This constant turning has two effects. First, it further dries the barley, already naturally drying itself by the actual process of germination. Secondly, it spreads it more thinly on the malting floor. These two processes are synergistic—that is to say, the more they work together, the better they work together. The whole process also produces a heavy, sweetish, smell, hard to describe but quite unmistakable.

One of the problems facing the distiller is nature's refusal to conform to man-made time scales and, just as the steeping period can vary, so can malting. Sometimes it can take as little as eight days, sometimes as long as a fortnight. All that can be said is that when the rootlet has reached about an eighth of an inch this is a sign that all the available starch in the grain of barley has been converted into the necessary soluble sugars for the next process, and that germination must now be stopped before the baby barley plant begins to use these to fuel further growth.

By this time, too, the continual turning of the heap of barley has reduced it from its original two feet thickness to five or six inches. It is in every way more easily manageable and is now ready for the next process, known as kilning. Traditionally, the malted barley was conveyed to the kiln in an ingenious cart known as a malt barrow. It looked something like an ancient chariot. Even more primitive was a two-man hod which was heaped with malt and carried by hand. Mr Colman, the deputy manager at Glenkinchie Distillery at Pencaitland, tells us that when he was a young man it was a favourite trick of the maltmen to conceal a 56 pound weight amongst the barley. In those days malt men were strong men with a strong sense of humour. They had to be.

Other methods of malting

The traditional malting-floor method of making malt is a back-breaking as well as a highly skilled job and it carries its own natural risks. It is not surprising, therefore, that engineers have given considerable thought to alternative methods of malting which would cut the drudgery and eliminate chance. Two methods have been evolved and these have now almost totally replaced the traditional methods of the maltmen.

The first, the Saladin method, was invented by a French engineer called Charles Saladin. It consists of a long trough into which the steeped barley is poured and spread. Through this trough travels a rotating paddle which slowly and thoroughly turns the germinating barley at exactly the right speed to complete the malting process safely and painlessly.

The second, the drum method, achieves the same result by exactly the opposite means. Here the wet barley is fed into enormous perforated drums which slowly revolve while cooling air is blown through them from a central vent.

Both methods allow a much more closely controlled malting process and both have the additional advantage of being totally independent of the weather. This control of temperature and humidity also means that the malting process can be speeded up, and it is now usual for the malting process to be completed within seven days.

The history and chemistry of malting

For the distiller, malting is the chemical process by which the starch in a grain of barley is converted into soluble sugar by the action of enzymes produced in the grain itself, triggered by the presence of water. The distiller can then dissolve out these sugars and ferment them to produce the alcoholic liquid he needs for distillation.

Malting is one of the oldest of all the agricultural arts and it was certainly well known and understood long before the written word was invented. Certainly, the Ancient Egyptians used malt to make beer and the yeast derived from beer to leaven bread. Interestingly, the shovels they used to turn and aerate their malt are almost identical to those used by today's remaining maltmen, which means that the basic technology of malting has hardly changed in recorded history.

Understanding the chemistry of malting is obviously a much more recent discovery, although alchemists and experimenters during the last millenium have tried to work out what actually happens. While the full story is still unknown, we know enough to be certain of the outlines. The ripe barley grain consists of a tiny plant embryo and a much larger store of starch which is destined to nourish the new seedling until its root and stem system have developed enough to support themselves. Until the grain is moistened the embryo is dormant. Water brings it to life. At this point the food store is unavailable because its hard insoluble starch form is necessary for durability and protection. This main body of the grain is made up of a densely but regularly packed mass of starch cells, each cell enclosed in a tough, cellulose membrane.

The moment the embryo is activated by moisture two enzymes begin to be produced—cytase and diastase. Enzymes are substances made by all living organisms— from mosses to mankind—to help them dissolve and digest their food. Human saliva and internal digestive juices are rich in them. All enzymes function by breaking up and making soluble the materials that living creatures need to live and grow.

In the case of barley, the cytase breaks down the cellulose walls of each starch cell and allows the diastase to reach and break down the starch within. This it converts first into soluble starch of dextrin and then the dextrin into soluble sugar or maltose. It is this maltose that the distiller is after, because he can ferment it into alcohol.

Another method of malting uses mechanical revolving blades to spread and aerate the malt.

Kilning and peating

At the end of malting, the malted barley still contains a considerable amount of moisture and each individual grain is busy using it in its natural ambition to develop into a full grown barley plant. Part of the same process has also been the production of enzymes and by now these have converted nearly all the original starch of the barley into sugar. If the distiller were not to intervene at this point, the growing plant would now begin to draw on these sugars for sustenance until its new roots were big enough to feed the plant by themselves. But, alas, these infant aspirations are nipped in the bud. The distiller now kills the baby barley plants by drying them in a kiln. In this way the sugar they have laboured to produce becomes available to him for his own future purposes of fermentation.

This drying process is known as 'kilning' or 'peating' and it drives off all but a tiny percentage of the moisture remaining in the malt. The distiller achieves this in a kiln with a perforated metal or wire floor about halfway up over a furnace. In the old days this would have been a natural draught furnace but now forced draught furnaces are common.

On this metal floor the 'green' malt is spread. It is impossible to generalize about the thickness of the malt layer because it varies so much according to the shape and size of the kiln, but depths of as much as three feet and as little as eight inches have been recorded. The furnace is now lit and the kilning begins.

In the old days the furnace would have been fuelled by peat and peat only, but today anthracite and other solid fuel is used with peat as a flavouring agent. The pungency of the mature spirit depends on the amount and type of peat used at the beginning of the kilning process and how long the peat is burned. The rule would be the more and darker the peat, the smokier the mature spirit.

In all cases some peat would be used. This burns very slowly and smokily so that its fumes are drawn through the malt by natural draught to discharge themselves through the 'pagoda', characteristic of all malt distilleries. This picturesque design is not particularly efficient as a chimney, but it is perfectly adapted to ensure that the essential peat smoke is diffused slowly through the malt. In fact, every aspect of this ancient design is devoted to ensuring that the maximum amount of peat flavour is imparted to the maximum amount of malt. The inference, clearly, is that our grandfathers preferred their whiskies stronger-tasting and smokier than we do today, with our current emphasis on lightness and smoothness.

However, while this preliminary peating is taking place, the whole area of the distillery is suffused with the 'peat reek', highly agreeable and evocative at a distance but distinctly unsympathetic at close quarters. It is one of the distiller's oldest tricks to open the furnace door and invite the unwary visitor, who admires the 'peat reek', to take a good close sniff. He seldom does it twice.

The barley on the kiln floor is turned over occasionally so that it is evenly dried and peated. After the required degree of peating is achieved, solid fuel only is used and the temperature of the kiln is slowly raised until the malt is fully dried and cured. It now looks and feels exactly the same as when it first entered the distillery

These beautiful pagoda chimneys are now seldom in active use as most distillers buy their malt already peat-dried. But nearly all the malt distilleries still retain them and they remain a distinctive feature.

but a few grains chewed will demonstrate that some remarkable changes have taken place. The malt is now crisp and friable with a sweet and slightly smoky flavour and it is not difficult to imagine from this the taste of the far distant mature whisky. This cured malt is now stored for a minimum of six weeks to allow it to cool down. If this does not happen the yeast is badly affected during fermentation.

This traditional way of curing malt is now, alas, uncommon, with more and more distillers turning to mechanical methods which can be more closely controlled and are quicker. A new method, for instance, blasts in hot, peat-flavoured, smoke so that the malt is cured in less than 24 hours. Even faster, most distillers are finding it both convenient and economic to buy their malt already fully kilned and peated. Professional large-scale maltsters will guarantee to supply them consistently with high-grade peated malt to their exact specification, which means that they can be assured that the quality of the finished whisky will always be at least as high as if they kilned the malt themselves. It means, though, that the traditional pagoda has already become a purely decorative feature in most distilleries and that the famous 'peat reek' so familiar in malt distilleries has now largely disappeared forever. Few lovers of Scotch whisky can view this prospect with any pleasure.

Peat being fed to the distillery furnaces. Malt, which is spread out on a wire mesh floor above, absorbs the smoke from the peat, and gives the Scotch its unique flavour.

Dressing and grinding

A modern mash tun in operation. Huge paddles constantly revolve, mixing the malt thoroughly.

At the end of the peating process the fire is allowed to die down, the malt to cool and the last wisps of smoke to disperse. The peated malt is now taken from the kiln floor to yet another set of storage bins. Here it awaits the next stage which is to prepare it for mashing into the 'wort' that is later fermented to produce the alcohol.

The first process is dressing. This gets rid of the useless dead rootlets which have nothing further to contribute. A measured batch of peated malt is carried from the store to a dressing machine which shakes and beats the grains about until the lighter rootlets are rubbed off from the heavier grain and can easily be screened—a process not unlike winnowing. Dressing machines can clean several tons of malt in two hours.

The dressed malt is then carefully weighed and a measured amount sent to a grinding machine. Here it is coarsely milled (it was discovered many years ago that if malt is milled too finely it releases substances which adversely affect the flavour of the finished whisky). The malt grist is then carried to the malt grist hopper, immediately above the mash tun.

Dressing and grinding are dusty, noisy, businesses and certainly the least appealing of all the processes which go to make malt whisky. Nevertheless, they get the care and attention typical of all stages.

52

Mashing

Mashing is the steamy and smelly process which leaches all the available sugar from the malt grist and makes it ready for fermentation. It is a process exactly analogous to that of making beer and, indeed, up to the point of distillation any competent junior brewer could cope with the operation of a distillery.

Mashing takes place in the mash tun which can vary in construction in its details, but basically remains a large metal circular tank with a perforated base which can be kept watertight and drained at will. Set on a central shaft are a set of revolving paddles and discharging into it are the malt grist hopper and an outlet for hot water.

Mashing begins when the man in charge of this part of the distillery allows a measured quantity of malt grist to fall into the mash tun. At the same time he lets a measured amount of hot, but not boiling, water pour into the tun. He sets the paddles turning and waits until the whole porridgy mess is thoroughly mixed. When he considers the mixture is properly and thoroughly infused he drains the liquor off through the perforated bottom into big storage tanks known as underbacks. When this is done, he lets a second flow of even hotter, but still not boiling, water into the mash tun, repeating the whole process and eventually drawing off the liquor into the

underback, a large tank which stores the wort before it is pumped through the cooler or refrigerator into the fermenting backs.

Because the mash of crushed barley and hot water becomes partially gelatinized, some distillers pump in hot water through the base plate of the mash tun before pumping in the hot water from above. This is known as 'underletting' and breaks up the mash so that it can be thoroughly infused by the hot water.

This process is repeated twice more but at the end of it he returns the much weaker liquor to the original hot water storage tank, where it will be used for the first mash of the next batch of malt. Every last trace of available sugar will now have been extracted. These last two weak liquors are called 'sparges'. The liquor that is now in the underback is called 'wort' (pronounced 'wurt'). This is a sweet smelling, sweet tasting, translucent liquid, amber in colour and sticky if rubbed between the fingers. It is also hot and must be cooled before it can go forward towards the next process, which is that of fermentation itself. Any temperature other than lukewarm would kill off the delicate yeasts needed for fermentation so the temperature of the wort is reduced by simple refrigeration to about 70°F (21°C).

This mash tun was in operation in 1845. Although the basic process has not changed since then, the appearance of the machines certainly has.

From wort to wash

It is hard to imagine that the insipid and cooling wort will ever result in a liquor as strong and pungent as raw whisky, but the next process, fermentation, takes it an enormous step forward. For now alcohol first appears. Economics appear, too, for it is in the completeness and effectiveness of the process known as fermentation that the amount of alcohol produced depends. And the amount of alcohol from any fermentation affects not only the distiller who, in the end, needs to sell it. It affects the exciseman, too. At the end of fermentation both he and the distiller can meet and calculate the amount of actual spirit that should be produced.

The wort, from the underback, cooled to about 70°F (21°C) by refrigeration or other form of cooling, is now run into enormous vats called washbacks. These were traditionally made from Oregon pine or larch but now are often made from stainless steel. They vary in size but a 10,000 gallon capacity is quite usual and even a small distillery would have four of them. Big distilleries would have a dozen. These washbacks are filled three quarters full and a measured amount of specially-chosen and prepared yeast is added—a really large vat would take more than three hundredweight.

Fermentation then begins almost immediately. On this scale it is a surprisingly noisy and violent business and the whole surface of the fermenting wort seethes and bubbles. Occasionally the whole washback can vibrate. It is the responsibility of the brewer in charge of the washback— incidentally, the most important and highly paid of all the craftsmen working in the distillery—to see that this crucial process is properly controlled and that the fermenting mass does not overflow. To prevent this happening, he has mechanical agitators fitted to each washback which, when used judiciously, release excess carbon dioxide and slow down over-fast fermentation. Before these mechanical stirrers were fitted the brewer's assistants would arm themselves with birch canes and lash an over-enthusiastic ferment as though it were a living creature. The amount of carbon dioxide produced in fermentation is very large, which is why the washbacks are always very well ventilated, with open windows to disperse the heavy gas. Being heavier than air, the carbon dioxide flows down over the side.

About 40 hours after fermentation, depending on temperature and humidity, the alcohol already produced by the yeast inhibits its further activity, a natural self-regulating mechanism. Fermentation is now complete.

The bubbling, frothy, mixture slowly quietens down and is finally still. The brewer now tests it for gravity, before it goes on to its final stage. What had started two days before as sugar-water has now been transformed into a beery liquid known as 'wash', a solution of yeast, alcohol and a few traces of other and unimportant chemicals in water. The alcoholic content will vary but will certainly be about five percent by volume and ten percent proof.

This wash is now pumped out of the fermenting backs into a large storage tank known as the 'wash charger' for the very final process of distilling. Single malt Scotch whisky is now ready to be born.

A typical wash charger.

Yeast

The antiquity of yeast is indicated by the discovery of fungi in certain fossilized plants dating from the Devonian period of the Paleozoic era, some 340 million years ago.

Egyptian tombs of the 11th Dynasty have yielded evidence of the use of yeast in the making of bread and beer. Prescriptions containing yeast are found in the earliest medical documents of the 16th century BC. We know that yeast was used for fermenting long before it was used as a leavening for bread, so we can be confident that the production of intoxicating liquor is one of the oldest skills that is known to man.

Yeast itself is a plant, one of the higher fungi. The particular yeast used in making whisky is classified as an ascomycetes, and its full Latin title is *Saccharomyces cerevisiae*, a simple minute organism. This particular yeast—and there are many hundreds of varieties—has an interesting history because it is the only one bred and developed by man, like a breed of cat or a variety of rose.

Over many centuries, brewers fermented their beer by taking a small quantity of yeast from their previous fermentation to start the next. They were not really interested in *how* it worked—all they knew was that it did. But over the years it became apparent that some yeasts fermented better and more quickly than others and, very gradually, a single strain was evolved. This became known as 'beer yeast' or 'brewer's yeast' and the yeast we use today is a descendant of this original strain.

The trouble was that until the last century even this brewer's yeast could be tricky to use. In transporting it from one vat to another it could easily be contaminated by wild yeasts (all yeasts other than brewer's yeast are known as wild yeasts) floating in the air, and these could affect the quality of the brew. So maintaining a pure yeast culture was largely a matter of luck.

Pasteur pioneered the change from chance to scientific control. The distillers of Lille, who made alcohol from sugar beet, were having a bad time during the middle of the 19th century. Their fermentations were being ruined by the persistence of wild yeasts and, in 1857, they called on the great French chemist to help them. Pasteur became fascinated and spent most

A mixture of malt grist and water is fermented. As the yeast attacks the sugar in the malt extract, the whole body of the wash bubbles and boils like a witch's cauldron.

of the next 20 years exploring the mysteries of fermentation and yeast. He soon distinguished the difference between the wanted and unwanted yeasts and was able to advise the distillers of Lille how to solve their problem.

But it was a contemporary of Pasteur, a Dane called Hansen, who devised the method by which a pure brewer's yeast culture can be maintained. He constructed a special yeast propagator which ensured that the yeast was grown under sterile conditions and propagators made on the same principle are used in British breweries today. So the whisky distiller can be sure that the yeast he uses is going to behave in exactly the same way as the yeast he used last time and will still be using on the day he retires.

What he needs is maximum sustained fermentation in the shortest possible time, and to achieve this he often uses two sub-varieties of brewer's yeast. One is the traditional kind, usually liquified. The other is dried baker's yeast. The former is fast-working and produces immediate and furious fermentation. The latter works more slowly but, once fermentation is induced, it helps to sustain it until all the sugar in the wort is converted into alcohol.

Distilling

The enormous, shining, onion-shaped copper vessels known as 'stills' are the heart of a distillery and the source of its greatest pride. It is within these stills that the final character of the whisky is shaped and its quality determined. If anything goes wrong here all the hard work and skill of the preparatory stages will have been wasted.

Because of this a considerable mythology now surrounds the stills and every stillman has his own idea of what goes on in the dark and sweltering interior of his burnished charges. Certainly, if a distillery is to be enlarged the distiller will insist that the new stills are as near as possible perfect replicas of the originals, even to the extent of purposely duplicating the dents and imperfections of the old ones.

The shape of the stills is crucial to the character of the finished whisky and, for instance, the shape of the relatively high and narrow stills at Glenmorangie certainly play some part in forming the extraordinary delicacy and sweetness of that particular whisky. Mr Peter Striach, the manager at Macallan and scion of the Kemp family who have owned and operated the distillery for generations, is emphatic that the shape of the still is the most important single factor in deciding the quality of the whisky, followed—in this order—by the heating method, the quality of the cask and the nature of the warehouse and, finally, the water from which the whisky is made. By usual standards this is a highly idiosyncratic opinion but the magnificent (and many

Wash from the wash receiver passes first into the stills to be distilled into low wines. It then passes through the spirit safe on the right into the low wines receiver.

56

would call it unsurpassed) quality of the whisky he produces means that his view deserves serious attention.

The complex problem of reflux—'molecules misbehaving', as someone put it—is another obsession with some distillers. Reflux is what happens in the neck of the still when violently agitated gases swirl about above the surface of seething and frothing liquid in the still. Some alcoholic vapour is forced back into the body of the liquid and this process affects the operation of the still. One distiller went so far as to provide for it by fixing a special arm to his still which allowed vapour from its upper part to be circulated directly into the main body of the still. Alas, there is no evidence that this interesting experiment had any effect, one way or the other, on the eventual finished malt whisky.

The inside surface of the still can be yet another factor in deciding the character of the individual whisky. The fierce processes of distillation produce a thick and uneven deposit on the walls of the still and this plays some subtle part in forming the whisky, possibly aiding heat retention. Mr Bob Gordon, the manager at Bunnahabhain says it is like the staining on the inside of a teapot. 'You never get a good cup of tea from a new teapot. It has to be used a number of times before you get a decent cup of tea. It's exactly the same with a still and whisky.'

Every distillery will have at least two stills and usually more. The larger is known as the 'wash still', the smaller the 'spirit still' or low wines still. They vary in shape, but all have a tapering neck which bends sharply to convey the vaporized alcohol away. Wash from the wash charger is run into the wash still. This can have a capacity of anything from 750 to 5000 gallons, although 3500 would be about average. The still is then heated. Individual distillers have strong views about which forms of heating result in the best whisky and have been known, when taking over a new distillery, to rip out their predecessor's installation and replace it with their own. But there are basically two forms—external heating by coal, gas or oil and internal heating by steam coil. Coal, gas or oil-fired stills are heated directly by a fire underneath the still. In this case there is a danger that the heated wash may stick to

the bottom and burn. To prevent this, base-heated stills have inside them a revolving 'rummager', the arms of which rotate and drag a copper chain mesh over the bottom to prevent any sticking. On the other hand, there are those distillers who claim that a little burnt wash not only does no harm to the distillate but actually improves it. There are as many views about heating stills as there are distillers.

Below: Almost 200 years have passed since this receiver and spirit safe were in use.

Bottom: The modern distiller has a number of low wine receivers. The distilling process is controlled by the switchboard in the background.

The alternative way of heating a wash still is by internal steam coils. These are becoming more and more popular because they are easier to control and maintain and are gradually replacing many of the older and more traditional coal fires.

Once the wash still is charged and the heating begun, the wash begins to heat up quite rapidly. Nowadays, in fact, it is common practice to preheat the wash before charging the wash still so that distillation begins almost immediately. Because alcohol has a lower boiling point than water it vaporizes first and fumes off to the top of the still. Here the narrow neck turns down sharply to pass, often through the stillhouse wall, to a condenser or worm tub. The modern condenser is a highly efficient heat exchanger which condenses the vaporized alcohol into its liquid form. The old fashioned worm tub is a coiled copper tube of diminishing diameter, enclosed in a large tub of cold water. This has continually to be renewed, either from a reservoir, storage tank or burn flowing near the distillery.

From the condenser or worm tub the alcohol is run off into a storage tank known as the 'low wines charger' via the spirit safe. This is an ingenious device which allows the stillman to test the strength of the distillate by remote control. The spirit safe looks rather like a big glass box containing a number of jars which can be charged with alcohol by moving spouts by means of external taps. Distilled water can also be added in a similar fashion. (Impure spirit goes cloudy when distilled water is added.) In each jar is a hydrometer for measuring the specific gravity of the contents of the jar. This means that the stillman can judge exactly what is happening at every stage of this first distillation.

The spirit safe is called a safe because it is guarded by enormous brass locks to which only the exciseman has the key. The spirit safe, in theory, is only opened and inspected when the distillery is closed down for its 'silent season' or annual overhaul. This normally takes place in summer and lasts about four weeks.

The 'low wines' spirit that passes to the low wines charger is weak and impure and needs to be redistilled to get true whisky. It contains only about 30 percent alcohol and obviously it needs to be refined and strengthened by redistillation before it

even approximates to the eventual finished malt whisky.

The second, smaller, spirit still is now charged from the low wines charger and heated. This time the alcohol vapour goes once more through the spirit safe and after this it proceeds to the final collection vessel, the spirit receiver. At this point, the resident exciseman is taking a great deal of interest and he will also be busy seeing that the amount of spirit, mutually agreed between the distiller and himself, that the wash will produce, is, in fact, going into the spirit receiver.

Because this is the final distillation, the stillman takes much more trouble with it than the first. One of his problems is that the character of the finished whisky depends to a certain extent on the congeners or 'impurities' present in the low wines. If no traces of these were left in the final distillation, whisky would be a far less

interesting and taste-full drink than it is.

Once the alcohol begins to vaporize in the spirit still, the stillman is busy at the spirit safe. He knows that the first liquids to appear—the 'foreshots'—are not, in fact, true ethyl alcohol at all but the more volatile or lighter alcohols, esters, aldehydes and acids. These he directs back to the low wines charger for further distillation. But he watches the spirit safe carefully until he sees that these substances no longer cloud the distilled water and that pure ethyl alcohol is being vaporized from the low wines. When he judges that this is so he turns the tap that feeds the distillate to the spirit receiver.

After a while all the true alcohol has been driven off and the higher temperature in the still begins to vaporize the heavier constituents of the low wines such as the fusel oils. These are known as 'feints'. These, too, must be eliminated and these,

too, are redirected back to join the fore-shots in the low wines and feints receiver for redistillation. In theory the stillman now has the true, pure spirit—the 'middle cut'—in the spirit receiver and the whole distilling process has been completed—or so it would appear.

But it is not quite as simple as that. The precise moment when the stillman decides that the foreshots have all gone—or nearly all gone—or that the feints have not yet appeared, or not appeared in too great a quantity, are matters for fine judgment. The relative proportions of these con-geners—aldehydes, furfurol, fusel oil, and so on—present in the final distillate is one of the most important factors which differentiates every single malt whisky from any other. The skill and judgment of the stillman determines what the mature whisky is going to taste like in five, ten or even twenty years in the future. Many

INTERMEDIATE SPIRIT RECEIVER

The intermediate spirit receiver, normally known as the low wines receiver, where dilute spirit goes from the wash still.

distillers believe that their stillmen operate as much from intuition as from the visual evidence available to them in the spirit safe.

Mr Harry Cockburn, the manager of Bowmore distillery, told me of a new complication to distilling which would never have occurred to William Ross and perhaps it is better that the old man never lived to hear of it. It is enshrined in the UK in the Equal Opportunities Act and means that distillers can no longer advertise for a stillman. Today it has to be a 'stillhouse operative'.

The final colourless spirit in the spirit receiver is finally run to the spirit store where it is reduced from 115°–118° proof to about 110° proof by adding distilled water. It is now ready for casking and for the long sleep of maturation.

A problem of disposal

When distillation is over, both the wash stills and the spirit stills remain charged with hot liquid, some thousands of gallons of useless dross which has, in the most literal sense, given up the spirit. The turbid gruel left in the wash still, a solution of dead yeasts and other carbohydrates, is called 'pot ale' or 'burnt ale'. The liquid left in the spirit still is almost pure water and is known as 'spent lees'. These liquid wastes are now run off into a receiving tank while the stills are cleaned. There they cool down. The problem now is what to do with them.

Originally these liquids were just pumped back into the stream below the distillery. This did not matter much when the distilleries were small. A few hundred gallons of soupy liquid once a fortnight made little difference. But tens of thousands of gallons a week or more, and several times this amount when a number of distillers draw on the same stream, would be quite unacceptable to Scottish trout and salmon fishermen, and, indeed, anyone else who cares for Scotland's rivers.

So the distilleries have come up with a number of solutions to the problem of liquid waste. D.C.L. recently invested £6 million in a multi-distillery effluent disposal scheme which produces pure water and 250,000 tons of high-protein animal food-stuffs every year. Some distilleries take it in tankers to the nearest sewage works. Others pump it directly into the sea, a practice increasingly frowned upon by local health authorities. Perhaps the most in-genious scheme is at Mortlach which pumps its liquid water under pressure to a nearby hillside and there ejects it as a fine spray. Could this be called the original Scotch mist, perhaps?

Casking and Maturing

A single malt whisky straight from the still is an impressive drink—raw, powerful and uncompromising. At 110° proof, a little is more than enough. But drink the same spirit five years later and an astonishing transformation will have taken place: the whisky will have mellowed and altered almost beyond recognition the palate is no longer outraged or the throat scorched. Another ten years and the malt will have flowered into a liquor that could only be equalled by a very fine Grande Champagne V.S.O.P. cognac. Most malt experts consider, with some justice, that no brandy made can equal a fine old malt whisky at its best.

But what makes the difference? What actually happens over those years when the cask sits in the whisky warehouse quietly preparing itself for its apotheosis on the palate of some future happy connoisseur? The first thing that has to be said is that nobody really knows. The chemistry of maturation remains a mystery and no one has been able to devise any acceptable measuring tools nor to define what it is that is to be measured (see footnote—p. 65). Yet, the difference is there—and greatly there. Even a totally untrained palate can detect it effortlessly and instantly. So what has happened can be described but not explained. Nor can the process be hastened. Up to a point, whiskies get better the longer you leave them in cask and there is no way of shortening this period artificially. From time to time stories circulate about methods of instant ageing—by electricity, by ultrasonics, by vibration, by incantation—but all of them prove to be without foundation. The fact

Casks of Macallan's whisky during its long sleep. If the casks were to be released from bond they would, at the time of writing, be liable to duty of £3,000 each.

The miracle in the barrel

In the cooperage at the Glen Moray distillery. Here, barrels are repaired by highly skilled craftsmen.

remains that at the end of a certain number of years raw spirit has been transformed into a rounded, smooth and mellow drink. But although we have no scientific scale by which to measure, or even an agreed vocabulary to describe, maturation we do know that there are three major factors which play their part—the whisky itself, the cask it matures in and the climate in which maturation takes place.

The whisky itself is the most intractable to deal with. If a chemical analysis of raw malt whisky is made it can be broken down into ethyl alcohol, pure water and traces of a number of organic compounds—esters, aldehydes, fusel oil, and so on. An analysis of the same spirit 15 years later shows exactly the same ingredients in exactly the same proportion— except for a gain or loss of water and perhaps the addition of an almost undetectable trace of sherry from the cask used for maturing. The slightly different

proportion of water is easily explained by evaporation or its reverse, but the addition or subtraction of distilled water could not effect the taste in any case. Neither could the trace of sherry possibly explain the difference. The sherry theory is finally squashed by the fact that some malt whiskies mature magnificently in plain oak casks which have never been within a thousand miles of Spain. All that can be said is that the elements of which malt whisky is constituted interact with each other over the years in some in-explicable way and that if science cannot detect this interaction, the palate can.

With the cask we are on easier ground. Here it is not difficult to describe and explain exactly what happens. The most important thing to remember is that the oak casks in which malt whisky is matured are not solid and impenetrable but porous and permeable. Over the years the spirit 'breathes' through them and

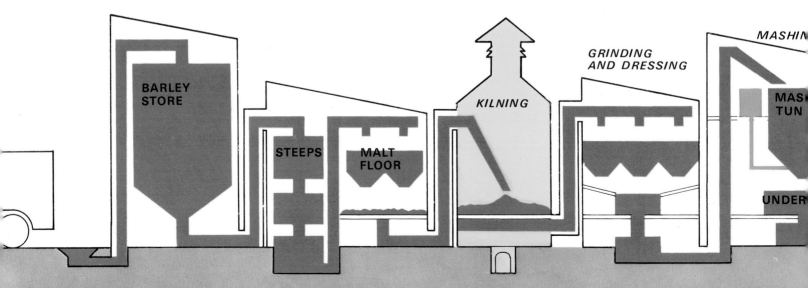

BARLEY STORE

STEEPS

MALT FLOOR

KILNING

GRINDING AND DRESSING

MASHIN

MAS
TUN

UNDER

there is almost conclusive evidence that the reverse process takes place, too. In fact, some experts claim they can tell a whisky that has been matured near the sea because they can detect the sea air that has breathed into the cask. But these are the realms of mysticism beyond the grasp of normal mortal whisky drinkers.

What is certain is that there is a loss both of volume and strength as the whisky matures. This might appear puzzling at first glance. Commonsense would seem to dictate that if the spirit reduces in volume it must become more concentrated and strong: this view is very widely held. But it is based on a false assumption about what is actually happening. In the first place, proportionately more volatile alcohol than water breathes itself out through the cask. Anyone who has ever entered a whisky warehouse will immediately be aware of the strong and pervasive smell of whisky. This disproportionate loss of alcohol explains the reduction in both volume and strength. Another factor is the humidity of the warehouse. A really damp warehouse will not only inhibit water getting out of the cask but, by absorption, actually diffuse some in. Conversely a really dry warehouse will lose more volume by evaporation but lose less in strength: it makes sense that under these circumstances the whisky would lose more water. Distillers universally favour the damp and cool warehouse rather than the warm and dry. They also universally agree that malt whisky naturally reduced both in strength and volume in this way is the better for it.

The customs and excisemen formally recognize this natural and inevitable loss from evaporation. They allow an overall two percent loss a year plus a further two percent for whisky in butts of 110 gallons or a further three percent for whisky in hogheads of 55 to 65 gallons. They estimate that a whisky can lose up to 15 percent of its volume before it is bottled—millions of gallons of delicious Scotch wafting into the air every year (Scotch mist again!). This process of evaporation is not, of course, progressive: otherwise, after a few decades in cask, there would be no whisky left. Experience shows us that casks a century old are still awash with spirit, although what it would taste like is another matter.

The size of cask also influences the speed of maturing. As the allowances for evaporation made by the excisemen would seem to indicate (and as in wine) the smaller the cask the faster the maturation. Thus, a single distillation of a malt whisky might be at its peak after ten years in a hogshead but only at 15 in a butt.

The nature of the casks is important too. By tradition oak casks are used for maturing whisky, used sherry casks being particularly favoured. In fact, the demand for used sherry casks among distillers exceeds supply by a very wide margin. This has inevitably resulted in increased prices and today the cost of sherry casks is a significant factor in the costings of the distilleries that use them.

The use of sherry casks has been established for more than a century. No one knows who first introduced them but, ironically, it seems probable that they were used because they were cheaper than new oak casks. In any case, it was soon found that they gave an inexplicable but unmistakable roundness and smoothness to whiskies matured in them. They also gave whisky some of its colour. Finos and Amontillados impart a pale tone, Olorosos

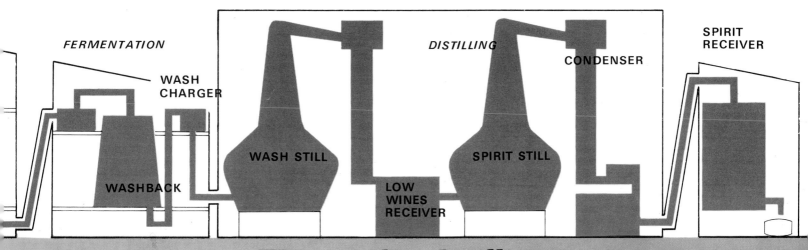

FERMENTATION   *DISTILLING*   SPIRIT RECEIVER

CONDENSER

WASH CHARGER

WASH STILL

SPIRIT STILL

WASHBACK

LOW WINES RECEIVER

The complete distilling process

a darker. Similarly, new sherry casks will give a deeper colour than those that have already been used. The shortage of used sherry casks has forced some distilleries to seek alternatives. The most popular of these are American oak casks previously used for maturing American whiskey. These casks arrive at the distillery as bundles of staves broken down from the original casks to be reassembled. On site this makes repairs and replacements simpler. These casks, too, will give colour to the finished malt whisky.

The whole business of the colour of whisky is full of pitfalls, mainly in the fields of psychology and aesthetics. It is a question of what people are used to and what they like. The colour of whisky has no influence whatsoever on its taste and Grants, in fact, make a magnificent malt which is quite colourless. But the people who buy whisky demand a familiar amber colour and, to this end, blenders will add small quantities of caramelized sugar to bring their over-pale whisky up to the shade that popular taste demands. By tradition, single malts are not artificially coloured, but as malts leave the distillery in casks and, as it is the business of bottlers and blenders to cater for their markets, it is possible that this tradition is more honoured in the breach than in the observance.

Once acquired, sherry casks are used over and over again and, indeed, when single staves are damaged or become decayed, they are replaced with staves cannibalized from other casks or with specially-made new ones. A veteran sherry cask can end up with less than half its original staves and some distillers genuinely have no idea just how old some of their casks are.

The third obvious influence on maturation is climate and it is probably the Scottish climate which ensures that Scotland and only Scotland can produce real Scotch. Sometimes harsh and raw, sometimes warm and soft—but nearly always moist—the Scottish climate provides ideal conditions for that subtle interchange of air and spirit through the permeable oak which gives the finished whisky its unique characteristics. Paradoxically, Scotland's climate seems to produce its opposite. From where it is most forbidding and inhospitable—from the windswept shores

The casks for maturing Scotch whisky must be made of oak. Originally, sherry casks were used but demand for them has now outstripped supply, so American oak casks are now used almost universally.

of Islay and the rugged glens of Inverness —come the deepest flavoured and most seductive malts. Conversely, the grain distilleries, with their crystalline and less characterful whisky are concentrated almost entirely in the milder lowlands.

Humidity is the key. And whatever the succession of hot dry summers it is certainly true that a malt aged ten years in casks will have spent most of its life in an atmosphere charged with moisture. Some distillers go even further than this, claiming that the very cycle of the Scottish climate—long wet winters, cool damp springs and autumns and short dry summers—itself plays a part in bringing a malt to perfect maturity. Here again we are in the realms where belief is more important than proven reality.

Another vexed question is that of the best age for malts. When are they at their peak and can they be too old? This must always be a highly subjective matter but although even among experts there are disagreements a number of general judgments emerge. First, best age varies from malt to malt. Some—very few—are drinkable at five years. David Daiches, in his book *Scotch Whisky*, says he has sampled several 'eminently drinkable' five-year old whiskies. Nearly all will improve in casks up to 10 years and many up to 15. Some of the heavier Islay malts improve up to 20 years and even longer. But most distillers would agree that a malt at 12 to 14 years old is a very splendid drink. After this, if it improves, the improvements are marginal. Broadly speaking the lighter-flavoured Highland malts mature earlier than the peatier Islay malts, but individual taste, in Scotch as in anything else, must take preference over received opinions.

If a single malt is left too long in the cask it can begin to deteriorate. It seems that it absorbs deleterious substances from the cask itself and acquires a 'woody' flavour, losing finesse and palatability. Like much else connected with malt whisky, the chemistry of this is obscure but its effect is unmistakable. Again, there are puzzling exceptions. Casks over a century old have been breached and the whisky inside found to be in excellent condition, if a little faded. But these would be exceptions. Distillers are occasionally asked to inspect and sample ancient casks of malt discovered in some forgotten

corner of a cellar. Almost always they are undrinkable: they will have completely lost the smoothness that sets malt whisky apart from all other drinks; the delicate flavour of the peat, the malted barley and wood will have disappeared entirely. The aftertaste will be an insult to even the most underdeveloped palate.*

Scotch, like any other spirit, does not age in bottle, although here again there are fanatics who claim they can detect differences in malts that have been in the bottle a very long time. Bottles of these antique whisky vintages turn up occasionally and can be regarded as much as curiosities as potable spirit. The truth is that there are, and can be, no yardsticks. And a reverence for great age itself can induce a psychological conditioning attuned to discovering merits that are only subjectively present. The best advice to anyone discovering an ancient bottle of whisky would be to drink it gratefully rather than bother about its ambience.

Nevertheless, there are some very distinguished old malts and I have personally sampled a 42-year old Glen Grant that commonsense dictated should not have been allowed to remain in cask for that length of time. But in this case it had worked. It was an astonishing drink; silky and mellow and with harmonies that lingered on the palate for a very long time. I was not allowed very much of it and I was profoundly glad it had been bottled when it had, and the risks of allowing it another year in cask not taken. But for normal times and purses it would be hard to improve on a 15-year old malt. Daiches has enjoyed a 68-year old Longmorn.

Personal taste must remain the final arbiter. While the great whisky savants of the Highlands might pontificate on the incomparability of a Speyside whisky of 15 years, a less sophisticated palate might prefer a younger and less sophisticated malt. *Experimentia docet*!

---

*One or two distillers are experimenting with gas chromotography as a possible research tool. This is a modern and highly sensitive method of discovering the constituents of a substance even to minute traces. It can then easily detect changes almost undetectable by other means. The trouble is that the technique provides a highly complex profile of whisky and no-one yet has found out a useful way of determining which are the significant peaks and valleys of the profile.

3 THE JOYS OF MALT WHISKY

The River Spey at Craigellachie in Banffshire. The distillery at Craigellachie produces whisky which is used in the blending of White Horse, one of the most popular blended Scotches. The river itself supplies the water for many of the most famous distilleries in Scotland, which are scattered along the length of its banks.

Pure malt whisky, served generously and neat, uncontaminated by the barbarities of ginger ale, soda or lemonade, and with its subtleties unmurdered by ice, is a noble drink, idiosyncratic, powerful, reflective. This is true of the whole spectrum of malts, from the smooth and silky lightness of a Glenmorangie to the pungent grandeur of a Laphroaig, from the mellow grace of a Linkwood to the organ notes of the mighty Glenlivet of Glenlivets—*The Glenlivet.*

Yet all have some things in common. Pure, clear water, whether it be from the rushing burns of Speyside or the quiet lochs of Islay; the best barley in the world, be it English, Indian, Australian or—in the case of D.C.L.—Scottish; and peat, black and brick hard or dun and crumbling, but Scottish peat, formed and ripened by a million Scottish summers. The Scottish climate helps, too, with mild dry summers and long wet winters, perfect for transforming a harsh and powerful new spirit into a glowing masterpiece.

Finally, there is the skill and devotion of the servants of malt whisky, the men who make it; the peat-cutter piling his turves, the maltman turning his barley, the brewer tending his washback, the stillman controlling his stills. Their mind and muscle inhabit every ounce of malt whisky.

All these—and much, much more—make Scottish malt whisky the spirit it is. It can never be a majority taste like the blended whiskies—excellent as these are—because not enough of it is made. It is a mere drop in an ocean of less demanding spirits. But for those of us who love it, it will remain the drink of drinks.

Classifying single malts

There are traditionally four types of single malt whisky, based on the four areas of Scotland where they are distilled. But, in fact, the whiskies taste different enough, category by category, to enable the expert blender to place them quite easily. This is not to say that there are not great variations within each category, but that the whiskies within each have enough common characteristics to announce their presence clearly.

As in all matters of taste, pronouncing judgement on a whisky or a group of whiskies is a highly subjective matter: 'I like what I know and I know what I like'. Nevertheless, where there is a long-received opinion about the way a particular whisky should taste there is generally some substance to it. When such an opinion has been held over several generations, then it is usually fair to assume that it has a solid basis in fact.

We have—to look at a parallel situation in a different field—no way of telling what the great clarets and burgundies of the 19th century actually tasted like, and we never can have. But we can allow ourselves to believe that we have a fair idea because we make wine today in very much the same way and use the same words to describe it. Similarly, we can never tell what a whisky such as Mortlach or Ardmore tasted like a century ago. But we know what people said about it and it sounds very much what we would say today. On the evidence available on those very rare occasions when a really ancient and unspoiled bottle of malt whisky turns up from some forgotten corner and is duly and reverently sampled, it seems that distillers have not changed the basic character of their whiskies much over the years. What small differences can be discovered are usually attributed to the quality of the barley. Ancient Scottish barley did not produce as rich a malt as modern imported barleys and old whiskies tend to be a fraction drier than their modern counterparts. But the peating and maturing, the processes which give whisky its precise and local character, seem to have remained very much the same.

One final and fascinating reflection of this continuity of character of individual malt whiskies is the surprising frequency of continuity of trade of the people who actually make it. In many Scottish distilleries there is a strong family tradition going back for generations—not only a tradition of working in the same distillery but of actually working in the same job. So you will find malting families, brewing families, stillhouse families all with memories—and usually photographs to verify them—going back into the remote past of their Scottish town or village. Their traditions of loyalty to a particular distillery is another intangible but memorable extra that comes free with every glass of malt whisky.

The four types of malt are, in order of seniority if not size, Highland malts, Islay malts, Lowland malts and Campbeltown malts. All have their afficionados, although it is fair to say that most malt whisky drinkers would admit that the crown must go to the Highland malts and, more especially, to the Speyside malts. Among the Speyside malts, superb individually and as a group, the crown of crowns is usually accorded to those malts which describe themselves as 'Glenlivets'.

Gilbey's Glenspey-Glenlivet distillery which was established in 1885 in the town of Rothes. It produces a fine malt whisky which is used in the blending of Gilbey's Spey Royal.

The Highland malts

The great bulk of single malts comes from the Scottish Highlands. This area embraces distilleries as far north as Old Pulteney in Wick, as far west as Oban in its namesake, as far east as Glenugie at Peterhead and as far south as Glengoyne in Killearn. This enormous area (which conventionally includes Island whiskies such as Talisker and Highland Park, although these have been separately treated in this book) produces an extraordinary range of malt whiskies, including all the well-known and most popular. Many of these are light and fragrant with none of the overpowering peatiness which makes some Islay malts a specialist and minority taste.

There are several rather confusing sub-divisions of Highland malt. One describes West Highland malts as Islay and Campbeltown malts, which is patently a misnomer. On the other hand, Eastern malts is well accepted as a general description of those whiskies distilled in Banffshire and adjoining parts of Aberdeenshire and Morayshire. But unless they are to be left out altogether you have to include distilleries in Inverness-shire, Ross-shire, Sutherland, and places even further afield. My own belief is that 'Eastern malts' is a kind of shorthand for the great concentration of malts on and around the river Spey. Of these, Speyside malts proper form a sub-division, with the Glenlivets an even further sub-division.

Even within these sub-divisions there are enormous variations of type, flavour and quality. Two distilleries next door to each other and drawing their water from the same stretch of river can turn out malt whiskies which seem to bear no relation to each other. Distilleries 100 miles apart can produce whiskies which are remarkably alike. It is all rather odd.

Choosing between them is bound to be invidious because personal taste plays such a large part in deciding. With malt whisky there is no 'cru' system as with French clarets, with first, second, third, fourth and fifth growths. But perhaps there ought to be.

Not surprisingly, the experts do not agree. In his classic book *Whisky* written in 1930, Aeneas Macdonald nominates his 12 great malts: The Glenlivet, Glen Grant, Highland Park, Glenburgie, Cardow, Balmenach, Royal Brackla, Glenlossie,

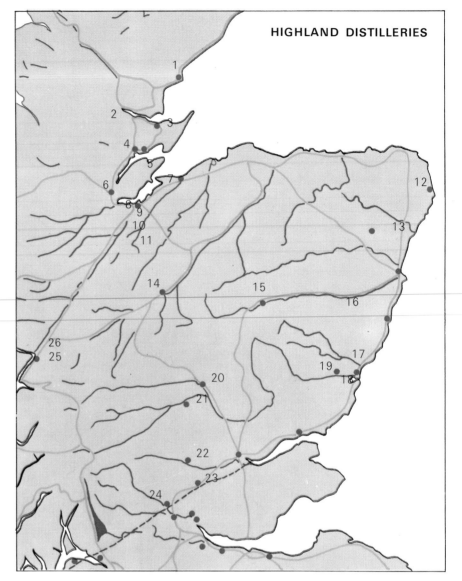

HIGHLAND DISTILLERIES

Longmorn, Macallan and Linkwood. The twelfth he divides between Clynelish and Talisker. Apart from Talisker and Highland Park, both Island malts, all the others are near or about Speyside, and eight of them are Glenlivets. Interestingly, there is not a single Islay malt in Macdonald's valhalla. Professor R. J. S. McDowall in his book *The Whiskies of Scotland*, first published in 1967, would add Mortlach, Strathisla and Glenmhor. Neil Gunn in *Whisky in Scotland*, 1935, favours both Glenmhor and Old Pulteney. David Daiches in his more recent and much more comprehensive book praises— among others—Glenmorangie, Dalmore, Glenmhor, Linkwood, Longmorn, The Glenlivet, Glen Grant and Macallan. I would not disagree with any one of these, but would add a personal plea for Glendullan, first bottled in 1972.

1 Brora-Clynelish
2 Balblair
3 Glenmorangie
4 Dalmore
5 Ben Wyvis
6 Ord
7 Royal Brackla
8 Glen Albyn
9 Glen Mhor
10 Millburn
11 Tomatin
12 Glenugie
13 Glengarioch
14 Dalwhinnie
15 Lochnagar
16 Glenury Royal
17 Hillside
18 Lochside
19 Glencadam
20 Blair Athol
21 Aberfeldy
22 Glenturret
23 Tullibardine
24 Deanston
25 Ben Nevis
26 Glenlochy

The Glenlivets

If there is one name which conjures up all that is finest and best about Scotch whisky, this is the one—Glenlivet. It is redolent of the grandeur of wild and desolate Highland mountainsides, the delicate music of burns cascading over granite boulders, the crisp bite of Scottish autumn mornings. Yet Glenlivet itself encompasses none of these things, being merely a smallish river valley following the course of one of the many tributaries to the Spey, itself a small river by all but the most parochial standards.

Yet the name Glenlivet still resounds and has still been found worthy of incorporating into lesser names to give them an added power and authority. True, some are now rather sheepishly dropping 'Glenlivet' from their title because they feel they can survive on their own merits without it. But there was a time when men felt that a whisky that wasn't a Glenlivet was hardly a whisky at all, and whiskies whose owners had never been within a day's march of the Spey had it hurriedly added to their name. Thus we reach the ironic conclusion that while we can say that all Speyside whiskies are good, and those Speyside whiskies which are also Glenlivet whiskies are exceptionally good, the name Glenlivet does not necessarily and in every case denote that absolute level of quality that it is often deemed to do. This situation is saved in many cases by the fact that many of the hyphenated Glenlivets are never bottled and are only used in blending. But I have always been curious to taste some of these pseudo-Glenlivets to test if my suspicions are correct.

Having said that, there is no question at all that, as a class, the true Glenlivets stand head and shoulders above all other malts. Individuals may have their own special favourite malts; my own, I admit, is not a Glenlivet but the light and delicate Glenmorangie from 50 miles farther north, but few would disagree with Aeneas Macdonald's judgment which puts two-thirds of the dozen best whiskies under the Glenlivet title. Among these, it is true to say, are some which are shedding the Glenlivet title: Macallan has already done so, as have Glendullan, Linkwood and Balmenach. I have already classified these as simple Speyside malts—and the rest are seldom referred to in the double-barrelled way. But the name Glenlivet clings, giving its royal accolade to the finest malt spirits the world has ever tasted or ever will taste.

To add to the confusion every writer on malt whisky has his own firm conviction as to what is or is not a true Glenlivet. Hugh McDiarmid says 'Of the Glenlivets only seven have survived to appear now as single malts. Most are used for blending only'. Even more puzzling, he includes Tomatin and Cardow among his Glenlivets. Daiches lists no less than 30. The variously edited book *Scotch Whisky* has 16 and this includes two that Daiches does not. McDowall has 23; he also claims that only seven of these are bottled when from his own list I can see 15 that I have sampled from the bottle. Perhaps D.C.L. are showing the way by withdrawing the name from all those malts they own that have traditionally used it. In the meantime I gladly leave the resolution of this problem to some future historian.

Glenlivet did once get the royal accolade in a very direct manner. In 1822 George IV visited Scotland and asked for Glenlivet. Elizabeth Grant, of Rothiemurchus, tells

All distilleries are dependent on constant supplies of water. As a distillery expands its operations the line of buildings will normally follow the course of the river, as here at Convalmore.

The best of the best

the tale: 'Lord Conyngham, the Chamberlain, was looking everywhere for pure Glenlivet whisky; the King drank nothing else. It was not to be had out of the Highlands. My father sent word to me—I was the cellarer—to empty my pet bin, where was whisky long in wood, long in uncorked bottles, mild as milk, and the true contraband gout in it. Much as I grudged this treasure it made our fortunes afterwards, showing on what trifles great events depend. The whisky and 50 brace of ptarmigan all shot by one man, went up to Holyrood House, and were graciously received and made much of.'

Finally, James Hogg the Ettrick Shepherd says—'Gie me the real Glenlivet, and I weel believe I could mak' drinking toddy oot o' sea water. The human mind naver tires o' Glenlivet, any mair than o' caller air. If a body could just find oot the exac' proportions and quantity that ought to be drunk every day, and keep to that, I verily trow that he might leeve for ever, without dying at a', and that doctors and kirkyards would go oot o' fashion.'

The Glenlivet. It sometimes seems that history distributes her favours unfairly. There is no reason why the first should necessarily be the best. The historical accident which led the proud and pugnacious George Smith to take out the first official licence for a distillery in 1824 should have no bearing on the spirit he distilled. Nevertheless, Smith's Glenlivet, then and now, remains one of the supreme examples of the distiller's art.

To be sure, the distillery had much going for it. As Robert Bruce Lockhart says, 'It has a superb site and stands on a pleasant brae half way between Ballindelloch and Tomintoul in the heart of the remote and still unspoilt Highlands.

'Apart from its beauty, the glen provided all the essentials of good whisky. The fertile fields of the Laichs of Banff and Moray were made for barley. The Livet which waters the place runs down in a sparkling liquid stream from the Cairngorms. A few miles away is the renowned Faemussach mossy moor with its almost inexhaustible deposits of the finest peat. The air makes you feel as if you were walking on top of the world. As for the distiller... there was, towards the end of the 18th century, a wider knowledge of distilling in the Glenlivet–Tomintoul area

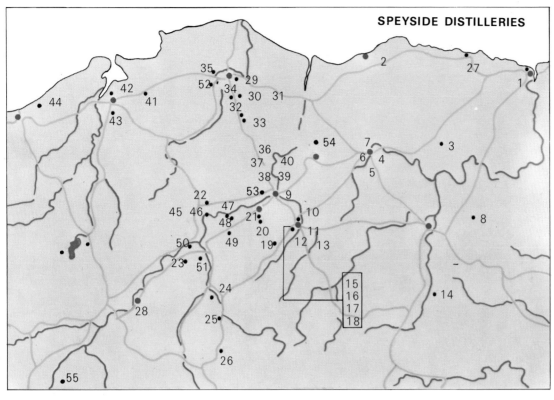

than in any other part of Scotland'.*
These few sentences sum up the natural
advantages that the original Glenlivet
distiller started with. But there are other
distilleries, as finely placed, with as good
water and peat as rich, which yet cannot
reach the same heights.

Of course, this has been the case for at
least two centuries. Certainly the malt
whiskies of Glenlivet were famous long
before they were legal.

George Smith's new and legal distillery
prospered mightily and the reputation of
its whisky, already great, quickly spread
across the whole of Scotland. This fact did
not escape the attention of other distilleries
who saw a shortcut to prosperity by
adding the name to their own malts. None
of these drew their water from the Livet
and some of them were far from the Spey.
Torrents of whisky calling themselves
'Glenlivet' poured from the Highlands and
the Smiths began to fear for their reputation. Nasty stories circulated that Glenlivet was the longest glen in Scotland.
Finally, in 1880, the distillery went to court

with a test case. Could anyone call their
whisky Glenlivet, or should the name be
restricted to the one and original glen?
The court met Smith halfway. Only the
original distillery could call itself *The*
Glenlivet. The others could only use it
hyphenated with their own names. Many
of them chose to do so and have continued
to until today.

Glenlivet itself lies on the road between
Tomintoul and Dufftown; and the Livet
burn, fed by a number of smaller burns
from the surrounding hills, runs nine miles
approximately northwest to join the River
Avon which itself joins the Spey a few
miles further downstream.

A very great deal indeed has been
spoken in praise of Smith's *The* Glenlivet.
A century ago Barnard said: 'Smith's
Glenlivet has become a household word
and the whisky is appreciated in every
country.' Others are less modest in their
praise, 'a great whisky', 'the premier
whisky of the world', 'Smith's Glenlivet
knows no superior, if any equal, in its own
country', 'full and sophisticated', 'one of
the very finest of Highland malt whiskies
and indeed has a claim to be considered
the champion of them all'. '*The* Glenlivet
whisky has a deep mellowness and a ripe
fullness of flavour together with a delicacy
of aroma which is easy to recognize. It has

---

* Lockhart was right at that time, but today Smith's
Glenlivet distillery draws its water from local wells
'where peat and granite are not conspicuous', and
imports the peat, as do some other distilleries, from
Pitsligo in Aberdeenshire.

Opposite: The distillery at
Convalmore is one of the
Glenlivets which occasionally
bottles its malt.

Two more glens and three more whiskies

a subtle peatiness without being agressively peaty and a gentle sweetness without any loss of freshness'. 'At its best Smith's Glenlivet combines a teasing subtlety of flavour with a distinctive "nose" and fullness', 'the sweetness mingles with the peatiness and the fullness in a most intriguing way'. It is bottled at eight, 12 and 15 years old and at 70°, 80° and 100° proof. It's an amazingly complete whisky, with a delicious nose and deep undertones of flavour, both of peat smoke and of the original barley. But in fairness there are at least two other Glenlivets—Macallan and Linkwood—which I personally find at least its equal.

Let the last words be spoken by an anonymous poet whose old rhyme speaks the truth again:

> *'Glenlivet it has castles three*
> *Drumin, Blairfindy and Deskie*
> *And also one distillery*
> *More famous than the castles three.'*

Glen Grant. After Glenfiddich, Glen Grant is probably the most widely distributed and popular single malt whisky. The distillery is at Rothes and has been established there since 1840, although the two Grant brothers who founded it had been distilling at a nearby farm for six years previously. Most of the whisky distilled today goes for blending but the small percentage left is bottled at a surprising number of ages. I myself have sampled five, eight, ten, 12, 15, 21, 25, 35 and 38-year old Glen Grant from the bottle, and on one occasion a dram of 42-year old from a private source. Glen Grant also matures some of its malt in new oak casks which produce a completely colourless whisky which, although it must be regarded as something of a curiosity, is nevertheless a first class and very drinkable malt. Because there are so many varieties of Glen Grant, there are a number of opinions about this fine malt. R. J. S. McDowall says 'Glen Grant whisky at its best has a distinction and flavour which is different from the other Glenlivets. Before the War many would have said that it was the best malt and I have some without a date of smooth almost unbelievable quality'. Daiches thinks that the 15-year old is the best but that the ten-year old is a fine whisky and the eight-year old 'eminently drinkable'.

He also goes on to say: 'How does Glenlivet compare with Glen Grant? In general character they are not dissimilar; each has that smooth integration of peatiness, softness and full sweetness (or almost sweetness) that needs age to bring out. Like Glenlivet, Glen Grant is conspicuously better at ten, or better still, 12 years old than at, say, five (and it is available at five years old). There is a sharpness about a young Glen Grant that belies its true potential. I once compared a 17-year old Glen Grant with a ten-year old, and I noted in my whisky scrap book that it was not the first sip of each that showed the real difference, but after a steady comparative sipping the superior mellowness of the 17-year old as against the ten-year old became evident.

'A well-matured Glen Grant has a splendid smoothness; it is not perhaps, such a complexedly patterned whisky in the combination of nose, taste and after-taste that is found in Glenlivet at its best, being more of a single minded whisky.'

I find it one of the most pleasant of all malts to drink although not of outstanding distinction. It also happens to be the single malt I am offered most often.

Tamnavulin. This brand new distillery was built in 1966 at Tomnavulin, a few miles upstream from the original Glenlivet distillery, on the site of an old mill; the name itself means 'the mill on the hill'. It is a true Glenlivet, although the rather stark concrete construction of the building contrasts strongly with its older and more rambling neighbour. Tamnavulin draws its water from local springs and the River Livet. It uses 'plump' barley for malting and, although this is reputed to produce a less smooth and flavoured whisky, it is a little early to judge the quality of the finished future malt. Certainly it was tested for some five years before and, in 1974, it was considered to be fit to bottle at 75° proof. Experts are sure it will improve greatly as it matures.

Glenfarclas. This distillery was established in 1836 at Ballindalloch on the lower slopes of Ben Rinnes, not far from where the Avon joins the Spey. The name is supposed to mean 'Glen of the Green Grassland'. Originally Glenfarclas malted its own barley and kilned it with local peat but since 1972 it has bought its barley ready peated. The distillery draws

The distillery at Glendullan began bottling its malt in 1972 and has already established itself so firmly that the suffix 'Glenlivet' has been dropped from its name.

its water from the Green Burn and its stills are gas heated. It has now been modernized and has a purpose-built reception centre and museum which features a confiscated illicit still and rich panelling from the Liner SS *Australia*. It bottles its whisky at various strengths—70°, 80°, 100°, and 105° proof. It is very popular with blenders and has been described as 'a forceful Highland malt', 'a fine full flavoured malt' and 'full bodied and assertive'. Daiches says he would regard it as an after-dinner, rather than an all purpose, whisky and I have always found it a little overpowering both in nose and flavour.

Aberlour. At Charlestown of Aberlour, overlooked by the two peaks of Ben Rinnes and Ben Aigan. It draws its waters from the River Lour, which comes from the side of Ben Rinnes and the distillery itself is the site of the Well of St Dunstan. There has been a distillery on the site from 1826 but, after a disastrous fire, it was totally rebuilt in 1880. In recent times the demand for its malt has increased so much that the distillery has had to treble its output within 20 years. The whisky it produces is

'smooth, sound and has a distinctive flavour', 'a light-bodied malt of individuality'. It bottles its whisky at nine years old and 70° proof. I find it typically Speyside, rather dry and light.

Longmorn. This distillery is just off the main road about halfway between Rothes and Elgin, on the track of an old and disused railway, although, in fact, it is still connected by a small, private railway to its sister distillery Benriach, just up the road. It draws its water from a local perpetual spring and it also cuts its peat locally. It heats its wash stills by coal and its spirit stills by steam. Strictly speaking, it is some little way from the Spey although it is one of Macdonald's chosen twelve. It was built in 1894 and bottles its malt at ten and 12-years old and at 70° proof. Longmorn has been recognized as one of the truly outstanding Glenlivets. 'Famous for its terriffic bouquet, which can stand comparison with that of a glass of the finest after dinner brandy' . . . 'it has an outstanding bouquet worthy of a brandy glass after dinner' . . . 'full, virile whisky with a fine nose'. Longmorn must be one of the longest-lasting whiskies in history. Daiches tells of the occasion when he drank 68-year old Longmorn: 'I recently drank, at Longmorn distillery, whisky from a cask that was filled in April 1899 and broached in 1967. By all the rules it should have gone "woody"—and indeed, it should have evaporated, because a loss of two percent per annum over 68 years should yield less than nothing. But in fact it was not woody at all: it had lost strength and body, but it was pleasant and mellow though (surprisingly perhaps) without the character of a much younger Longmorn.' An astonishing story.

Tamdhu. This charming little distillery at Knockando is overlooked by its big neighbour, Cardow. It was built in 1897 by a syndicate who very quickly sold it to Highland Distilleries who have owned it since before the turn of the century. It malts its barley by the Saladin method. Much of the whisky it produces is exported but a certain amount goes into bottle at eight years old and 70° proof. Its whisky is 'typically Speyside with a good flavour and not too peaty'.

Tomintoul. In 1800 Tomintoul was described as a place where 'everyone made whisky and everyone drank it', which seems a very satisfactory state of affairs. It was also described as 'a wild mountain village where drinking, dancing, swearing and quarrelling went on all the time'. Perhaps there is a connection.

Whatever the history of the village, Tomintoul has the distinction of being the highest distillery in Scotland, at more than 1,100 feet above sea level. Before this time, this honour belonged to Dalwhinnie; Mr Duncan, the new distillery manager there, showed me a rather sad photograph where this fact was proudly proclaimed in enormous white letters on the roof of his distillery.

It is also one of the very newest distilleries, building being started in 1964; work to double production was started in 1974. It lies on the Lecht road between Grantown and Ballater on a pass between four hills, drawing its water from the spring of Ballantuan, about a quarter of a mile above the distillery. This was closely observed for a year before the decision to build was taken. Tomintoul first bottled its malt in 1972 at 70° proof. It is a standard Glenlivet, a little lighter than most.

Flavours, full and fragrant

Strathisla. This is believed to be the oldest operating distillery in Scotland. It has certainly been working since 1786 and may have been producing malt whisky long before that. A stone in its wall bears the date 1695. It is situated just outside the historic town of Keith and until recently was known as the 'Milton' distillery. Its water comes from a spring sited above the distillery and is collected in a reservoir. Strathisla malt is bottled at eight, ten and 12 years old and at 75° and 100° proof.

In 1950 the distillery was bought by Chivas Bros, a subsidiary of Seagrams. Strathisla single malt whisky is the basis for the famous Chivas Regal blend. But Strathisla whisky itself is a very distinguished malt. McDowall says that Macdonald's famous dozen is an unfair classification today because there are several whiskies now, including Strathisla, which are every bit as good. Other opinions are 'full and fragrant, somewhere between Glenlivet and Mortlach', 'a rich, full-flavoured whisky in the best tradition of Glenlivet'. I find it a pleasantly, mellow and forceful malt with an excellent nose.

Dufftown. Not surprisingly, one of Dufftown's seven. A new distillery, Pittyvaich-Glenlivet is now in operation next to it. The town itself is served by two burns, the Fiddich and Dullan, both beautiful burns in beautiful glens. It is in the latter that the Dufftown distillery is situated, although it actually takes its water from Jock's Well, a bountiful source of water that is ideal for distilling. The distillery itself was built in 1887 and it produces 'a typically peaty Speyside malt that is much sought after by blenders'. Someone else describes it as 'a fine example of Speyside whisky'. It is bottled at eight years old and at 70° proof.

Glenrothes. Built in 1878 just outside Rothes, the distillery is sited a little way up the Glen of the Rothes Burn, the source of which is in the Mannoch Hills. This soft and brown-tinged water—perfectly pure and clean—is ideal for the purpose of distillation. The distillery has recently been totally reconditioned. Most of its production goes for blending but some is bottled at eight, ten and even 20 years old and at 70° proof. 'A strong peaty "nose", if not the subtlest, one of the fullest of

Eastern malts, a whisky of great character'. Another writes about it as 'a typically delicious Speyside whisky'.

Glenburgie. At Forres, a long way west of Speyside it still classes itself as a Glenlivet. The distillery was first founded in 1810. It bottles some of its malt and it is included in Macdonald's great dozen.

Glenlossie. An Elgin distillery, it is also named by Macdonald in his list of twelve. It is named after the River Lossie.

Glenallachie. A new distillery built in 1967 at Aberlour in Banffshire. It was totally designed by the same company which also helped build Tullibardine and Jura. It bottles its malts at over eight years old.

Glen Moray. This distillery is sited a few miles north of Elgin. It bottles its malts at ten years old and 70° proof.

Glen Elgin. Sited a little south of Longmorn. It is architecturally interesting because of its six external worm tubs. It bottles its malt whisky at 12 years old and 75° proof.

Miltonduff. Another Elgin distillery, founded in 1824. It has recently been completely rebuilt to double its capacity to two million gallons of spirit a year. The distillery retains a picturesque waterwheel as a memento of a more romantic past: it was water-powered until Hiram Walker took it over in 1936. Miltonduff is bottled at 12 years and 75° proof. Its sister distillery is Glenburgie.

Other malts which have used the name Glenlivet and may occasionally bottle their own malts are: Benriach, Speyburn, Benromach, Coleburn, Convalmore, Cragganmore, Craigellachie, Glen Keith, Imperial and Braes of Glenlivet.

Opposite: Dufftown-Glenlivet malt whisky is a fine Speyside malt. The distillery was established in 1896 and purchased by Bells in 1933.

Glenallachie is a comparatively new distillery with little of the faded antiquity of most malt distilleries. Yet there is nothing young or new about the mature malt whisky it produces.

Speyside malts

The Spey is Scotland's second longest river, famous for its fishing—salmon, salmon trout and brown trout—and for the never-ending variety of the natural beauty that accompanies it from its source and the sources of its tributaries, until it discharges itself into the cold and choppy waters of Spey Bay on the Moray Firth. The main stream rises in the vicinity of the Corrieyairack Forest a few miles north of Loch Laggan in central Scotland. From here it flows north and east, first through bare and mountainous scenery that gradually gives way to picturesque valleys and thickly clustered woodlands.

The Spey is also Britain's fastest-flowing river and this may well be a contributary reason for its other great claim to fame. Along its beautiful banks and those of its tributaries are concentrated more distilleries than anywhere else in the world. Oddly enough, very few of them draw their water directly from the Spey, preferring to use nearby wells and numerous small burns that flow into the main river. But they do use the river to discharge their used water into and it is a sign of the care they take with this that the extensive (and expensive) fishing beats along the river do not complain.

The River Spey, the fastest flowing of all Britain's rivers, is the 'father' of many of the finest malt whiskies. The river rises in the Corrieyairack Forest west of the small Loch Spey from which it takes its name. The water is ideal for distillers' purposes—cold, clear and pure.

By common usage Speyside whiskies include not only those which are actually on the river itself but all those in its general area. They share the same scenery, the same climate, the same general conditions. So they permit themselves to describe themselves as Speyside malts.

There is no common quality that infuses all the Speyside malts except quality itself. These are the aristocrats of whisky (and some would say of all spiritous liquors), many with lineages going back into the mists of Scottish history. Some have a noble simplicity, a robust distinction born of the bleak glens which produced them. Others have the subtle and complex character of ancient Scottish townships and only release their secrets as they expand on the palate. Yet others have a sweet and gentle delicacy that can mislead the unwary drinker who forgets the solid alcoholic punch they all carry. No two are alike. They can share the same water, the same peat, the same barley. They can lie side by side in the same soft Scottish air, quietly maturing together. Yet at the end of ten years one will be a perfect and mellowed masterpiece and the other will only have just started on its journey to greatness. All that can be said is that every Speyside malt that is bottled repays the most careful and respectful attention. For the true malt lover the only tragedy is that about half of them are forbidden to him in that they go straight from the distillery to the blender's vat. The possible glories of these as single malts remain the privileged knowledge of those few people who actually make them.

The whiskies described here are in no particular order of merit and they do not include any of the Glenlivets, which we have already dealt with. Glenlivets, of course, are Speyside malts by definition.

Caperdonich. Built in 1897 alongside its sister distillery of Glen Grant. For some extraordinary reason, the excise authorities of the time insisted that the whisky distilled at the new Caperdonich distillery be piped to the the Glen Grant distillery next door, where the two whiskies were mixed. The whisky was pumped from the one to the other by a pipe which ran under the main street of Rothes and was known as the 'Whisky Pipe'. All too soon the new distillery fell into serious trouble. It became involved in the great slump which

followed the crash of Pattinsons in 1898 and in 1901 it had to close its doors.

However, in 1965, in view of the rapidly increasing world demand for whisky, Grants reopened the derelict distillery and in 1967 completely modernized it. It is now probably the most automated malt distillery in Scotland, with every process controlled by a central control panel. Its new stills are heated by steam coils and the new distillery buys its barley ready malted.

Because of its newness, Caperdonich malt whisky in bottle is only just beginning to be fit to drink. Nor is it yet bottled in great quantity. All that can be said is that it shows many of the qualities of Glen Grant while being a noticeably different spirit, fresher and slightly sharper and without the noted floweriness characteristic of Glen Grant.

There are very few bars that do not have at least one vintage of Glen Grant malt whisky on their shelves. This is the label from a bottle of ten-year-old whisky, but the distillery bottles at various ages.

Cardow (Cardhu). This famous malt distillery is magnificently sited at Knockando, with a superb view over the Speyside valley of Craigellachie, itself the home of another famous distillery. It was originally founded by a man called John Cumming in 1824 on the site of a long established illicit still. At that time it had a most peculiar leasing arrangement which expired every 19 years. This meant that the owners had no incentive to invest in any mechanical handling equipment and so for many years the distillery was operated by hand in a very primitive fashion. Barnard records that 'the establishment was originally built on the farm of Cardow, without any title to the building, beyond the currency of the lease, which periodically expired every 19 years. When we saw it, the buildings were of the most straggling and primitive description and, although water power existed, a great part of the work was done by manual labour. It is wonderful how long this state of things continued, considering the successful business that was carried on for so many years.' But changes had taken place. Barnard adds: 'Previous to the time of our visit a feu had been obtained to a piece of ground in close proximity to the old work, and an entirely new distillery had just been built on the most approved plan with all the latest improvements and appliances.'

Barnard, in fact, was in at the birth of the new distillery. In the year previous to his visit (1886), what little plant there was left from the old distillery was bought from the Cumming family for £120 by a certain William Grant, who carted it off and used it as the basic material for building a new distillery at Glenfiddich. The Cardow distillery seen by Barnard was bought from the Cumming family in 1893 by John Walker and Sons, the blenders of Johnnie Walker.

It is only comparatively recently that Cardow has been bottled again, usually at 12 years old and at 70° proof. Daiches describes it as 'a pleasing if not world shattering Highland malt'. McDowall says that it is 'a good Speyside whisky but does not claim to be a Glenlivet'. Both, I think, underrate Cardow, which I consider to be a great deal better than some malts which do claim to be Glenlivets. I side with Macdonald who placed it in the top 12. Cardow is a full, clean tasting, whisky with a beautifully controlled fire and an excellent nose. People who know better than I say it goes exceptionally well with haggis.

Tormore. This big and handsome distillery was the first completely new Highland malt distillery to be built this century. The architect was Sir Albert Richardson K.C.V.O., past President of the Royal Academy, and it was planned for maximum productivity and ease of operation from the very beginning. Tormore has eight big stainless steel washbacks automatically cleaned by a device with the nickname 'Sputnik'. Its two wash stills and two low wine stills are coal-heated but automatically stoked. It was completed in 1958, and is situated near the village of Advie on a tributary of the Spey a few miles north of Grantown-on-Spey. It has a curling pond, a mock watermill and a chiming clock which plays the tune 'Highland Laddie' every hour.

The distillery itself dominates the road at the base of its slope and is named after a big hill nearby. It draws its water from the Loch of Gold. The whisky itself can be described as a full-flavoured rather than as a refined one, although it maintains its Speyside character. As it is a comparatively new whisky, time may well be on its side. It is bottled at ten years old and 70° proof.

Tormore was the first of the modern generation of distilleries and was purpose-built for the efficient production of whisky, using the minimum work force.

Glenfiddich. More people have drunk Glenfiddich than any other single malt whisky. It is the largest selling of all the malts and can be quite easily found in most parts of the world. It accounts, in fact, for about half of all malt whiskies exported. Glenfiddich was also for many years the only malt whisky to advertise although this is now a bandwaggon a growing number of malts are joining.

The distillery was founded by William Grant, a man of humble origin who was born in 1839. He started his working life as an apprentice shoemaker but later became manager of a lime works. He set himself on the road to fame and fortune when he joined the Mortlach distillery as a clerk in 1866. He worked there for 20 years, learning all about how to build and run a distillery and developing a growing obsession that he wanted to build and run his own. In 1886 his chance came. A site in Dufftown by Fiddich Burn became vacant and he and his son John bought it. They were also fortunate enough to buy the equipment of the old Cardow distillery for £120 and the two of them, with some help from his five other sons, literally began to build the distillery by hand. They started late in 1886 and the first whisky ran from his stills on Christmas Day the following year, burning peat cut by his daughters.

William Grant was not yet a wealthy man, so operating the distillery had to be very much a family affair. Three of his sons worked there while typically attempting to complete their classical Scottish education. On the occasion of the first visit of the supervisor of excise to the new distillery, he was interested to find scholarly textbooks on Latin and mathematics scattered over the tunroom and stillhouse. On enquiring where the unusual books came from he was told that they belonged to the maltman, the brewer and the stillman. Two of these scholarly workmen went on to make distinguished careers while the third, after a career as a schoolmaster, surpassed even these by taking over the Glendronach distillery. The supervisor of excise said that he had never visited a more remarkable distillery.

William Grant deservedly prospered and five years later he built a second distillery, close to the first in Balvenie Castle. Both distilleries share the waters

The barrel store at Glenfiddich distillery. Glenfiddich is one of the few distilleries to bottle at the plant. Every year, more than 4,000 visitors are given a free dram after they have been conducted round the distillery.

of the Fiddich, both use very similar basic materials to produce malt whiskies which are not in the least alike.

Glenfiddich was greatly enlarged in 1955 and with its 27 pot stills is now one of the biggest malt distilleries in Scotland. Its stills are comparatively small and this gives the finished whisky its unique flavour. It also heats its stills directly both by coal and gas oil and its stills have rummagers. It buys its barley ready malted and, with Springbank, is one of the only two malt distilleries which bottle their own malts at the distillery. The original buildings have now been turned into a museum and reception centre, staffed by more than a dozen guides, some in Highland dress. These cope with nearly 50,000 visitors in the course of the year. Glenfiddich is bottled at eight and ten years old at 70° proof in its familiar triangular bottles. It has been described as 'dry yet flowery', 'a good fruity Glenlivet—like whisky with a distinctly peaty flavour', 'cream-smooth', and 'a pleasing dry fragrance'. My own view is that it is so popular because it is one of the most perfectly balanced of all single malts and thus has something to offer to everyone without any particular element being overstressed.

'One of the greatest'

Mortlach. This distillery, another of the famous Dufftown seven, is situated at the southern end of the town near the church of the same name. The name means 'bowl-shaped valley' and the site is reputedly the scene of a famous victory by King Malcolm II of Scotland over marauding Danes.

The distillery was built in 1823 and much of it was rebuilt quite recently. This was not, as is usual, to increase its capacity, but simply because it was falling apart. It draws its water from the Conval Hills to the west and a well-known 'Priest's Well'. It has a unique method of disposing of its liquid wastes by spraying them over neighbouring hills. The distillery buys two thirds of its barley ready malted but malts the remainder itself. It has three wash stills and three low wine stills and uses traditional coal fires to heat them. The whisky itself is 'a fine full Eastern malt, with a rich but not especially peaty flavour'... 'full and fruity but with little of the taste of peat', and, contrarywise 'most fruity and lush, with more peat than it used to have'. I myself have not detected any increase in peat and have always found Mortlach a rich and flowery malt without a particularly strong nose.

It was at one time designated 'Mortlach-Glenlivet' but, like Macallan and one or two other top quality malts, it now finds it can stand on its own feet without the protection of the famous Glenlivet name. It bottles its malt at 12 years and 70° proof.

Knockando. The distillery stands on the northern bank of the Spey at Cardow and has been producing malt since the turn of the century. The name in Gaelic means 'little black hillock'. It has only begun to be bottled quite recently and the label is unusual in that it states the year of distillation as well as the age of the malt (usually 12 years) and the 70° proof. Knockando is a typical Speyside malt, clean, robust and with a most pleasant aftertaste.

Macallan. Universally agreed to be one of the greatest of all malt whiskies. The distillery is on the west bank of the Spey by a ford near Craigellachie, on what was once the main north-south cattle droving route. It is certain that malt whisky was being distilled here long before the Macallan distillery was first licensed in 1824, thus becoming one of the earliest legal distilleries in Scotland. From its earliest days it was famous for the quality of its malt whisky and even in the worst of times has had little trouble in selling all it makes. But the demand grew to such an extent that a primary expansion in the 1950s proved to be not really great enough. Between 1964 and 1966 a second distillery had to be built, effectively doubling the output. It is bottled at 70°, 75°, 80° and 100° proof, never less than ten years old, but also at 12, 15, 17, and 30 years.

Macallan has always insisted on small stills because the owners have always believed that small stills, directly heated, produce a superior whisky. They also insist that all their whisky is matured in sherry casks for precisely the same reason. They have calculated that they lose the equivalent of 3000 bottles of Macallans a day by natural evaporation. The distillery is also unique in that, before casking, it stores its whisky in two enormous glass-lined cylindrical tanks, the biggest of their kind ever made. This means that any slight differences between the whiskies produced by the two parts of the distillery are evened out.

During the 1954 visit to Great Britain of Khrushchev and Bulganin, Macallan malt whisky had the honour of being offered as an alternative to the finest cognac at the Mansion House dinner. This testifies to the high regard in which it is held, echoed almost universally—'one must approach a Macallan with great reverence', 'a whisky of quality in the best Speyside sense; indeed, many consider it now the best. It has a smooth richness of flavour quite its own', 'rich and smooth in flavour, ranks very high among all the Scotch single malt whiskies', 'a Speyside whisky of great individuality. The 100° proof...has a powerful nose which proclaims very accurately the flavour to the palate, which I find difficult to describe as its special kind of richness is neither peaty nor flowery, but something in between'. Personally, I find Macallan a simply delicious whisky, rich and fragrant, although I would advise approaching the 100° proof with some caution. Macallan, once Macallan-Glenlivet, has sensibly decided, after 140 years, to drop the 'Glenlivet'. It does not need it.

Balmenach. Another great whisky and also one of Macdonald's chosen twelve.

On 29 December 1879, the same storm which ravaged the distillery at Balmenach demolished the Tay Bridge, many miles away.

The night the roof fell in

The distillery itself sits at the foot of the Hills of Cromdale, about three quarters of a mile south of the village of Cromdale itself. It was one of the earliest distilleries to take advantage of the 1823 Act and take out a licence, an unpopular move in the locality because the whole of this area of Speyside was a hotbed of smuggling and illicit distilling, as Barnard recounts at some length. The whisky produced here found favour very early on and, in the 1820s, buyers included the Duke of Bedford.

The distillery grew over the years but had a narrow escape in 1879. On the even-ing of 28 December of that year, the same storm that brought down the Tay Bridge also blew down the distillery chimney. A heavy rain of bricks crashed through the roof of the stillhouse and ruptured the stills which were working at the time. Hot and volatile spirit poured down into the fires below and a fire started. If it had not been for the cool-headedness of the still-man who opened the discharge cocks and allowed the stills to empty into the sewers, a serious fire would have destroyed the whole distillery. As it was, the damage was only temporary.

Sir Robert Bruce Lockhart, the famous diplomat, spent his childhood at the distillery, which was owned by his family, and he devotes a chapter of his book *Scotch* to Balmenach. Balmenach was also the whisky supplied to Queen Victoria when she visited the area in 1878. Balmenach malt is a deep amber spirit which combines a powerful flavour with a surprisingly soft nose.

Linkwood. This is another of the great Speyside whiskies, although geographically the distillery itself is nowhere near the river. It lies to the southeast of Elgin in a small wood. Linkwood was first built in 1821 and was named after an old mansion house that once occupied the same site. It was rebuilt in 1873. This fine malt owes its good name to the efforts of Roderick Mackenzie who ran the distillery for many years. He was a fierce traditionalist and refused to make the slightest change in the distillery in case it altered the quality of the whisky he distilled. He even refused to have spiders' webs removed. This extreme caution seems to have paid off because Linkwood is acknowledged to be one of the best by nearly all connoisseurs. Professor R. A. S. McDowall says that it is 'a pleasant light whisky with a typical Glenlivet flavour

although it reminds me of the Lowland Rosebank'. My view is that it is an excellent and mild tasting malt but that it could be said to lack a little character in comparison with other Speyside whiskies distilled by the river itself. Linkwood is another malt which has dropped Glenlivet from its name. It has recently been modernized with what is effectively a brand new and bigger distillery built alongside the old.

Aultmore. This distillery, again, is not strictly speaking on the banks of the Spey, being situated in a rather isolated position on the road between Keith and Buckie. It was started in 1895 and the first whisky flowed in July 1897. The distillery was modernized in 1972. It draws its water from springs in the hills to the north. Aultmore is bottled at 12 years old and at 70° proof. It has been described as 'an excellent malt' and is now becoming much more available.

Balvenie. (The original Gaelic is 'Balbheineibh', meaning a small hillock in the field.) Sister distillery to Glenfiddich, it was built five years later in 1892 and in close proximity. This is as far as proximity goes because the whiskies that each produces are very different. The distillery is sited near the old Balvenie castle from which it derives its name. It draws its water from the Robbie Dhub spring, and is one of the few distilleries that still malts its own barley by hand. It is bottled in the familiar green triangular bottles, similar to those used by Glenfiddich, at eight years old, and 70° and 75° proof. Professor McDowall mentions a bottling at 106·4° proof but I have not encountered this formidable malt. Balvenie is a smooth but strong tasting malt with a pleasant but pungent nose.

Glendullan. Another Dufftown malt. The distillery itself was the last of the seven to be built there, being completed shortly before the turn of the century. Before 1972 it all went for blending but in that year it was first bottled and is now rightly becom-ing known as an exceedingly distinguished Speyside malt. As one writer said, 'It is indeed a really grand whisky, robust and full of character and flavour, but mellow'. If it continues to be produced at this level of quality it could well find itself in the company of the greatest Speyside and Glenlivet single malts. Glendullan has recently been modernized with a brand new and bigger distillery built alongside.

Other Speyside Malts. There are a number of Speyside malts which may occasionally be bottled but which nearly always go to the blenders, such as Strathmill, Glen Spey, Glentauchers, Benrinnes, Speyside, Dailuaine, Allt a'Bhainne and Pittyvaich.

The distillery at Dailuaine is licensed to the company which owns the Talisker distillery.

Other Highland malts in bottle

Apart from the magnificent concentration of superb malts around and about Speyside and Glenlivet there are, of course, some dozens of other malt distilleries scattered the length and breadth of the Highlands. Some produce very distinguished whisky indeed. Some of this is bottled; much of this seldom travels very far from its place of origin and so has only a local reputation; but some of it is freely available and is well known all over the world. The whiskies listed here are not in order of merit or by geographical location.

Glenmorangie. Located at Tain, the east coast town on the Dornoch Firth in Rossshire. This makes it one of the northernmost distilleries in Scotland. It is right on the foreshore and on the site of an ancient brewery, once famous for its fine ale, but in 1843 this brewery was replaced by a distillery which was itself replaced by a newer one in the late 1880s. The Glenmorangie Distillery Company itself was formed in 1887. In the grounds of the distillery there is an enormous boulder, a relic of the glaciers of the last ice age: for some unknown reason it bears the inscription 'The immortal Walter Scott ob. 1832', which was probably inscribed by one of the builders of the brewery. On this account Sir Walter used to appear on Glenmorangie labels, although he has now been replaced by a picture of the distillery.

The distillery at one time used local peat but it now brings it in from Pitsligo in Aberdeenshire: it draws its water from springs in Tarlogie Hill. The Glenmorangie distillery has exceptionally tall pot stills which have been heated by steam coils since the 1880s and the special quality of the whisky is, in part, attributed to these facts. The whisky itself has always been a favourite—'fragrant and delicate', 'delicate and fragrant', 'it has a special kind of floweriness, a delicate yet unmistakable fragrance', 'a gentle but delicate whisky with some resemblance to a Lowland malt', 'delicate and mild, like a Lowland malt', 'a honey sweet flavour'. It is bottled at ten years and 70° proof and many people prefer it above all other single malts.

Clynelish. The distillery was founded by the Marquis of Stafford, later the Duke of Sutherland, in 1819. He chose to built it at Brora, a small coal-mining port on the east coast of Scotland, to provide an outlet for the barley produced by farmers

he had evicted from his enormous estates in the interior and resettled in new farmland in the vicinity. The whisky it produces is highly idiosyncratic and the favourite of the great Victorian scholar and connoisseur, George Saintsbury. Macdonald says of it, 'Clynelish whisky is certainly the most fully-flavoured whisky outside Islay and one is tempted to think that the peat moors from which the peat is obtained used to grow seaweed. It is a little reminiscent of Laphroaig but less peaty. It is a man's whisky but not to everyone's taste. I find it fruity and delicious'. Other people confirm this view: 'richly dour Sutherland whisky', 'mellow and fruity', 'fine, full, mellow whisky'. It is bottled at 12 years old at 70° and 80° proof.

Old Pulteney. This is the most northerly of all mainland Highland malts; it is distilled at Wick, the county town of Caithness. It was established in 1826, although it closed its doors during the slump years between 1926 and 1951. It is now owned by Hiram Walker. It draws its water from the heavily peated Loch of Hempriggs although, curiously enough, little of this comes across in the finished whisky. This

The whisky boom saw an enormous expansion in the production of Scotch whisky. This picture of 1888 gives some idea of the scale of operation at just one plant.

84

is bottled at 85° proof at eight years and is then fully finished, as Old Pulteney is one of the fastest-maturing of all single malts. It has many admirers, Neil Gunn being among the foremost; of it he said that 'it had some of the strong characteristics of the northern temperament. It has to be come upon as one comes upon a friend and treated with proper respect'. It was, in fact, his own local whisky. Others speak highly of it: 'Old Pulteney has a peatiness that is subtle and not too strong. It is a whisky with a fine bouquet', 'it has a splendid fruitiness (as distinct from a peatiness), the tasted flavour fulfilling most interestingly the promise of its nose', 'a whisky of considerable distinction having a succession of flavours and not noticeably peaty'. Old Pulteney, with the two previously mentioned whiskies, Glenmorangie and Clynelish, are sometimes known as 'the northern malts'.

Inchgower. The small town of Buckie on the Spey Bay was once the home of the biggest herring fishery in Britain. Now the herring have gone through overfishing, and the town is only famous as the home of the Inchgower distillery. It had at one time been an extremely popular malt whisky, both in Great Britain and her overseas possessions, but it fell out of favour and it was only in 1972 that Arthur Bell and Sons Ltd., the owners, began to bottle it again. The original distillery was founded in 1871 and Barnard described the whisky it produced then as 'clean and mellow to the palate and much appreciated by connoisseurs'. Today it is bottled at 12 years old and 70° proof; it remains mellow but distinctly peaty, supposedly from the peatiness of the water from which it originally comes.

Tomatin. The biggest single malt distillery in Scotland, and thus in the world, with a capacity of more than five million gallons a year. It was founded in 1897 at the small village of Tomatin (pronounced like 'satin'), on the main Perth-to-Inverness road about 16 miles south of Inverness. Tomatin is Gaelic for 'the hill of bushes'. Not only is the distillery the biggest but it is also one of the highest, at an altitude of 1,028 feet above sea level. It has yet another distinction in being one of the very few malt whiskies, outside the D.C.L. group, to be owned by a company quoted on the stock exchange.

The workforce at Tomatin in 1916. Today the distillery produces more than five million gallons of malt whisky every year.

It draws its water from the Alt-na-Frith ('free burn' in Gaelic) which, in the classic manner, passes through peat and over red granite. The distillery has been enlarged several times since it was founded, although the workforce has only increased by eight—from 22 to 30—in over 20 years. This is due to the introduction of automation wherever possible. Tomatin malts some 60 tons of its own barley every week although it still needs to buy a great deal ready malted from maltsters. It has 11 stills (six wash, five low wine) and 12 stainless steel washbacks. Each of these is capable of holding 10,000 gallons. Tomatin also has the capacity to store and mature up to ten million gallons. So Tomatin distils malt whisky on the grand scale. And excellent whisky too—'a light bodied and peaty flavoured malt, not unlike Glenlivet, but with a more emphatic taste of peat', 'a good example of a dry single malt well matured, although its flavour, which is not unlike a Glenlivet, is somewhat obscured by the peat', 'light yet peaty'. I have always found it a good malt but the similarity to Glenlivet escapes me. It is certainly much peatier than any of the classic Glenlivets I have tasted. It is bottled at five and ten years old at 70° proof.

Ord. The shortest named of all single malts, situated at Beauly on the river of the same name—famous for its salmon—just as it broadens into the Beauly Firth. Barnard tells of a fascinating but gruesome story of Beauly which, even if not strictly relevant to the whisky, may give the malt drinker a frisson as he raises his glass of Ord:

'On a Sunday morning, in the 16th century, a numerous body of the Mackenzies were assembled at prayer within the walls of the old chapel, when they were surprised by a strong party of Glengarry men, bent on revenging the death of Angus, the son of their chief, who had been killed during a foray into the Mackenzies' country. Fastening up the doors, and placing his followers so as to prevent all possibility of escape, Allan, the chief, gave orders to set the building on fire. The miserable victims were without a single exception—man, woman and child—swallowed up by the devouring element, or massacred by the swords of the relentless Macdonalds; while a piper marched round the church playing a pibroch, until the shrieks of the Mackenzies were hushed in death. The Macdonalds did not, however, escape with impunity, for the funeral pile of their clansmen roused the whole tribe of the Mackenzies to vengeance, and they immediately started in pursuit, dividing their force into two bodies, one commanded by Murdoch, and the other by Alexander Mackenzie. The latter came upon a large party of the Macdonalds at the burn of Altsay, who were nearly all extirpated, while a still more severe retribution befell the other party, who were pursued to Inverness by Murdoch Mackenzie. They were overtaken and shut up in a wayside inn, where they had been carousing, which was set on fire, and the whole party, 37 in number, perished by the same agonising death they had inflicted on the Mackenzies.'

Ord distillery itself was founded in 1838 on the site of an older and illicit still. It stands on the slope of a gentle hill and draws its superb water from the Oran burn which flows from Glen Oran and from two lochs in the hills of Knockudas. Ord malt whisky has been described as 'very agreeable to the palate' and is, indeed, a well balanced malt, not too peaty and not too dry. Heather is traditionally mixed with the peat before kilning, just as with Highland Park.

Oban. This distillery is a long way away from any other, in its lovely position on the west coast and, indeed, was there before the town was founded; it was first constructed in 1794 when Oban was only a small fishing village. Oban water comes from two lochs in Ardconnel just above the town. These drain extensive peatfields. This is reflected in the flavour of the malt which is highly individualistic, combining mellowness and pungency with quite a strong peaty nose. Barnard called it a 'self whisky' and this is not a bad description, although the term today tends to be used for malt whiskies generally. It comes in a curiously shaped bottle, not to everybody's taste.

Dalmore. This has a beautiful site on the shores of the Cromarty Firth, looking over to the Black Isle. It was founded in 1839 and has made a practice of bottling its malt whisky almost from the beginning. It is particularly well served, having both its own pier and railway siding, and, not surprisingly, Dalmore is one of the more readily available malt whiskies. The distillery has been almost completely modernized in recent years and now uses the Saladin method of malting as well as mechanized stoking. During the First World War it was commandeered, first by the American Navy and then the Royal Navy, as a factory for making mines. By accident it caught fire and was very badly damaged; whisky production was only started again in 1922. Two stills dating from 1874 survived the blaze and are, surprisingly, still in use in one of the most up-to-date distilleries of them all. It draws its water from the River Alness which flows from Loch Morie. It is a particularly soft and pure water, naturally filtered by gravel. It also has no trouble with its effluent, simply discharging it into the sea. Dalmore is known to be a quick-maturing whisky, and some have found it drinkable at the minimum of three years old. The distillery itself, however, insists on a minimum of eight years and bottles its malt whisky up to the age of 20 years. Dalmore is a 'good solid dry whisky with slightly peaty flavour, a little reminiscent of Cardow', 'a heavier whisky . . . peatier, full bodied . . . robust . . .', 'an excellent after dinner drink'. I would describe it as

The chimney of the distillery at Oban towers above the main street and harbour of this thriving commercial and tourist centre.

pleasantly aggressive, not to be refused.

Balblair. This distillery lies at Edderton a few miles due west of Glenmorangie and, like it, also overlooks the Dornoch Firth. One problem Balblair does not have to face is the availability of peat. There is so much of it in the area that Edderton is known as 'the parish of peats'. The distillery was founded in 1790 although its history has been traced back as far as 1749 and claims to be the second oldest in Scotland. It has certainly changed its position

Regicide!

at least once. The peat it uses is soft and crumbly and the flavour of the finished whisky may well owe something to this, being very delicately peaty and at the same time highly scented. McDowall says 'a more flavoured whisky, almost without any peat but very slightly aromatic'. Daiches says it is 'a pleasing, light-bodied whisky of distinctive flavour'. Both play down its aroma, which some consider its most attractive and individual feature. It bottles its whisky at ten years and 100° proof.

Fettercairn. Bottled as Old Fettercairn. The town has a curious story attached to it concerning the ruins of Fennella's Castle. Barnard tells us:

'This castle, which stands on an eminence near Fettercairn, was the scene of the murder of Kenneth III, King of Scotland.

He ascended the throne in the year 970, and occasionally resided at a castle about a mile distant on the east side of the village. The king excited the deadly hatred of the royal lady, Fenella, daughter of the proud Earl of Angus, for having legally put to death her son, Crathilenthus. She invited him to the castle, where she had prepared an "infernal machine", which consisted of a brass statue, which threw out arrows when a golden apple was taken from its hand. It stood in a handsome apartment, surrounded by rich drapery and curious sculptures. Under pretext of amusing the king with this curiousity, she conducted him to the apartment, and courteously invited him to take the apple. The king, amused with the idea, did so, when instantly he was pierced with arrows

The gentle and undulating landscape around Blair Athol typifies the smooth malt whisky to which it gives its name. In fact, the distillery is situated some distance from the town.

'Famous since time immemorial'

and mortally wounded. The attendants, on coming for their royal master, could not gain admittance to the castle, from whence the assassin had already fled. However, they forced open the doors, and found to their horror and consternation the king weltering in his blood. So much for a woman's vengeance.'

The distillery itself was founded in 1820, but four years later this site was abandoned and a new building erected on the banks of the River Esk. It was the first distillery to heat its stills with oil. It originally malted its own barley but now buys it ready malted. The whisky itself has been described as 'the best of the eastern malts now available, with a full dry flavour'. It is bottled at eight years old at 75° proof.

Blair Athol. A showpiece distillery where visitors are always welcome. It is a small distillery, beautifully sited and maintained but, geographically speaking, nowhere near Blair Athol itself which is a dozen or so miles to the north. Blair Athol Distillery is sited, in fact, at Pitlochry in the Vale of Athol. Some of its water comes from Ben Vrachie, and the waters which flow through Pitlochry are generally so good that they are widely used for 'cutting' the newly-distilled whisky. The distillery was founded in 1826. The malt whisky it produces is rightly famous: 'one of the best single malts', 'famous from time immemorial'. It is, in fact, a gracious mellow malt, very full and flavoury, and with a fine nose. It is bottled at eight years old and 70° proof.

Glen Mhor. An Inverness distillery, sited on the bank of the Caledonian Canal. Glen Mhor means 'Great Glen' and, indeed, the whisky is named after the Great Glen that slashes Scotland in half from Inverness to Fort William. It was built in 1892 and draws its water from Loch Ness. It was the first malt whisky distillery to use the Saladin method of malting and the stills are heated by steam coils. The whisky itself is very fine, one of Macdonald's immortal dozen. Mac-Dowall is full of praise—'there certainly will never be a glut of delicious Glen Mhor. While it cannot be said to have any outstanding flavour, it has an honest, subtle richness and "fatness", reminiscent of the patina of old furniture, which it owes to the care with which it is made and the fact that it is well matured before it is sold.' This is a feature which the

demand for whisky makes rare. To appreciate Glen Mhor at its best, I advise taking it after one of the standard blends. Then one appreciates the words of Neil Gunn, the Scottish novelist, just after speaking of Glen Mhor, 'that until a man has the luck to chance on a perfectly matured malt, he does not know what whisky really is.

'Like Blair Athol, it is not really a Glenlivet but can be conveniently put in the same class. It can be described as a little more robust. A little added to John Haig makes a lovely smooth drink, the cheapest de luxe . . .' I must admit I have never had the courage to take that final eccentric hint. Elsewhere it is 'one of the truly great post-prandial whiskies, full rich and mellow, slightly less peaty than Dalmore and with a smoother finish . . . a "bigger" whisky than a characteristic Speyside whisky, but it has some of the qualities of a Glenlivet'. It is bottled at six years old at 70° proof and ten years old at 75° proof. A sister distillery, Glen Albyn, owned by the same company, is no more than 100 yards away, using the same water and very similar equipment. Its whisky, of course, is totally different.

Glengarioch. At Oldmeldrum, about 15 miles northwest of Aberdeen, and one of Scotland's oldest distilleries, being founded in 1797. It lies at one end of the valley of the Garioch, traditionally the finest barley growing area in the whole of Scotland. Ironically, it is one of the latest to bottle its malt whisky, the first batch appearing in 1972. The distillery draws its water from springs on Percock Hill, as well as local springs. Glengarioch uses the heat from its effluent to warm greenhouses which, I am assured, produce some of the finest tomatoes grown anywhere in the country.

Glengarioch describes itself as 'having a magnificently robust nose, flowery, not very smokey; it is surprisingly mild on the palate and it is this quality which could well become the Glengarioch signature. A crisp, rather than a bland finish, with a good fine aftertaste'. I find it an excellent malt with a slightly aggressive nose and I will watch its development with interest.

Deanston. One of the southernmost of the Highland malts; the distillery being situated just outside Doune, about seven miles

Blair Athol malt, one of the best Highland malts.

northwest of Stirling. Pure, clear water flows down from the Trossachs and it was this that led to the construction of a cotton mill here in 1785. This building was converted into a distillery in 1965. Deanston Mill whisky, the name under which it is bottled, says of itself that it has a 'spirit of hidden vigour and an elegant palate'. I think it is a mildish malt with a delicate nose, soft and a little sweet. It is bottled at 70° proof.

Tullibardine. This quaintly named distillery is at Blackford in Perthshire, not far from the famous Gleneagles Hotel. The hotel actually stands on the Tullibardine Moor from which the whisky takes its name. Until 1949, the distillery was a brewery but it was then converted to produce whisky rather than beer. It was, incidentally, at a brewery in Blackford that ale was brewed for James IV of Scotland on the occasion of his coronation in 1488. This says something for the loch water. The new whisky is reputed to have a 'quite outstanding, almost wine-like flavour'. It is bottled when it is ten years old and at 70° proof.

Glendronach. Built in 1926 at the small town of Huntly in Strathbogie. The distillery is also fortunate in being the site of a large and noisy rookery; this is traditionally supposed to be lucky and certainly the distillery looks attractive and prosperous enough. It draws its water from the Dronach burn which has previously made its way through rich peat beds. This gives the water—which is totally pure—a beautiful golden brown tinge which the distillers find invaluable in forming the taste of the finished malt whisky. This colour led to trouble with the Common Market (EEC). In Brussels some 'experts' said the water was 'contaminated' and thus should not be used, to the astonishment and fury of the Scots. Fortunately it all came to nothing. Glendronach is bottled at eight and 12 years and 80° proof. It has been described as a 'pleasant malt but not a distinguished whisky'. Local drinkers strongly disagree with this judgment.

Lochnagar. It is sited at Balmoral about a mile away from the Royal Castle. The distillery was built in 1825 by a certain John Robertson, a notorious smuggler, and it was sold in 1845 to John Begg. Three years later came his moment of glory. He records:

'I wrote a note on the 11th of September to Mr G. E. Anson (Her Majesty's Private Secretary) stating that the distillery was now in full operation and would be so until six o'clock the next day and, knowing how anxious H.R.H. Prince Albert was to patronise and make himself acquainted with everything of a mechanical nature, I said I should feel much pleasure in showing him the works.

'The note was handed in at Balmoral Castle about 9 pm. Next day about four o'clock, whilst in the house, I observed Her Majesty and the Prince Consort approaching. I ran and opened the door, when the Prince said, "We have come to see through your works Mr Begg". There were besides H.R.H. the Prince of Wales, the Princess Royal and Prince Alfred, accompanied by Lady Cumming. I at once conducted the Royal party to the distillery.

'On entering the works, the two young princes at once ran away among the casks, like any other children, whereupon Her Majesty called to them "Where are you young children going?" on which I laid hold of one in each hand and held them during the time they remained.

'I endeavoured to explain the whole process of malting, brewing and distilling, showing the Royal party the bere (barley) in its original state and in all its different stages of manufacture until it came out at the mouth of the still pipe in spirits. H.R.H. tasted the spirits with his finger from both the still pipes. On going downstairs H.R.H. turned round to me and said (looking at the locks on the stills) "I see you have got your locks there". On my replying, "These are the Queen's locks", Her Majesty took a hearty laugh.

'When we came to the door I asked H.R.H. if he would like to taste the spirit in its matured state, as we had cleared some that day from bond, which I thought was very fine. H.R.H. having agreed to this, I called for a bottle and glasses (which had been previously in readiness) and, presenting one glass to Her Majesty, she tasted it. So also did His Royal Highness, the Prince. I then presented a glass to the Princess Royal and to the Prince of Wales and Prince Alfred, all of whom tasted the spirit.

'H.R.H. the Prince of Wales was going to carry his glass quickly to his mouth. I checked him, saying it was very strong, so he did not take but a very small drop of it. Afterwards the Royal party took their departure, I thanking them for the honour of the visit they had been so generous to pay to the distillery.'

After their visit, the enterprising Mr Begg was allowed to call his distillery the 'Royal Lochnagar' and he was appointed distiller to the Queen by Royal Warrant. Royal Brackla is the only other whisky allowed to use the 'Royal' prefix. This privilege was granted to Captain William Fraser, of Brackla distillery, in 1835 by William IV.

The distillery draws its water from a burn which flows down the mountain from which the whisky takes its name. It is an excellent whisky—'Royal Lochnagar is indeed a wonderful whisky with a subtle flavour of sherry from the cask in which it has been matured—a flavour which cannot be imitated by putting a little sherry in any whisky. It is a privilege to have tasted such a rich whisky'. It is indeed a very full and rounded whisky. I have heard it described as 'liquid velvet'. It bottles its whisky at 12 years old and 70° proof.

Glenury Royal. It is at Stonehaven on the east coast of Scotland, some 15 miles south of Aberdeen. The suffix 'Royal' does not indicate royal patronage as in Lochnagar. The distillery was founded in 1836; it bottles at 12 years old and 70° proof.

Glendevron. One of the very few whiskies that are named differently from their distilleries. Glendevron is distilled at the Macduff distillery on the east coast of Scotland in Banffshire. It is named after the River Devron which flows into the sea here, and from which the distillery draws its water. It is a very new distillery, built in 1960 after the discovery of the exceptional quality of the water from a local spring. Glendevron is bottled at five years and 75° proof. It is very lightly peated and for some obscure reason very popular with the Italians.

Glenturret. This small distillery was first established in 1775, two miles northwest of the Tayside town of Crieff. The site was a well known haunt of smugglers (smugglers meaning illicit distillers), who chose it for the magnificent quality of the water.

Inside the Ben Nevis distillery, founded by 'Long John' Macdonald.

This—the River Turret—rises in Benchonzie, a mountain over 3,000 feet high where the snows lie unmelted until into June. From here it drains into Loch Turret and there runs five miles to join the Earn. So for most of the useful distillery year, the water is not only pure and clear but ice-cold. The present distillery was built on the same site in 1959 and its production has quadrupled in its first ten years. The whisky produced 'has a somewhat flowery flavour, a little reminiscent of Glenmorangie'. It is a curious but likeable whisky with a slightly lemony flavour that fades very quickly on the palate. In 1922 it won the silver seal at the International Wine and Spirit Competition in London.

Ben Nevis. Founded in the shadow of Britain's highest mountain in 1825 by John Macdonald, a man of such great size and superb physique that he was known as 'Long John', a name which has descended to us in the shape of Long John Distilleries Ltd. It is sited a couple of miles northeast of Fort William. The water it uses comes from the heights of Ben Nevis, from an opening called Buchan's Well, the highest spring in the whole of Scotland. This water is extremely pure and thus perfect for the purposes of distillation. There is a grain distillery alongside.

Glengoyne. This distillery, the southernmost of all the Highland malts, is situated in a small glen in the Campsie Hills in the south of Stirlingshire. It was originally called Glenguin and appears thus in Barnard. It was originally built in 1833, close to a beautiful waterfall. It has been extensively modernized. Marshal of the Royal Air Force, Lord Tedder, was born here; his father was Excise Officer at the distillery and later went on to play a famous and important part in the whisky trade. Glengoyne, bottled at eight years old and 70° proof, is 'a very pleasant, sweetish and gentle malt, with no outstanding flavour. Although the whisky is technically just a Highland malt, it is fair to say that in many instances it is bought and used as a Lowland malt for blending'. My own view is that it should be classified as a Lowland malt whatever the niceties of geography dictate. It bottles its whisky at eight years old and 70° proof.

Glenallachie. A comparatively new distillery built near Aberlour. Its entire output goes for blending, although I have tasted an eight-year-old Glenallachie. It had a faint tarry taste which I found very remarkable and by no means unpleasant.

Other Highland malts which may occasionally be bottled or may be tasted at the distillery, but which almost certainly all go to the blender are: Aberfeldy, Banff, Ben Wyvis, Dallas Dhu, Dalwhinnie, Edradour, Glen Albyn, Glencadam, Glenglassaugh, Hillside, Knockdhu, Loch Lomond, Lochside, Millburn, North Port, Strathmill, Teaninich, Auchroisk, Glenlochy, Mannochmore, Glen Foyle and Ardmore.

Islay and Island malts

Islay is a small and beautiful island off the west coast of Scotland, remarkable for its remoteness, its superb scenery, the fact that Gaelic is still a living language—and that it possesses eight distilleries. This may in part be due to the fact that Islay is also an island of peat and it is the peat of Islay—dark and densely-textured—that gives its malts their unique and inimitable quality. Every blended Scotch whisky that you drink has a greater or smaller proportion of Islay malt in it; it is absolutely necessary to the 'bite' of a blend. Islay whiskies are the 'whiskiest' whiskies. This is why some people—even most people—find most Islay malts overpowering, too strongly flavoured, too pungent. But some will drink no other.

The Islay peat bogs are some of the thickest in Scotland. Thousands of years of cutting for domestic fuel and, latterly, for distilling have hardly scratched the surface of the huge deposits which cover much of the island. Stacks of drying peat are one of the commonest sights on the island and each distillery has its own private and favourite peatfield for cutting its own fuel. Islay peat is different from almost any other, too, in that it contains substantial amounts of seaweed and other shore plants. This means that Islay peat burns with a particularly dense and strongly-flavoured smoke. This permeates the malt to such an extent that it is carried over very powerfully in distillation. Connoisseurs of malt whisky claim that they can detect iodine—the smell of the sea—in all Islay malts, especially the heavier ones like Laphroaig or Ardbeg.

All Islay distilleries are situated on the coast of the island and all of them command views of exceptional natural beauty. Until

Bringing in the peat on Skye.

'The most extraordinary whisky'

comparatively recently, Islay could only be reached by a lengthy—and often extremely uncomfortable—journey by steamer, but today there is a daily air service from Glasgow. This means that the scenic delights of Islay are more accessible —and with them the delights of Islay malts. So, although they will always remain a minority taste, it is a minority taste that is bound to increase over the years.

Islay malts cannot be classified in any order of merit, but geographically they can be classified as to where they lie on the island's one and mainly coastal road, running approximately from east to west.

Ardbeg. The easternmost distillery, looking over the sea to the Kintyre peninsula due east, and the Island of Jura due north. It was established in 1815 and, as Barnard points out, this was 'a noted haunt of smugglers' before that date. It draws its water from Loch Uigeadail and Loch Iarnan, both noted for their softness and purity. Ardbeg whisky is soft and powerful, with a pronounced smokiness. It nearly all goes for blending, although some is bottled at ten years and 80° proof.

Ardbeg uses local peat and has only two, albeit very large, stills. It malts its own barley. It was in 1977 acquired by Hiram Walker and there has been some speculation as to their intentions. However, Ardbeg is such an individual whisky that there is no doubt whatsoever that, whether as a single malt or as a component of a blend, it will continue to give pleasure to malt whisky drinkers.

Lagavulin. Just to the west of Ardbeg and three miles east of Port Ellen. The name means 'The Mill in the Valley'. At one time Lagavulin was the home of a feudal chieftain who had the curious habit of employing a bodyguard with enormous feet whose job was to walk through the dew before his master so that the latter should not get his feet wet. The water for Lagavulin comes from numerous small waterfalls which trickle down the hill of Sholum. Here there are also two small lochs. The malt whisky produced is milder in flavour than most Islay malts, although it retains its typical peatiness. It is bottled at 12 years old and 75° proof. Lagavulin matures some of its whisky in the ruined Lochindaal distillery across the bay from Bowmore. The distillery offers some

charming advice to Lagavulin drinkers— 'as a general guide to drinking Lagavulin we recommend the use of unchilled water with a 50:50 dilute, and drunk within a reasonably short period after dilution.'

Laphroaig. Probably the most extraordinary whisky distilled in the whole of Scotland. Luckily, it is fairly easily obtainable—although there have been periods of drought—and anyone interested in whisky should experience its unique charms, or otherwise. It arouses strong passions and strong language. It has been described as 'medicinal', 'powerful and for strong men', 'something like an antiseptic', 'an oppressive peaty flavour', 'a thick and pungent spirit'. In a recent catalogue it was said of Laphroaig, 'a marked peaty flavour with a pungency some love and others cannot take'. Obviously, a spirit to be reckoned with. I freely admit to finding it rather hard to take but I know many who prefer it to all other malts.

The distillery itself is on the seashore a mile east of Port Ellen. It is an exceptionally attractive building with a beautiful garden maintained by a retired employee. Until quite recently it was one of the very few distilleries run by a woman. It malts its own barley and cuts its own peat which is dark, hard and exceptionally smoky. A very pronounced smell of seaweed pervades the distillery and it is easy to imagine that this fragrance in some way comes through in the final whisky.

The distillery at Ardbeg was recently acquired by the Canadian firm of Hiram Walker.

Port Ellen. This small town is the capital of the island. The distillery itself was the site of some of the earliest experiments in continuous distillation and both Stein and Coffey, the originators of grain distilleries, worked here at some time. Port Ellen distillery also pioneered the export of whisky to the United States. The distillery closed down in 1930 during the slump and was reopened by The Distillers Company Limited in 1967. Its whisky goes for blending. It also contains a large malt plant from which it supplies other distilleries on Islay and even on the mainland.

Bowmore. About ten miles north of Port Ellen, past the small airport, this distillery is right on the foreshore overlooking a beautiful bay. Bowmore is one of the few independent distilleries still in operation and is owned by the Glasgow whisky broking company of Stanley P. Morrison Ltd. They have only recently begun to bottle their own malt whisky. Bowmore is powerful and pungent but distinctly milder than both Laphroaig and Ardbeg. It ages exceptionally well and the 18 and 21-year-old Bowmore, now, alas, in short supply, are superb examples of Islay whisky at its best. It malts and kilns its own barley and bottles its whisky at eight years old and 70° proof. The distillery recently opened its own reception centre in a splendid hall, which is highly popular with the people of Bowmore for parties and celebrations.

Bruichladdich. This distillery is sited on the other side of Loch Indaal from Bowmore and has an equally spectacular outlook. It is a very small, rather pretty, distillery and was first built in 1881. It, too, closed down during the slump which followed the whisky boom but it was reopened, enlarged and completely remodelled during the 1960s. It does not now malt its own barley as in the old days but buys it ready malted from a wholesale maltster, so the familiar pagoda chimneys are no longer in evidence. Some of the malt whisky it produces is bottled for local use although it can be found from time to time in specialist shops and stores south of the border at 75° proof. It is a typical Islay malt, strong and peaty, but softer and gentler than Laphroaig.

Caol Ila. This D.C.L. distillery, first built in 1846 and recently modernized to double its output, also looks across the Sound of Islay. Barnard says that it stands in the wildest and most picturesque country that he had ever seen, and things have not changed much since his day. Caol Ila whisky, again, is characteristically peaty and with an excellent 'nose'.

Filling the casks at the Caol Ila distillery. The distillery, which was built in 1846, produces whisky with a strong peated malt flavour.

Bunnahabhain. This distillery is situated in the remotest part of Islay, looking across the Sound of Islay to Jura, a magnificent view. It brings its malt in by sea but takes its whisky out by road, on 40-foot trucks, as Mr Bob Gordon, the distillery manager, assured me. I needed this assurance as I found the narrow, twisting and sometimes alarmingly steep track, hardly shown on the usual Ordnance Survey map, difficult enough to negotiate even by car. Like all distillery managers, Bob Gordon is proud of his whisky and told me something I did not know before. This is that if the feints are allowed to distil over in any quantity they make a whisky 'leathery'. His own whisky was excellent and surprisingly lightly peated for an Islay malt. I thought it was also distinctly sweeter than the other Islay malts, a big whisky, well rounded and with a slightly sweet

aftertaste. It is bottled at eight and 12 years old and at 70° proof, although, sadly, the whole of the current bottling is destined for Japan. Bunnahabhain also exports some of its whisky in bulk to Ecuador. The distillery also contains its own 'dark grains' plant for the production of animal foodstuffs.

Island Whiskies. Although Islay whiskies are recognized to be worthy of a classification of their own on account of their special and unparalleled qualities, there are a number of other island-born malt whiskies with special individual qualities. For convenience, they are all classed as Highland malt whiskies but, in my view— now becoming more widely shared—they should have a class of their own. If the classification of Campbeltown remains for historical reasons, Island whiskies should have their own for practical reasons.

The exterior of the distillery at Caol Ila. The building has been modernized and in the process lost its pagodas. It now looks more like a factory than a malt distillery.

Whiskies from Scotland's islands

Jura. There are records of a distillery on Jura as early as the end of the 17th century and, by the 19th century, it had developed into a very substantial distillery indeed, with a sea frontage of more than 500 feet. Be that as it may, it fell upon hard times, and this original distillery finally closed down in 1904.

The new distillery has nothing to do with the old one at all, and was completed in 1963. Although it is geographically very near Islay, the whisky it produces is much lighter, and with little of the heavy peatiness of the whiskies distilled on its sister island. Some malt drinkers go as far as to say it reminds them of Glenmorangie, perhaps the lightest of all Highland malt whiskies. It is very drinkable at an age when Islay whiskies would still be unformed. There is no doubt it will become more popular as it becomes more widely known and distributed.

Talisker. This splendid malt comes from the only distillery on Skye and must be regarded as one of the remotest and most inaccessible of all malt distilleries. Ships bringing in the malt and taking out the whisky have to travel right round the north of Scotland. The distillery itself is in the village of Carbost on the shores of the beautiful Loch Harport, a sea loch on the west of the island. The small settlement of Talisker from which the distillery takes its name is six miles even farther west. The malt whisky produced is very distinctive and fortunately fairly widely available. It is a light but peaty malt with a flavour mildly reminiscent of Irish whiskey and with a very pronounced aftertaste. Daiches says that 'if you breathe the flavour out of your nose immediately after swallowing you get an aftertaste of a kind of oily smokiness which I find extremely agreeable'. It is bottled at eight years and 80° proof.

Highland Park. The better known of the two whiskies produced in the Orkneys. The great whisky expert Aeneas Macdonald pronounced it one of the very best single malts, in the company of Glenlivet, Macallan and Longmorn. The special quality of Highland Park may be due in part to the composition of the Orkney peat which was once considered so superior that it was transported to the mainland to be used in distilleries all over the north of Scotland. Another possible factor is that the distillery draws its water from two hidden springs and so the water it uses 'never sees the light from source to mash-dam'. The distillery is in the town of Kirkwall, the capital of the Orkney Islands, which has its own cathedral of St Magnus dating from the 12th century. Highland Park malt whisky is heavy and very full flavoured, although its peatiness is less pronounced and smoky than the Islay malts. It has been remarked that it has much in common with the finest vintage cognac. By tradition, a little heather is added to the peat when the malt is being dried. Also by tradition, this subtle addition can be detected in the taste of the whisky itself. I cannot find it myself but perhaps there are others who can.

Scapa. This is the second malt whisky of the Orkneys, produced at a distillery two miles from Kirkwall on the shores of Scapa Flow. Compared with some ancient distilleries it is comparatively modern; it was only completed in 1885. Until about ten years ago all the whisky produced went straight to the blender, but at that time it was felt to have proved its worth and it is now on the market, bottled at eight years old and 100° proof. It is a powerful and highly aromatic whisky with a crisp bite and an exceptionally good aftertaste. It is well worth bottling as the growing demand for it shows, and while it is not yet generally available, it can be obtained. It would be a very pleasant prospect if some of the other distilleries whose output goes straight to the blenders were to follow Scapa's lead. Who knows what delights there would be in store for us if this were to be the case.

Ledaig. This distillery, the only one on the island of Mull, was originally founded in 1823 at the port of Tobermory, overlooking the famous bay that conceals a sunken 16th-century Spanish galleon. It closed its doors in 1928 but was reconstructed in 1972. It draws its water from the 'Tobermory River' which flows into the sea close to the distillery. This burn drops down from Misnish lochs in a series of spectacular cascades, ending in a magnificent 60-foot waterfall close to the distillery. This distillery, alas, has been recently once more closed due to difficulties with planning and transportation. We can only hope that happier times will see it open again and in full production.

Isle of Jura malt is comparatively new on the market but is already establishing itself as a popular brand.

Campbeltown malts

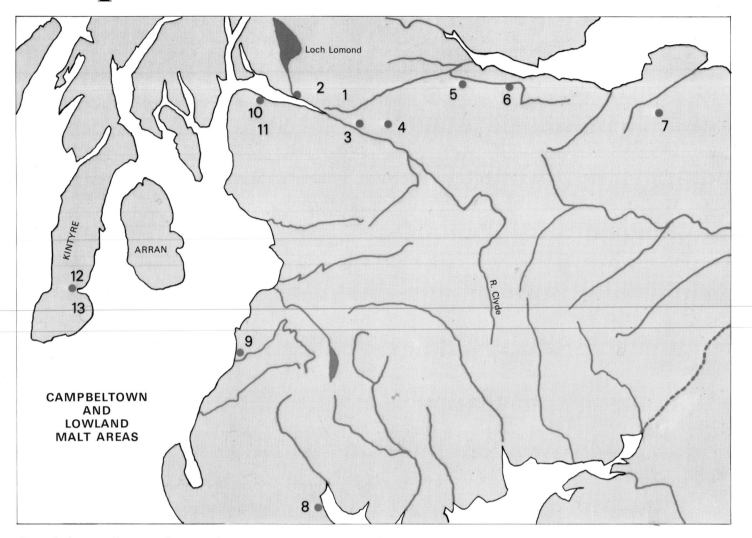

Campbeltown lies at the southwestern end of the Kintyre peninsula in the district of Argyll on the west coast of Scotland. It is an area of heath-covered hills and the town itself is beautifully situated at the head of its own bay.

Not long ago, the town of Campbeltown was the whisky capital of Scotland and thus of the world. During that time, this small town fostered no less than 32 distilleries. Even a century ago there were 21.

Their names were like a peal of bells—Hazelburn, Dalintober, Benmore, Ardlussa, Dalaruan, Lochead, Glen Nevis, Kinloch, Burnside, Glengyle, Lochruan, Albyn, Scotia, Rieclachan, Glenside, Longrow, Kintyre, Campbeltown, Argill, Springside, Springbank. Now only two are left—Springbank and Glen Scotia—to uphold a great and venerable tradition that ended in greed and disaster.

Campbeltown was—and is—ideal for making malt whisky. It has plenty of cold pure water. It has peat. It was even able to grow all the barley it required. It had skilled manpower and a tradition going back to the very beginning of malt whisky history. And for many years it did, in fact, produce large quantities of excellent whiskies, popular with blenders and malt whisky drinkers. Yet within a few years the Campbeltown whisky business collapsed almost totally. The story of the disaster is both sobering and instructive.

Campbeltown whiskies were famous for their quality and, at the beginning of the 1920s, it appeared that they just could not produce enough of them to meet the demand. This was the root of the trouble. As the 1920s progressed, the distillers began to increase production by cutting corners. They speeded up the process of distillation and thus reduced the quality of the original spirit that came from their stills. They cut back on the period of maturation and began to use cheap and inferior casks. In a seller's market it seemed they could not go wrong. It was

1 Auchentoshan
2 Littlemill
3 Kinclaith
4 Moffat
5 Rosebank
6 St Magdalene
7 Glenkinchie
8 Bladnoch
9 Ladyburn
10 Inverleven
11 Lomond
12 Glen Scotia
13 Springbank

A sorry tale of greed

a whisky boom and the advent of Prohibition in the United States meant there was an almost limitless market for anything alcoholic. Everything they produced they sold, so what was the use of wasting time and tying up valuable stock and capital if people did not care what they drank? Inevitably the whisky they sold became inferior and latterly very inferior. The distilleries were working flat out and large and quick profits were being made.

Then, quite suddenly, came the Great Crash of 1929, the economic depression that followed it, the end of the whisky boom and the repeal of Prohibition. Now whisky became hard to get rid of and a strong buyer's market emerged. In effect, the public stopped buying whisky because they couldn't afford it, and what little those who could afford to buy certainly was not the firewater that Campbeltown was now producing. More important, the blenders did not want to have anything to do with them either. They had the pick of the finest malts to choose from and why should they destroy their reputation by using the inferior spirit that was all Campbeltown was producing or had in cask? All the good Campbeltown whisky

had long since been sold. Campbeltown whiskies, once the pride of Scotland, had earned themselves a thoroughly bad name.

The results were quick and catastrophic. Nearly all the old distilleries soon went out of business. They could not sell what whisky they had and it was too late to reform. They could not afford to wait the decade or more it would have taken to rebuild their shattered reputations.

Of the two distilleries that operate now, only one—Springbank—had never compromised on quality for the sake of quick and easy profits, and it reaped its just rewards. Glen Scotia closed its doors between 1928 and 1933 but, since then, it has been back in business producing a heavy, peaty and pungent malt whisky, somewhat reminiscent of the Islay malts, just a short distance across the water. Springbank, which never closed, has always produced a whisky which was quite untypical of the Campbeltown malts of the past. It is unique in that it uses two spirit stills in the distilling process instead of the normal one. One is used for the low wines and the second entirely for redistilling the foreshots and feints. It is also unusual in that the wash still is heated by both coal and steam coils. This combination of stills produces a light but flavoury whisky, rather reminiscent of the Lowland malts. Springbank describes itself in rather endearing terms. 'The fullness of flavour and the absence of fire should be noticed. Notice also the even centre of the palate taste. This may be contrasted with the greatness of Islay whiskies, which are concentrated on the back of the tongue, and those of the finest Highland (Speyside) malts, which seem to be split into two parts, one forward in the mouth and one at the rear.' Springbank shares with Glenfiddich the distinction of bottling its malt at the distillery itself at eight years and 80° proof. Traditionally, the old, dead Campbeltown malts were much more of Glen Scotia type.

It is not unreasonable to hope that if the demand for Scotch whisky—of all kinds—goes on rising at its present rate, some of the old Campbeltown distilleries might be reopened or rebuilt. Everything necessary to make malt whisky is to hand and it is sad to see the once flourishing whisky capital of Scotland so fallen from its former glory.

Strangely enough, during Prohibition in the United States, where anti-drink rallies such as this were not uncommon, the world demand for whisky soared and the Campbeltown distilleries started to sell substandard malts. When the crash of 1929 occurred, no one wanted the Campbeltown 'fire-waters' and many of the distilleries in the area were forced to close.

Lowland malts

Very large quantities of malt whisky are produced by Lowland distilleries, nearly all of which are found near Glasgow and Edinburgh. This means that the location of the distilleries tends to be less picturesque than that of the Highland and Islay malts. Some Lowland distilleries in industrial areas are, in fact, ugly and in ugly surroundings.

But the materials they use are as fine and the skills of their craftsmen as great as at any Highland distillery. The trouble is that nearly all the whisky they distil goes straight into the cask for blending. Very little is bottled. This is a pity because some extremely drinkable Lowland malts are produced, although it must be admitted that none of them approaches the sunny majesty of the greatest Highland malts.

Possibly there is some element of snobbery in the anonymity of all the Lowland malts, a reflection of the belief that the Highlands are romantic and fashionable and the Lowlands mundane and dowdy. But whatever the reason may be, Lowland malts are hard to come by and only very few—Rosebank being the best known—ever seem to be exported.

Rosebank. The most easily come by— a very light, sweetish whisky; slightly flowery and without a great aftertaste, bottled at 70° proof. The distillery itself is on the banks of the old Forth and Clyde canal, not far from Falkirk. It is not a pretty sight, and the supposed bank on which roses once grew is not readily in evidence. A century of industrial development has seen to that.

Glenkinchie. This, on the contrary, is beautifully sited in a small glen at Pencaitland in East Lothian. It is meticulously maintained and very much a favourite of D.C.L. The gardens are quite lovely and there is even a bowling green for the workforce. Glenkinchie goes straight to the blenders but David Daiches was lucky enough to be given a bottle by an Edinburgh blending firm. In his excellent book *Scotch Whisky*, he describes it as 'a very agreeable whisky, slightly sweeter and perhaps just a trifle sharper than a Rosebank.' The distillery manager, Mr Alistair Munro, has also built a most fascinating museum of many historical distilling tools and machinery. He also found an exquisite model of a distillery from the 1925 Empire Exhibition at Wembley which he has lovingly rebuilt.

Ladyburn. This distillery is at Girvan, on the coast between Stranraer and Ayr, looking due west to Ailsa Craig and northwest to Arran. It is a close neighbour of Grants' enormous grain distillery, which is itself called Girvan.

Littlemill. Situated at Bowling, in Dunbartonshire, about 12 miles to the northwest of Glasgow. It was built in the middle of the 18th century as a brewery but was certainly producing whisky by 1820. It takes both its water and its peat from above the Highland line which separates the Highlands from the Lowlands, although it is classified as a Lowland malt.

Auchentoshan. Halfway between Littlemill and Glasgow, this is unique for the way it produces its mash. Instead of the normal three or four infusions with hot water, there is one charge which is stirred for 20 minutes and then left for an hour. The drained wort then goes straight into the washback while the residue is used to sparge the next batch of mash. The distillery claims that this gives a better wort for the all-important brewing.

The distillery was founded in 1825 and, like Littlemill, draws its water from above the Highland line. It also triple distils its spirit. Auchentoshan is another Lowland malt which is bottled, a light textured malt whisky, rather dry but, again, very drinkable at an early age.

Inverleven. Another close neighbour of Littlemill, actually sited inside Hiram Walkers' enormous Dumbarton blending plant which also, incidentally, encompasses their giant Dumbarton grain still.

St Magdalene. This is at Linlithgow, 17 miles to the west of Edinburgh. At one time, Barnard records, there were five distilleries in Linlithgow. An artesian well supplies most of the water necessary for whisky making.

Bladnoch. At Wigtown on the West coast, the southernmost distillery in Scotland, which produces one of the finest Lowland malts. R. J. S. McDowall says in his book *The Whiskies of Scotland* that 'in its heyday this was a very good whisky with a wonderful bouquet but the old mature variety is no longer available. Fortunately, I have a bottle over 30 years old which now smells like the best cognac although it is tasteless.' The distillery closed down in the 1930s but it was reopened in the 1950s and came back into production during the 1960s. Barnard mentions its red woodwork: this remains.

Other Highland malts are Lomond, Kinclaith and Moffat. Daiches' words on Lowland malts as a whole are worth remembering. At the very end of his book he says, 'I should like to beat the drum a bit for Lowland malts. They have been

overshadowed in the literature of whisky and in the esteem of single whisky drinkers by Highland malts, which have more romance in their story and the best of which, it is true, are whiskies of greater character and grander flavour. But a well-matured Lowland malt is—especially for those who do not prefer a heavily-peated whisky—a pleasant and civilized drink of distinctive quality and makes a good all-purpose whisky.'

The Lowland malt distilleries are not nearly so attractively situated as their Highland counterparts, but the whisky they produce is not to be dismissed lightly. Here, barrels are being taken into St Magdalene distillery at Linlithgow.

Vatted malts

Although nearly all malt whisky ends up in the blender's mixing casks, a few barrels are reserved for 'vatting'. Vatted malts are, simply, single malts mixed with other single malts to produce a blend of malt whiskies with no admixture of grain whisky. There is no clear record of when the practice first started but it appears that during the 19th century distillers occasionally blended malt whiskies from the same distillery but of different ages to produce a more consistent whisky or, brutally, to disguise or improve a poor malt. Then someone had the bright idea of mixing malts from two different distilleries and vatted malts were born.

They have always been uncommon and some purists disagree with them. R. J. S. McDowall says: 'For the most part they are gimmicks made to satisfy the demand for more flavoured whiskies and, of course, at considerably higher price than most blends . . . I am afraid that too many contain immature whiskies. Some are quite smooth but somehow the mixture of flavours is wrong, as if one took a mixture of different kinds of chocolate into the mouth at the same time. The result would be an indeterminate taste.'

This seems a bit hard. The vatted malts I have tasted have all been whiskies of considerable character and interest. George Saintsbury's famous recipe of half Glenlivet and half Clynelish produces a princely drink. It was Saintsbury, incidentally, who had another formula for producing an accidental variety of vatted malts. He, along with many other connoisseurs, believed that whisky kept in the same cask for more than 15 years can become slimy (although I have personal knowledge of many splendid exceptions to this rule). It was his practice to fill a barrel with good malt whisky, stand it on end and insert a tap halfway down. As soon as the level of the whisky fell to that of the tap, the barrel was topped up with more good malt whisky. This process was continued indefinitely. It must have produced a fascinating series of vatted malts and it would be nice to know how often in a year the cask was topped up.

The most easily available vatted malt is Strathconon which is bottled by James Buchanan, the Black & White whisky people. Berry's make one called simply All Malt, Findlaters have a Mar Lodge

and Haig has a Glenleven. Highland Fusilier is a vatted malt supposedly bottled for the Royal Highland Fusiliers at Elgin. Other vatted malts are Glencoe, Hudson's Bay 1670, Old Bannockburn, Glen Douglas, Pride of Strathspey, Seven Star Special, Capercaillie, Dewars, Glensloy, Glenfairn, Royal Culross, Rhosdu, Inchmurriss, Connoisseur's Choice, Glen Drummond, Seven Stills, Kylemore, Cairnbrogie, Glen Gloy and Duncraggan.

There are also a few vatted malts which go for export only. Among them are Kiltarity, Justerini and Brooks 20 year old, and Glen Dew. Harrods of London used to make their own vatted malt but have stopped doing so quite recently. As with ordinary blended whiskies, the makers of vatted malt are exceedingly reluctant to say how much of what goes into them.

At the end of the distillation process, the raw spirit is piped into casks for the long period to maturation. After some years much of the produce of the malt distilleries is used in the blending of what is, without doubt, the most internationally popular of all spirits.

Right: Newly blended whisky rests in large, glass-lined tanks before it is finally bottled.

Mr Campbell of Tomintoul produces a rare and powerful vatted malt whisky. He admits that he uses six fine malts in the process but, very cannily, refuses to specify them.

4 GRAIN WHISKIES

The main thing to remember about grain whisky as distinct from malt whisky is its scale. Making malt whisky can be regarded as a craft. Making grain whisky can be regarded as an industrial process. The output of a big pot still can be measured in thousands of gallons. The output of a moderate sized patent still can be measured in terms of tens of thousands of gallons over a comparable period of time. This is an important consideration because it must be remembered that malt whisky is made by a batch process, with a start and a finish, while grain whisky is made by a continuous process. Malt uses expensive barley, grain the cheaper maize as well as barley. At one time malt whisky distillers refused to recognize that grain whisky was whisky at all. It was, they said, a neutral spirit fit only to be made into methylated spirit or redistilled into gin.

The controversy still rumbles on, especially in parts of the Highlands. Neil Gunn, writing in 1935, said, 'The product of the pot still contains the oils and aromatic substances that give true whisky its body and flavour. The product of the patent still is almost pure alcohol, flavour-less, and is mainly used for industrial and scientific purposes. . . . Now a patent still produces alcohol much more cheaply than a pot still and in vastly greater quantities. If, therefore, one can put upon the market a bottle of this patent still spirit, reduced with water to the usual retail strength and coloured nicely with caramel, a bigger profit would be obtained from its sale than from the sale of a bottle of pure pot still whisky.

'When the Highland and Irish distillers of the real *uisgebeatha* saw what was happening, they became alarmed. This trade of theirs, that they had been conscientiously building up for generations, was facing disaster, for of course the patent spirit (or "silent" spirit as it was called) was being alluringly labelled as fine old matured Scotch whisky. . . . It does seem hard on Scotland that one of her most distinctive products should be thus imitated throughout the world. The commercial loss, taking everything that is wrongly labelled "Scotch" into account, must be enormous; but as I suggest, it is surely more enormous that so fine and indeed so noble a spirit should be so vilely

Suffolk maize destined for the grain distilleries of Scotland. When the spirit is produced, it is kept for between three and four years before being blended with malt whiskies to produce standard blends of Scotch. On its own, grain whisky has been described as 'antiseptic' and 'characterless'.

treated.' Some would still agree with him.

In fact, the question is largely academic, because no one drinks grain whisky by itself anyway. It all goes into the blending vats to be mixed with the more pungent malt whiskies to produce the popular blended brands we see behind the bars in our pubs. The one exception to this seems to be the 'Choice Old Cameron Brig' grain whisky which is produced at Cameronbridge Distillery and bottled by John Haig and Co. It is sold only locally and was discovered almost by accident by David Daiches who found it 'clear and sharp in taste, almost antiseptic indeed, with nothing at all of what I would call whisky character'.

He goes on to say that an Edinburgh blending firm sent him a 17-year-old sample of grain whisky which had a 'sharp, pungent acidy smell ("like surgical spirit" my wife remarked as I passed the glass to her and she sniffed it). Its sharpness caught me at the back of the throat as I drank. It seemed to have little or no body, but all surface flavour, and that the flavour of a pungent sweet sharpness that makes one think more of a chemistry laboratory than

a bar. My own experience with patent still grain whisky, then, suggests that while it has a part to play in blends it is not a whisky to drink by itself, nor can it begin to compare as a drink with a pot still malt whisky. But it is clearly no mere "silent spirit": indeed, it is rather "noisy".' This seems to me to be definitive. I myself have sampled both North British and Port Dundas grain whisky. North British I found had a distinct if evanescent lemony flavour. Port Dundas was harsher.

Although grain whiskies possess less of the complex characteristics that make it so vital that malt whisky be properly matured, they still have to be aged in the same way. They are reduced in strength by the addition of distilled water, filled into barrels and left to mature in properly bonded warehouses. Because of their comparative simplicity they mature much more speedily and it is unlikely that many of them are given more than a few years in cask, except those needed for the rarer and much more expensive blends. Three years is the minimum period for maturation but four years is standard. There is agreement that they do not improve beyond that time.

The patent or Coffey still

The still used by most Scotch grain whisky distillers remains essentially that invented and patented by Aeneas Coffey around 1830. Although working on totally different principles to the pot still, the inherent distillation characteristics of the Coffey still nevertheless ensure the presence of the necessary congeners in the spirit vital to grain whisky character.

Modified versions of Coffey's still can be incorporated into even more complex distillation systems which completely remove all those congeners essential to grain whisky character and flavour. A 'neutral' spirit is thus produced suitable for gin or vodka, or indeed any flavoured beverage liquor.

More complicated enlarged distillation systems are also used to produce industrial alcohol, much of Europe's enormous wine surplus, for example, being so distilled to produce alcohol for industrial use.

The principle of the patent still is that of a heat exchanger, the refinement here being that cold wash is heated by hot alcoholic vapour which, in turn, it condenses to produce grain spirit.

The most common type of patent still consists of two 40–50-foot connected rectangular columns, each subdivided horizontally by a number of perforated plates. One column is called the analyser, the other the rectifier.

Wash is prepared as at a malt distillery but on an incomparably greater scale. Even a moderately sized grain distillery will have 16 washbacks producing a million gallons of wash a week. The difference is that it is a wash made from unmalted grain and malted barley rather than wholly from malted barley as in the malt whisky distilleries. The unmalted maize is cooked under pressure in big steam boilers for about two hours until its starch cells burst and then a proportion of ground malted barley is added. The enzymes in the malt go to work on the starch of the unmalted grain when it is mashed in mash tuns in the normal manner, and a sweet wort is thus obtained which can be fermented in the normal way. The alcoholic wash produced then goes to the top of the analyser via the coils of the rectifier.

Steam from an outside boiler is fed into the bottom of the analyser and hot wash into the top. The steam heats the system as it rises and the wash heats up and begins to give off its alcohol as it descends. The alcohol-laden steam this process produces rises to the top of the column while the spent watery wash, which boils at a much higher temperature than the alcohol, runs down the column to be drained away. The alcoholic steam is now piped to the base of the rectifying column where it begins to rise. It now begins to condense on a long coil that runs through the rectifier. This coil carries wash down through the column, cold when it is pumped in from the washbacks at the top but progressively hotter as it travels down. At a predetermined point, where sufficient spirit has accumulated, the horizontal plate has a duct which carries the liquid off to the spirit receiver. The beauty of the system is the heat exchange process whereby the alcoholic steam which needs to be condensed is made to do it by the cold wash which it, in its turn, heats. The more volatile vapours (the 'foreshots') pass up to the top of the column and are led away. The less volatile vapours (the 'feints') condense farther down the column to be led away to the top of the analyser for further redistillation.

Although working the continuous process still is basically a mechanical operation, it nevertheless requires considerable skill. In a patent still house, the stillman stands on his platform near the top of the rectifier so that he can control the temperature and rate of flow of the wash and keep an eye on the spirit and other volatile vapours. Judgment is important here and his actions can significantly affect the quality of the grain spirit that he produces. The spirit pulled off a patent still is of considerably higher strength than that from a pot still—usually around 165° proof as distinct from 125° proof. But after this it is diluted and casked in exactly the same way.

This traditional way of producing grain whisky is now being adapted in various ways and one of the distillers has come up with a revolutionary new method called 'the whole mash system'. Here the mash is not drained to produce wort but goes on as a slurry to the washbacks. It is fermented in the normal way by the addition of yeast which appears to be quite unaffected by the presence of solids. The resultant alcoholic porridge goes straight to the analyser and rectifier and is treated as though it is normal mash.

This illustration of a long-defunct distillery of 1851 gives a highly stylized account of whisky distilling in the mid-19th century. The size of the washbacks shows that whisky was being produced in large quantities even then.

DISTILLERY THAMES BANK

WASH STILL

GRAIN MILL

MASH TUN

5 BLENDED SCOTCH WHISKY

When people talk about Scotch or Scotch whisky, 99 times out of a 100 they mean *blended* Scotch whisky, a combination of grain and malt whisky. Blended whiskies generally contain a larger proportion of the light grain whisky and a smaller proportion of the heavy and powerful malts. By far the larger proportion of all malt whisky produced goes straight to the blenders and only a relatively small amount ever finds its way into bottles. Roughly speaking, the better the blend, the higher proportion of malts. Blenders are very guarded about what goes into their blends and guesses range very widely. But it would be a very poor blend indeed that had less than 20 percent malt whisky in it. Really good ones are probably half and half. However, we just do not know.

You will notice that blended whisky advertisements commonly stress the High-land-Island-pot-still-age-old-craftsmen-rushing - burns - and - waving - fields - of-barley aspect of whisky and never the grain whisky that makes up the bulk of their contents. As a former composer of blended whisky advertisements for many years, I know this only too well. This again demonstrates the manufacturers' discomfort about people really knowing what goes into the whisky they buy. It is almost as if they feel guilty about it, or as if the ghost of the Islington judgment of 1906 still haunts them.

They are wrong. The brutal fact is that the vast majority of people prefer blended whisky. It is a lighter, more dependable, more standard, more digestible drink than single malt. It demands less. It does not mind being diluted with soda or ginger or more exotic mixtures. It thrives on being frozen with ice cubes or heated with honey or lemon. It enjoys being chased by beer or thrashed into cocktails. In short, a decent blended Scotch is a very good drink, and it has its own advantage: it is usually about half as expensive as a good malt whisky.

No one knows how many blends there are, although more than 5,000 separate names have been recorded, of which over 400 can be found on the labels of bottles on the market today. Scotch whisky is exported to almost every nation in the world and it is highly likely that some blends have many different names according to local preferences and idiosyncracies.

Blends vary in quality, too. This depends on two factors—the relative amounts of malt and grain, and time in cask. The greater the malt content and the age, the better the blend. From this you would gather that a blend like Chivas Royal Salute, heavily malted and 21 years old, would be a very good blend indeed. You would be right.

The actual process of blending is simple but usually done on a very large scale. The description of how one famous blend—Johnnie Walker—is made will serve for them all. There may be minor differences at some stages of the operation but they would not significantly alter the story.

The blending plant is a large empty shed with a concrete floor. Sunk into the floor are a dozen or so long and parallel stainless steel troughs about a foot wide and 18 inches deep. These all flow into a larger trough which lies horizontal to them. In the centre of this trough is a large circular hole which is, in fact, the opening to an enormous stainless steel blending vat.

Whisky is tested at every stage of the blending process.

Malt whiskies are delivered from the distillers and warehouses where they have matured and are rolled to one side of the blending floor; similarly grain whiskies go to the other side. The barrels are man-handled so that their bungs (circular wooden stoppers) are over the troughs. A small (tenth of a gallon) sample is taken from each cask by a large metal spigot and emptied into a special bottle to be sniffed to make certain the whisky is fit and not woody or contaminated.

A normal day's blending at Johnnie Walker would be about 40,000 gallons, so some hundreds of casks are involved. It is now the practice to bring in at least some of the grain whisky by tanker. This accomplishes considerable economies in handling at both distillery and blending plant. Of course, a number of grain whiskies and an even larger number of malt whiskies are involved. In Johnnie Walker at least three grain whiskies and several dozen malt whiskies are used.

At a given signal, the unstoppered casks are rolled over and begin to discharge their spirit into the troughs. As more and more casks are rolled, the flow of whisky grows until a veritable river of whisky is cascading into the horizontal troughs and thence into the blending vat. At this point a certain amount of colouring matter is added; in this instance, it is in the form of extremely dark molasses. This brings the colour of the blend up to the normal standard but the amount is so small in relation to the flood of whisky that it could hardly affect the taste.

When all the whisky to be blended is safely in the tank, it is 'roused' by having air pumped through it from perforated pipes in the base of the vat. This goes on for an hour to ensure that all the whiskies are thoroughly mixed.

The next process is to pump the newly-blended whisky into receiving vats, where they are once more 'roused' with com-pressed air. The whisky is then pumped back into barrels which now go for a final four-to-eight months 'sleep' in the wood before being taken to the bottling plant. This final maturing process smooths out any tiny rough edges the blend might have and ensures that a true marriage has been made. This takes place these days in huge, on-site warehouses where the barrels are stored on racks eight feet high. 'We like to see empty racks', said a blender, 'because that means we're selling our whisky.'

At all stages of this blending process, the ubiquitous excise officer is present, making his calculations and ensuring that

The casks which are used to store whisky are made of oak. Old sherry casks are preferred but most whisky is today kept in American oak casks. These are normally shipped in pieces and re-assembled at the distillery. Many of the casks have been repaired so often that little, if any, of the original barrels remain.

Black & White is one of the brand leaders in the blended whisky market.

the government gets its money. Enormous amounts of money are involved. The duty on a 110-gallon cask of whisky is £3000. The duty on any one day's blending at Johnnie Walker is more than £1,000,000. As one of the directors at the plant dryly said, 'If you were to sell all Scotch whisky in bond today, you'd wipe out the national debt'. It is not, then, strange that every whisky warehouse has its own excise officer and that all access doors need two keys to be opened or closed— one belonging to the distillery, the other belonging to you and me in the person of the excise man.

At the end of six months—or it could be as little as four or as many as eight months, depending on demand—the casks go from the blending plant to the bottling plant, from which the whisky finally emerges in the familiar bottles you see in bars or in wine merchants. Again, this process is so large and complex that it can only sensibly be described in industrial terms.

Every day hundreds of thousands of bottles arrive at the plant. In fact, the whisky industry's demand for bottles is so insatiable that it has made economic sense for D.C.L. to buy into the glass industry: to ensure supply they now own the majority of shares in the British United Glass Company.

The bottles arrive boxed in cartons already supplied to the glass makers. They are new and clean. But whisky blenders have to be absolutely sure, so the bottles are unboxed and carefully washed and sterilized with caustic soda, rinsed and dried before going onto the production line. Meanwhile, in another part of the plant, the whisky casks from the blending plant are arriving to be emptied into glass-lined storage tanks where the whisky is reduced to the required proof strength by the simple addition of water: different markets demand different strengths of spirit and, for the blenders, this is a comparatively simple job.

The whisky is then fed to the smaller receiving vats through a filter consisting of numerous porous pads. It is also chilled to take out those congenerics which might cloud the bottled whisky if it encountered really cold temperatures. It is then pumped through a bottling machine into bottles at a very high speed. At the Johnnie Walker plant there are some dozens of production lines because they bottle in over 60 different bottle shapes and sizes.

The 'old' bottling machines there can fill 6000 bottles an hour. A new machine they are testing can fill nearly 15,000 bottles an hour. After the bottles are filled, they are inspected against a light source to make sure that the whisky in each bottle is perfect. Rarely rejected bottles are recycled. Each bottle is then mechanically sealed, capsuled and labelled, and in some instances excise stamped. The completed bottle is then re-cartoned and is ready for dispatch. For export, dispatch is now usually done by container. The arrival, filling and departure of the containers is in itself an impressive business. In a normal bottling week, between one and two million bottles of Johnnie Walker will leave this one plant.

Famous the world over, the Johnnie Walker symbol is instantly recognizable in over 150 countries.

Born 1820
Still going
strong

The blender's art

Every blend is a combination of malts and grains. More than 40 separate and different single whiskies go into making some blends. How, then, did any particular blend come into being and how is its particular taste and flavour maintained? The answer is not simple. Most standard blends—the popular ones that are heavily advertised and are familiar in public houses—are of very respectable antiquity, going back well into the last century. A whisky blending company, deciding to market a new blend, would start a process of experiment, mixing various numbers and proportions of malt and grain until the blender had achieved exactly what he had in mind or, more precisely, what he thought would sell most successfully.

This happened in the 1960s when Americans developed a taste for 'light' whiskies. There is no need to enter into the long-standing controversy as to what exactly a 'light' whisky is. Experienced judges of whisky are quite unable to agree. It is enough that a demand arose, which was met by producing blended whiskies such as Cutty Sark and J. & B. which now sell extremely well in the United States, by far the biggest importer. These whiskies also sell well in Britain and have established themselves among the brand leaders. Certainly, the amount of money spent on advertising and promoting them seems to have paid off handsomely; and perhaps the most important person in their creation was the 'man with the nose'—the blender.

To achieve his ends, the blender has to take into account a number of considerations. The whiskies he uses must marry well: no single flavour must dominate. Secondly, he must attain a balance between the heavier, smokier malts and the sharper grains. Thirdly, there is cost: too much malt whisky in the blend and it becomes uncompetitive.

So—with his nose—he will reach towards the perfect compromise he is trying to achieve. He will very seldom—if ever—taste the whiskies he is creating; he may pour some on the palms of his hands, rub them together so that the spirit evaporates readily and inhale deeply from his closed hands. He takes careful account of exactly what proportions of which whisky must go into making the finished blend.

However, his troubles have not ended there. Although malt and grain distillers go to great lengths to bring their whiskies to the same exacting standard, there are bound to be small changes over the years and even from year to year. Making whisky is not an exact science and barley, maize, climate and cooperage are all susceptible to change and variation. So the blender has a continuing problem of consistency: he must concern himself to see that every bottle of his blend that

An average blended Scotch whisky can be the product of as many as 40 different malts and blends. Despite the extent of mechanization in the modern whisky industry, the head blender depends on his sense of smell to match the whiskies in his final blend. Here, he is 'nosing' the blend before giving his approval.

leaves the bottling plant is, over the decades, as nearly as possible a replica in taste, strength and colour of every other bottle.

The blender will test and sample his whiskies at every stage. Straight from the still, he will want to ensure for himself that the whiskies he may be using in the future are of good quality and not 'burnt', 'cooked', 'sour', or 'with background smell'. To do this he will use a special, tulip-shaped nosing glass, into which he will pour a measured ounce of spirit. This he will mix with two ounces of water,

shake vigorously with his thumb over the glass and then sniff. If he is satisfied (and he almost always is), he knows the whisky can be safely matured and will be of good quality when he needs it.

He will need to repeat this process again when the whisky is matured and ready for blending. If it is at full strength, he will again reduce it with twice as much water and shake and sniff every individual whisky. Finally, when it has been reduced in the vat before bottling, he will give it another sniff, this time adding only one measured ounce of water. Every individual

A selection of popular blended Scotch whiskies. Most blended whisky drinkers claim to have their own favourite which they can tell from any others. Perhaps some can, but whereas it is true that malt whiskies have individual characteristics and can, with a little practice, be identified by palate, aftertaste and nose, blended whiskies do tend to have a similarity that makes them more difficult to differentiate.

After the malts and grain whiskies have been blended in the troughs they are stored in barrels to 'marry' together. As with malt whiskies, the longer the blends are kept in the wood the better the whisky will be (within certain limits), but generally the quality of the final bottled blend will depend on the ratio of malt to grain spirit.

barrel is also sniffed before being poured into the blending troughs. Thus each whisky has been 'nosed' at least four times, if not more, before it reaches you.

The blender acts as a kind of quality control and his sense of responsibility is accordingly very great. Senior management is intimately involved and the sampling room at the bottling plant is the nerve centre of the whole process, as I saw very clearly on a visit to the Johnnie Walker plant in Kilmarnock in Ayrshire. What very few people know is what proportion of what whiskies go into each individual blend. This is the secret of secrets of Scotch whisky. No blender will ever divulge his formula to any but those few intimately concerned, nor will he divulge the adjustments he may make to that formula from time to time.

One or two facts emerge very clearly. There do appear on the market from time to time inferior blends which obviously have a very high proportion of grain whisky in them. From their sharp, almost bitter taste I would guess about four-fifths of such whisky is grain. Such blends may also use inferior or under-aged malt. Although the organized whisky trade is almost Calvinistic in its integrity it would be quite impossible for them to control every drop in the ocean of whisky produced. Whisky is a marketable commodity, like any other, and subject to the same

risks from people out to make a quick killing. It is only remarkable that such inferior blends do not appear more often.

Quality inevitably depends to a large extent on the proportions of malt. In my view, the standard blends have got it about right. I myself freely admit I drink them all (with one nameless exception) with equal pleasure. I would hate to be faced with the task of identifying which of the standard blends was which if presented with them in a dozen anonymous glasses. Much rubbish is talked by bar heroes on this subject, claiming that their own standard blend is the only one worth drinking and that they can always tell it from others. Wisely, the whisky merchant keeps quiet and takes their money.

Ageing, too, plays an important part. An older whisky is almost always a better whisky (subject to limits earlier described); it is smoother and deeper. A grain distiller told me that, in his opinion, grain whisky was about as good as it would ever be at four years old but that he had no objection to blenders keeping it for 20 years if they wanted to. But I can see the blender's argument that to mix a really venerable malt with a young grain would be to run an awful risk of losing balance. There is no doubt about it that the older, de luxe blends are better whiskies than their standard counterparts. You pay for the difference but it can be worth it.

Standard brands

These range from brands that would be familiar in any part of the world to those which would only be known in odd corners of Scotland itself. Of the familiar kind, White Horse claim, typically, that they can even be found in Alaska, Mongolia and in the wilds of Africa. Johnnie Walker, the largest-selling whisky in the world, can be found in 168 export territories. Up with these are Haig, Black & White, and Dewars. Not quite in the same league, but still enormously successful, would come Vat 69, Bell's, Teacher's Highland Cream, Long John, Grant's Standfast, Ballantine's, King George IV, 100 Pipers, Mackinlay's, Cutty · Sark, Queen Anne and Whyte & Mackay Special.

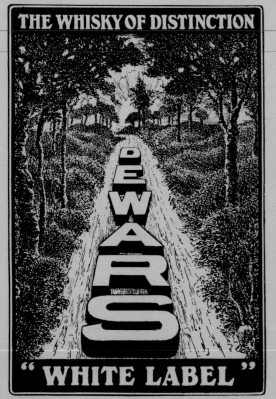

The inventive capacity of whisky advertisers seemed to run dry in the early years of this century when this was produced. Perhaps the message that Dewars was trying to get across was the longer the road, the shorter it seemed with Dewar's White Label. Dewars, of course, were one of the first blenders to 'export' to England and were one of the most successful whisky companies. They still are.

More specialized and localized brands are Royal Edinburgh, Red Tape, House of Stuart, Highland Mist, Crown of Scotland, Peter Prime, Blue Cap, Benmore, Highland Monarch, B.L. Gold Label, Shooting Lodge, Clark's Reserve, Campbell's Private Cellar, Scottish Prince, Murdoch's, Royal Strathythan, Crabbie

8 Year Old, Crawford's Three Star, Red Star, Curtis de Luxe 5 Year Old, Peter Dawson Special, Cairn's, Findlater's Finest Scotch Whisky, Ye Monks, Dew of Ben Lawers, Spey Royal, King William IV, V.O.P., Glen Crinan, Loch Fyne, Glen Rossie Special Reserve, Famous Grouse, Black Bottle, Glen Calder, Dew of Ben Alder, Avonside, Spey Cast, Glen Ghoil, Hankey Bannister, Harvey's Special, Red Hackle, Highland Clan, St Leger, Holt's Buff Label, Glen Garry, Old Mull, Auld Shepp, Coldstream Guard, Golden Glen, Highland Breeze, Inver House, Green Plaid, Kiltarie, J. G. Kinsey, Macarthur's, Munray, Old Blairmhor, Julian's, Monument, Camlan, Scottish Cream, Glenside, Lang's, Lauder's, William Lawson's, Longman, Highland Pride, Inverness Cream, Glendrostan, The Abbot's Choice, Q.E.2, McCallum's Perfection, Sandy Macdonald, Claymore, Highland Queen, Macgregor's, Scottish Heath, Macleay Duff Special Matured Cream, Glenfinnan Cluny, Martin's V.V.O., M. & D. Golden Crown, Heather Dew, Clan Roy, Rob Roy, Morton's Blended, Morton's Three Star Special Reserve, Dundee Cream of Scotch, Black Swan, Ben Macdhui, Strathaird, Oldfield's Blue Label, Johnny Wright's, Cockburn and Murray 4 Year Old, Yellow Label, Black Rooster, Black Shield, Wm. Maxwell, Isle of Skye, The Queen's Seal, King's Vat, Thistle, Rodger's Old Scots, Cream of the Barley, Queen's Own, Usher's Green Stripe, Usher's O.V.S., Jamie Stuart, Stewart's Finest Old, Old Smuggler, Gauntlet, Eight Reigns, Ambassador, Highland Cream, Beneagles, Robbie Burns, Big T, Watson's No 10, Baxter's Barley Bree, Ballochmyle, Black Bull, Highland Prince and Old Inverness.

There is no pretence that this is a complete list and there may well be hundreds of other locally-bottled brands that sell only in a few stores. It would be a herculean task to ferret them all out. I have sampled all the first and second rank standard brands and a couple of dozen or so local brands at various times and have survived the experience. It would be unfair to say that the standard was not surprisingly high and, in one or two of the half dozen or so really unpleasant whiskies I have tasted, I have suspected that what came out of the bottle may well not have been what originally went into it.

It must be assumed from this poster, that the future King George V of Britain was a lover of Black & White blended whisky.

Blends for home and abroad

Standard brands for export only

Export-only standard blended Scotch whiskies are:

King's Legend, The Real McTavish, Baird's, King Arthur, Marlboro, Duncan's Reserve, Tranquility, Campbell's Private Stock, Catto Gold Label, Catto Rare Old Scottish Highlands, King Edward I, Old Matured, Mary Stuart, Old Court, Gillon's G Blended, Sandy Tamson, Holt's Mountain Cream, Holt's Liqueur, Braebassie, Dalting, Dougherty's, Glen Mavis, Inver House Red Plaid, Kilt Castle, Glenrosa, Scot Royal, Talisman, Tam O'Shanter, Glen Eagle, Old Guns, Ben Cally, Green Tree, Dormy, Grey Label, Loretto, Clanroy, King's Favourite, King's Pride, Brae Dew, Macnish V.L., Doctor's Special, St Dennis, Marshall's, Malcolm Stuart, Munro's Square Bottle, Angus McKay, Glen Graeme, Liqueur Cream, Thistle Scotch, Huntley Blend, Scot's Own, Lord Douglas, Rodger's Special, Begbie's, Duncraig, Clan Stewart, King Charles, Glen Laggan, Highland Rover, Strong's Scotch Whisky, Strong's Genuine Highland, Strong's Real Mountain Dew, Gold Thimble, Huntingtower, Old Angus, Windsor Castle, The Kilty, Highland Fling, Jamie '08, Swing, Mackie's Ancient Scotch, Craig Castle, Red White and Blue, House of Lords, Fraser's, Royal Decree, Gun Club, Jockey Club, Noble Queen, Five Lords, Roderick Dhu, Premier, Special.

De luxe blended Scotch whiskies

These are the superior blends, older and more malty and also more expensive. Most Scotch drinkers will be familiar with one or two of them. Here, I believe, real preferences can and do emerge. All of them are good, although here again there are well known and little known brands. Among the best known and most popular are Johnnie Walker Black Label, Chivas Regal and Chivas Royal Salute, Dimple Haig and The Antiquary.

Others are House of Stuart Royal (8 Year Old), Specially Selected, Ballantine's de Luxe, Gold Cap, Bell's de Luxe 12 Year Old, Benmore Special Reserve, Berry's Best, St James 12 Year Old, Buchanan's, Royal Household, Old Rarity, David Ross de Luxe, Catto 12 Year Old Scottish Highland, Crabbie 12 Year Old, Crawford Five Star, Bene Vobis, Curtis de Luxe 12 Year Old, Old Curio, Ancestor, Ye Whisky of Ye Monks, Highland Nectar, Ye Auld Town, Perth Royal, Grant's Royal, Glen Ghoil (which also exists as a standard brand), Hankey Bannister 12 Year Old, Gold Label, Red Hackle de Luxe, Something Special, Navy Supreme, Glen Gagler 8 Year Old, Inver House Red Plaid 8 Year Old, Macarthur's 8 Year Old, Pinwinnie Royale, Islay Mist, Excalibur, The Monarch, Lang's 12 Year Old de Luxe, William Lawson's 8 Year Old, Longman 8 Year Old, Chequers de Luxe, McCallum's de Luxe, Mak' Readie, Old Parr, President, Highland Queen Grand 15, Legacy, Macleay Duff Antique, Glenfinnan Royal Liqueur, Grand Macnish, Martin's de Luxe, Martin's Fine and Rare, Old Highland, Royal Mile, King of Kings, Cockburn and Murray 8 Year Old,, Cream of the Barley 8 Year Old, Queen's Own 8 Year Old, Usher's de Luxe, Antique Jamie Stuart, Bank Note, Old Perth de Luxe, Laird O'Logan, King's Ransom, Whyte & Mackay Supreme, Whyte & Mackay 21 Year Old, Harrods' de Luxe, Harrods' 12 Year Old.

Some of these de luxe blends are very good indeed. Chivas Regal and, more especially, Chivas Regal Royal Salute are superb, although you pay a stiff price for them. The latter blend was the personal creation of Samuel Bronfman, the strange Canadian whisky genius who illuminated the Scotch whisky world in the years after the Second World War. Old Parr, for some reason, is especially popular with the Japanese.

De luxe blended Scotch whiskies for export only

Just as there are export-only standard brands, there are also export-only de luxe brands. I suspect that precisely the same reasoning lies behind the one as the other. Among the export-only de luxe brands are Haig Pinch, Royal Vat, Ne Plus Ultra, Spey Royal 8 Year Old, Royal Ages 15 Year Old, Piper, Long John 8 Year Old, Long John 12 Year Old, Glen Eagle 8 Year Old, Scottish Gold 12 Year Old, King's Favourite, King's Pride, Brae Dew, Ancient and Honourable, Angus McKay 8 Year Old, B.E.B., Liqueur Cream 12 Year Old, Huntly de Luxe, Willie's Choice, Ambassador Royal and Teacher's Royal Highland 12 Year Old.

6 AMERICAN WHISKEY

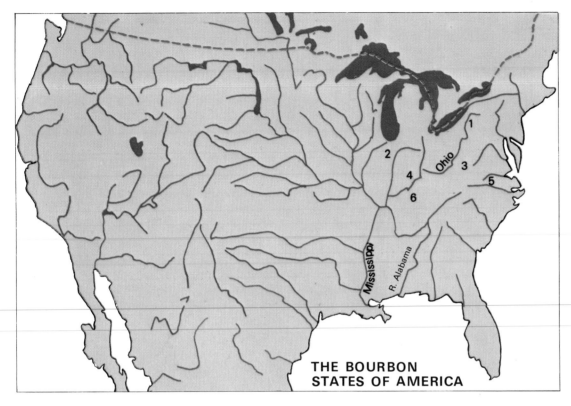

1 Pennsylvania
2 Illinois
3 Virginia
4 Kentucky
5 Maryland
6 Tennessee

THE BOURBON STATES OF AMERICA

The story of American whiskey is as complex as the country itself, mingling craftsmanship, science, geography, commerce, adventure and crime with a strong seasoning of violence. And so much popular mythology and folklore have crept into the story that it is often impossible to disentangle fact from fiction.

Typically, it had a fitful start. We know for certain that the first mention of a spirit distilled from cereal was in 1640 when William Kleft, the Director-General of the Dutch colony of New Netherlands, ordered that spiritous liquor be produced on Staten Island. The man who actually operated the still, Wilhelm Hendriksen, used both corn and rye to produce his mash. But after this solitary mention the attention of the settlers turned to rum and applejack. The West Indians, with a plentiful supply of sugar cane, made the former easily accessible and cider apples grew readily enough in the fertile soil of New England and Virginia. It was not until the arrival of Scottish and Irish immigrants that the art of distilling whiskey was imported and began to flourish.

The whiskey they produced was right for the time—a rough raw spirit with fire and strength, a drink for a man grappling with a huge and hostile nature, a drink for a pioneer breaking new ground in a new continent. As the new breed of farmers settled in their log cabins or behind their stockades, they built themselves the primitive stills they remembered from the glens and bogs of their distant homelands. These distilled spirits were highly functional too. Communications between these isolated homesteads and the tiny new townships were very poor, if they existed at all; most were mere tracks which dissolved into mudbaths when it rained. So, transporting heavy bags of grain on horseback would have been hard and heavy work. Transporting the product of many bags of grain in the form of a few barrels of spirit was both easier and more profitable so the early settlers built their stills and shared their experience until the distilling of whiskey was a widespread and flourishing domestic industry, mainly located in the states of Pennsylvania and Kentucky where most of the Irish and Scots had settled. The rum dealers of New York tried to prevent this new competition from coming into their state, but they were on the defensive from the beginning and the popularity of whiskey inexorably forced them out of business. The fact that the Revolutionary War cut off supplies from Cuba and the West Indies did not help the rum merchants of New York either.

By the end of the 1780s whiskey was

116

firmly established as the favourite spirit of the new nation. But then an event took place which was profoundly to affect the shape of the infant industry. The new American government found itself in financial trouble and Alexander Hamilton, the first Secretary of the Treasury, was casting round for ways of raising revenue. His eye lighted on distilled liquor and he calculated that he could raise as much as $800,000 a year from spirits, principally whiskey. In 1791 a new tax came into effect. The tax imposed a charge of between seven cents and 30 cents a gallon, which worked out at a third of the cash price of the spirit. Almost immediately tax inspectors were appointed and they went about their new task with enthusiasm. It could hardly be said that they were popular.

The settlers' reaction was swift and warm. Their spokesman in Congress, Representative James Jackson, claimed that the tax was 'odious, unequal, unpopular and oppressive, most particularly in the Southern states'. He had some justice—as well as a great deal of prejudice—on his side. Whiskey was widely held to be medicinal and essential to the health and well-being of men labouring in the southern parts of the country. The outcry in western Pennsylvania was particularly strong. Here cash was scarce and whiskey itself was frequently used as an article of barter—whiskey was, in fact, currency. So to settlers here, the new tax was a tax on money itself.

There is much evidence that Hamilton himself was uneasy about the whiskey tax. Some years earlier he had written that 'the genius of the people will ill brook the inquisitive and peremptory spirit of excise laws', an observation, incidentally, with wider application than to the American people alone. A meeting of aggrieved settlers in Pittsburgh in September, 1791, made the point very clearly. Here it was resolved that, 'it is insulting to the feelings of the people to have to have their vessels marked, their houses ransacked', and so on. And there was another obnoxious feature of the tax. If you were caught out and prosecuted for evading the new tax, you had to be tried at the federal courts. The nearest one to Pittsburgh was in Philadelphia 350 miles away. That length of journey could take a long time and this, too, worked out as an extra punishment to the victim, and one that was quite unavoidable.

In fact, the tax was a failure. The cost of collecting it was more than 15 percent of the money raised and this itself was never more than half the target. In May,

The negro servant of these Union officers of the American Civil War is carrying a demijohn of rye whiskey from the unit commissary. In those days, whiskey was recognized as an essential war supply!

The whiskey war

1792, Congress recognized the strength of feeling about the tax and cut it sharply, especially on small domestic stills. But even this was not good enough. The aroused armies of farmer-distillers became so angry and vociferous that President Washington himself was induced to proclaim that 'malcontents...desist from all unlawful combinations...tending to obstruct the operation of the laws'. But the sullen populace remembered that they still had to travel 350 miles if they were caught, and Congress finally had the good sense to repeal this part of the law and allow cases more than 50 miles from a federal court to be tried at state courts. Alas, this commonsense solution only added fuel to the flames. It specifically excluded 'distillers who had previously to its enactment incurred a penalty', and so gave a new grievance to the already aggrieved. The final blow came in 1794 when the federal court in Philadelphia prosecuted 75 distillers from western Pennsylvania in May but neglected to serve the writs until July. Federal law officers went to Pennsylvania to deliver the writs but they were set upon by angry crowds of settlers.

The leaders of this rebellious mob were farmer-distillers such as Albert Salletin and Henry Brackenridge, and populists like David Redford. Several unfortunate tax collectors were tarred and feathered and later in the month of July about 500 armed men surrounded the house of General John Neville, who was the regional chief of the excisemen, and burned it down.

Alexander Hamilton reacted swiftly. To him, this disorderly rioting was a dangerous rebellion against the new and fragile country, and he persuaded Washington, in his role of commander-in-chief, to raise an army of 13,000 militiamen to put down the mob. Washington agreed and Hamilton set off at the head of his citizens' army. When they got to western Pennsylvania, they found that the insurrection had collapsed of its own accord and the militiamen could do nothing more than temporarily arrest a hundred or so leading troublemakers. Hamilton felt he needed an example and two of the accused were tried and found guilty of treason. They were actually sentenced to death but Washington combined good sense and clemency and pardoned them. American

whiskey was saved its first two martyrs.

The expense of mounting this punitive expedition, set against a much lower return on the tax itself, probably gave the Treasury a net loss but Hamilton stubbornly insisted on maintaining his notorious tax on distilled spirits. His successors in many countries must bless his memory. Modern drinkers may not feel so benevolent.

The 'Whiskey War' or 'Whiskey Insurrection' was never as serious as it is often made out to be but it was an early and clear example of the strength of feeling that whiskey could arouse. It was also an example of the sturdy independence of American whiskey distillers, a characteristic that was to show itself in a less favourable light several times over the next two centuries.

George Washington was a gentleman distiller himself, with a commercial distillery situated near his farm at Dogue, near Mount Vernon in Virginia. He produced a rye whiskey of which he was very proud and, indeed, it had an extremely high reputation in its day. Could this have been because his steeps, tuns and stills were under the personal direction of one James Anderson, a Scot?

Thomas Jefferson also distilled his own rye whiskey. Thus, two of the first three presidents of the United States were whiskey distillers.

Typical scenes from 'the Wild West'. Whiskey had an important place in the society of the day. It went hand-in-hand with gold prospecting in the mining towns and there are many reports of hard won fortunes being lost over the card tables of the whiskey-selling saloons.

Thomas Jefferson was a skilled distiller and proud of the quality of the whiskey he produced.

THE DISCOVERY.

"WHISKY GOES"

FREIGHT FOR THE DIGGINGS.

"JUMPIN CLAIMS, IS YER?"

THE MILL.

MAIN STREET.

THE PACK-MULES.

"JOHN"

SUNDAY AMUSEMENTS.

Whiskey goes west

The provocative attempt by the federal government to tax American whiskey had another, and unpredictable, effect which was to contribute in a way to the growth and power of the new nation. Disgruntled farmers moved farther west, preferring the arrows and lances of hostile Indians to, among other things, the unwelcome attentions of the excisemen. As they moved they sought out the conditions they knew were essential to the distillation of good spirit—clear, pure, cold water, uncontaminated with organic matter but graced with a suspicion of lime. Water with these qualities wells up from deep in the earth through a purifying stratum of limestone and so it is no accident that the best American whiskies are produced over a vast bed of this rock that stretches from western Pennsylvania into Kentucky, Indiana and southern Illinois. A further outcrop appears in Maryland. Even today, 80 percent of American distilleries are to be found in these five states.

The first distillery in Kentucky is supposed to have been in production in Louisville in 1783, and the first whiskey to be distilled in Bourbon County, Kentucky, is usually attributed to the Rev. Elijah Craig who first casked his spirit in 1789. From some thousands of similar settler-distillers of the time few names have survived but among them are Jacob Spears, John Hamilton and Daniel Stewart. Men like these can be considered the founding fathers of the American whiskey industry.

The move west into the interior had another effect on American whiskey. Before this almost all native whiskey had been rye, which grew particularly well in Pennsylvania. But on their new homesteads the pioneers found that maize grew better and bigger and thus the transition towards the mellower, lighter kinds of whiskey was begun.

As the production of whiskey was refined and enlarged, another and unexpected outlet was found for it—the American Indians. There is an apocryphal story that Henry Hudson took Indians aboard his ship on his voyage to America

Whiskey was very often the most convenient currency in the remoter areas of North America. The owner of this trading post of the 1880s would have traded whiskey to Indians for the furs of beavers, arctic foxes and bears.

in 1610 and gave one of them so much strong drink that he fell to the deck helplessly drunk. When he came to he told his companions that he had visited paradise and experienced a series of heavenly sensations and after this, the story goes, it was impossible to keep Indians away from drink. A further extension of this highly improbable story says that the Indian word 'Manhattan' actually means 'the place of the first big drunk'.

Be that as it may, tragically the Indians soon developed a taste for spirits, a fact that was used quite ruthlessly by both British and French in their struggle for control over the sub-continent throughout the 17th and 18th centuries. The American Indians had never discovered the principle of distilling alcohol and had no experience of its effects. The sensations whiskey produced were beyond their control or understanding and their sole response to it was to get hopelessly drunk. There was a sad and simple reason for this. For centuries they had had the custom of sharing all their food and consuming it on the spot and they pathetically did exactly the same with a keg of whiskey—they shared it until it had all gone. This led to scenes of violence and

debauchery that the white man did little to discourage. It made dealing with them cheaper and dispossessing them easier.

An American trader of the early 19th century graphically records the effects of whiskey on Indians. He worked on a trading post for seven years between 1800 and 1807 and his journal records no less than 77 drinking debauches of large crowds of Indians. Sixty-five Indians suffered injury during these drinking parties, ranging from small wounds to death. He draws a picture of noisy brawling, sexual orgies, the wailing of neglected children, sometimes even knocked about by drunken adults, something previously unknown in Indian society. He recounts:

'I sincerely believe that competitive trade among the Saulteurs [a Great Lake tribe] is the greatest slavery a person of any feeling can undergo. A common dram-shop in a civilized country is a paradise compared to the Indian trade, where two or more interests are striving to obtain the greater share of the Indians' hunts—particularly among the Saulteurs, who are always ready to take advantage of the situation by disposing of their skins and furs to the highest bidder. No ties, former

The frontierswomen of the young United States came to loathe whiskey. They felt neglected and unprotected while their menfolk spent their free time in the saloons drinking and playing cards. Their feelings grew to such an extent that they became one of the bases of the prohibition movement of the early 20th century.

121

'We know it to be hurtful'

favours, or services involved, will induce them to give up their skins for a penny less than they can get elsewhere. Gratitude is a stranger to them, grant them a favour today and tomorrow they will suppose it is their due. Love of liquor is their ruling passion, and when intoxicated they will commit any crime to obtain more drink.

'But the Indians totally neglect their ancient customs and what can this degeneracy be ascribed to but their intercourse with us, particularly as they are so unfortunate as to have a continual succession of opposition parties to teach them roguery and destroy both mind and body with this pernicious article...? What a different set of people they would be, were there not a drop of liquor in the country. If a murder is committed among the Saulteurs it is always in a drinking match.'

The wiser Indians saw very clearly the destruction spiritous liquors were wreaking on their people. As early as 1698 a Delaware chief mourned:

'We know it to be hurtful to us to drink it. We know it, but if people will sell it to us, we so love it that we cannot refuse it. But when we drink it, it makes us mad, we do not know what we are doing; we abuse one another; we throw one another in fire. Through drinking, seven score of our people have been killed.'

This pitiful plea fell on deaf ears. Certainly the farmer-distillers of a century later who were pushing their way west into Indian territories and driving the original inhabitants out were not going to refrain from using this highly destructive and highly profitable weapon on their demoralized victims.

All that can be said of this sorry episode of American history is that the Indians may have had a long and subtle revenge. As whiskey flowed west, tobacco flowed east and so the coughs and cancers of the world that destroyed their culture with whiskey may be an historical recompense three centuries in the paying.

The spirit that these cowboys drank was rough, raw and harsh, in keeping with the times in which they lived. The saloons were the centre of social life in many small towns but were strictly for men only—apart from the saloon girls whose morality was sometimes held to be questionable.

The birth and adolescence of bourbon

The first true bourbon whiskey is popularly supposed to have been distilled by the same Rev. Elijah Craig we have already met, at Georgetown in Scott County in 1789. Scott County was then part of Bourbon County. Bourbon, Jefferson and Lincoln counties were the three counties of Virginia that made up the territory of Kentucky, which was then not a state in its own right. The new kind of whiskey distilled here was so different from the old-fashioned rye whiskies of Pennsylvania and the crude 'corn likker' produced by moonshiners that it quickly came to be called 'Kentucky bourbon'.

Bourbon got off to a fairly slow start. Up to the time of the Civil War few distilleries in Kentucky produced more than 1000 barrels of whiskey a year. Most were small domestic stills, some producing as little as 50 barrels a year. The method of making bourbon whiskey in those days was very similar to that used for making malt whisky in Scotland for generations. Corn and a varying proportion of rye were ground to a coarse meal and infused with boiling water in large vats to extract the starch. The mash would be vigorously stirred with wooden paddles to ensure that little soluble starch would go to waste.

The mixture would then be allowed to cool overnight. At this stage, malted corn, rye or, occasionally, barley would be added, so that the malt enzymes could convert the dissolved starch into fermentable sugar, the maltose familiar to the distiller of Scotch malt whisky. The sugary liquid drained from the mash would then be fermented in wooden tubs by the addition of yeast, usually contaminated with various wild yeasts, and the resultant wash heated in a pot still. The crude corn and rye liquor that fumed off was casked straight from the still and was sold with no further refinement. On the rare occasions when the first distillation was redistilled to produce a stronger and smoother spirit, this fact was made a great deal of—and the whiskey priced accordingly.

These rough and ready spirits—it is difficult to call them whiskey—were exactly what the rough and ready frontiersmen wanted, and there are no records of any complaints (although cynics have pointed out that there could be other and less reassuring reasons for this!). But it would be hard today to recapture the pungency and flavour of this kind of whiskey, the kind that General Ulysses Grant was known to be so fond of, or

After weeks on the range, the cowboys would arrive in town, their pockets stuffed with dollars, and head for the nearest saloon. After a good drink of whiskey they were easy prey for the card sharps of the time.

The root of all evil

that the cowboys splashed into their tumblers in the saloons of Dodge City. But it did have one curious virtue. At the time of the great westward expansion of the American nation there was necessarily little piped or purified water. The coarse spirit that was the ancestor of Bourbon certainly 'killed the bugs' in the river water, which was usually all they had to drink. Whiskey, in fact, was a pretty effective disinfectant.

Visits to the saloon, very often many miles away, was often the only solace of the farmer, hunter or woodsman, who spent his days in backbreaking labour, wrestling a bare living from the virgin soil of the American west. He had no theatres, no libraries, no concert halls, even in the unlikely event that he wanted them. But the saloon was there, where he could talk to his friends and take the edge off a harsh and unrelenting existence with a little soothing alcohol. The saloons he frequented were usually shabby, poorly furnished shacks with a bar, a few chairs and tables, and the statutory spittoons but it was a relaxation and the saloons were seldom empty.

The arrival of the saloon had another and unexpected long-term effect. If the frontiersman grew to love the saloon, his wife grew to hate it. It took her husband away from his home and family, leaving them unprotected from marauding Indians, it ate into what little money there was and it gave the man an enviable escape from the grinding realities of frontier life that she could never share. So she listened eagerly to the sombre warnings of the preachers and prohibitionists. They reinforced her belief that alcohol was the root of all evil. She *knew*. This belief, more and more widely spread through the women and the religious fundamentalists of rural America, was to have shattering repercussions in the next century.

Meanwhile, Kentucky whiskey went on being produced in the old traditional manner. People drank it—so that was that. There seemed no need for, no pressure for, improvement. Only a few of the more perceptive distillers realized that this was because they had no choice: there were no brands, no standards, no control. Those who read the future correctly realized that

The saloon girls were often as lethal as the whiskey sold.

124

the pioneers would be succeeded by a generation who would not have to work so hard, who would make more money, who would become more civilized. These people would demand better standards and a better way of life. And better whiskey would certainly be a part of that.

Up to the time of the Civil War, no one had bothered much about maturing their spirit. It had sold well straight from the still, either without colour or with added colouring matter in a childish attempt to make it look like brandy. No one was particular because there was nothing to be particular about. But already some anonymous genius, either by chance or experiment, had discovered that corn and rye whiskey kept even a short time in charred oak barrels took on an amber colour of its own and lost some of its fieriness. This discovery was to have significant results over the next few decades.

After the Civil War, the country was poor and in urgent need of revenue.

Whiskey was now a sizeable, even if unorganized, industry and the U.S. government—as all governments—saw in it a ready source of money. The resulting taxation had two effects: it meant that the government itself began to take a close and technical interest in what went into and what came out of American distilleries. And, because whiskey necessarily became more expensive, it became more reasonable to mature it. People would willingly pay more for a better product if they could then be sure of a consistent standard of quality. This fundamental rule of economics operated in the whiskey industry as it does in any other and the rationalization of the American whiskey industry got under way.

It started in Kentucky when individual family names began to be associated with individual drinks. The economies of scale and cost offered by the patent as distinct from the pot still had also not escaped the attention of American distillers, and

These Arizona oldtimers of 1880 would have been used to whiskey that was produced in crude local stills.

adaptations of the Coffey still were quickly built. The production of whiskey on this kind of scale and the steady introduction of maturation in charred oak casks familiarized new standards of quality, and distillers soon discovered that by relatively small changes in the technology of distillation they could produce a wide range of acceptable—and profitable—brands.

Not that the growth of the whiskey industry did not have its share of troubles. The freebooting nature of American business in the latter half of the 19th century led to many scandals, and whiskey was by no means immune from them. In the early 1870s, during the presidency of Ulysses S. Grant, a 'whiskey ring' was discovered which had defrauded the government of millions of dollars in taxes. Orville Babcock, a dandyish colonel who had served under Grant, had the key job of controlling access to the President and was discovered to be deeply involved in the fraud. Only the frantic intervention of the President himself on behalf of his friend saved Babcock from prison.

In the next decade another major scandal emerged with the discovery of the presence of a major 'trust' or cartel in the whiskey business. A trust operated where a group of competing companies appointed a board of trustees to control every aspect of the industry. In this way prices—and profits—could be fixed, supplies dominated, production controlled and competition eliminated. In some cases a trust like this, powerful by definition, could use its powers with the utmost ruthlessness. The formation of the whiskey trust, under the name of the Distilling and Cattle Feeding Association (cattle food was an important by-product of whiskey distillation, just as with Scotch whiskies) was followed by immediate and drastic action. Prices were selectively slashed to force competition either to join the trust or go out of business. If this didn't work, competitors were either bought up by trickery or forced out by violence and intimidation.

By the late 1880s, where once 83 distilleries operated, just over a dozen were in production, and the savings and profits accumulated from this concentration of power were high enough 'for purposes of contest with outsiders'. This whiskey ring effectively controlled the whole of the trade, deciding where and how much whiskey could be made, who should make it and how much it should cost. By February, 1888, only two sizeable independent distilleries out of 80 were still outside the trust. They were both in Chicago and one of them disclosed in the *Chicago Tribune* that it had caught an undercover agent of the trust in their distillery interfering with the valves on their vats. After this they were offered enormous bribes to sell out. Their refusal to come in had spectacular results in the following December when there was a mysterious explosion at the distillery.

'All the buildings in the neighborhood were shaken and many panes of glass were broken...there were 15,000 barrels of whiskey stored under the roof that was torn open, and if these had been ignited a terrible fire would have been added to the effect of the explosion. A package of dynamite which had failed to explode, though the fuse had been lighted, was found on the premises by the Chicago police.'

Truly, the growth years of the American whiskey industry were far from peaceful.

Old Forrester was first introduced in 1870, making it one of the oldest proprietary brands on the American market.

What is bourbon?

Bourbon lovers are just as passionately addicted to their favourite nectar as those who cherish the single malts of Scotland. It is true that they have a great deal more choice—nearly 3000 brands to choose from as against a few dozen available malts. It is also true that they drink a great deal more of it—and it is almost certainly true that it is the biggest selling single spirit in the world.

A true, classic, straight bourbon—the product of one distillation at one distillery, aged 12 years in a new charred oak cask and served neat—is one of the world's great drinks. It is mellow, sweet on the palate, with a fine clean 'nose' and a clear, light amber colour. It has enough hidden fire to warm the throat but without a hint of fierceness. Let one of the great experts on bourbon speak. Bernard De Voto writes:

'Our political institutions were shaped by our whiskies, would be inconceivable without them, and share their nature. They are distilled not only from our native grains but from our native vigour, suavity, generosity, peacefulness and love of accord.... The ideal is recognized everywhere—it is embodied in an American folk saying that constitutes our highest tribute to a first-class man. "He is a gentleman, a scholar, and a judge of good whiskey."'

Good whiskey, in this case, would certainly be a straight bourbon.

Bourbon is a drink you would expect to be offered in any civilized American home, just as it would be a rare and parsimonious Scottish manse that could not offer a guest a dram of malt. And bourbon is splendidly various, from a light, young, scarcely aromatic spirit drunk as a refreshing aperitif to a weighty odorous masterpiece, full of age and character, meant to be sipped thoughtfully at the end of the day.

Although bourbon is now made in several states in America—Virginia, Maryland, Illinois, Pennsylvania and Tennessee all make excellent bourbon—the true afficionado knows in his heart that Kentucky is the spiritual homeland of bourbon. Luckily this religious belief is reinforced by solid, pragmatic fact: more than half the bourbon distilleries of America still lie within the borders of the blue grass state. 'Kentucky Straight Bourbon Whiskey' on the bottle is a guarantee that you are getting the real thing.

Most bourbon lovers will take their bourbon straight—that is, undiluted—but if the time or the palate are not right, a little pure water is permissible: 'bourbon and branch water'. Ginger ale, soda water, ice and other diluents are strictly out of bounds for the dedicated bourbon lover. This is not to say that they are not added and enjoyed by millions who enjoy bourbon better this way. Indeed, there are standard bourbons which would not suffer from this sort of mixing overmuch, a thousand or more middle-range bourbons, perfectly respectable drinks which serve their everyday purposes admirably. But a straight, matured Kentucky bourbon demands a special respect and should be treated accordingly.

It is, perhaps, invidious to select out a few individual bourbons but some are so well known as to be familiar in bars many thousands of miles from their points of origin. Bourbons like Old Grandad, Old Forester, Jim Beam, Old Charter, Old Taylor, Old Fitzgerald, Yellowstone and C. W. Harper can be enjoyed from Singapore to Santiago and the true bourbon lover can be assured of finding his necessary solace almost anywhere he goes.

Bernard De Voto deserves the last word:

'True rye and true bourbon make delight like any great wine, with a rich and magical plentitude of overtones and rhymes and resolved dissonances and a contrapuntal succession of fleeting aftertastes. They dignify man and enoble his soul as shimmering with the response.'

The name Kentucky on a bottle is a sure sign of quality. Kentucky whiskey is held in as high regard in America as the Speyside malts are in Scotland.

American whiskey

The last half of the 19th and the first decade of the 20th centuries saw an increasingly bitter and sterile argument both inside and outside the whiskey industry as to what the various types of American whiskey actually were. There seemed to be as many schools of thought as there were drinkers, each with his own set of beliefs and prejudices about the rye, bourbon, blended, bonded, straight, grain or light whiskey he was drinking or thought he was drinking. The picture was further complicated by some unscrupulous distillers who had no compunction about telling downright lies as to what went into their bottles. This practice, backed by heavy and mendacious advertising, was bringing the whole industry into chaos and it was patently time to do something about it. The large whiskey companies had been putting pressure on the government for many years and this finally paid off.

The true definition of the various types of American whiskey was established in 1909 during the presidency of William H. Taft:

Whiskey: 'Whiskey is an alcoholic distillate from a fermented mash of grain distilled at less than 190° proof, in such a manner that the distillate will have the taste, aroma and characteristics generally attributed to whiskey, and withdrawn from the cistern room of the distillery at not more than 110° proof and not less than 80° proof, and is further reduced before bottling to not less than 80° proof.'

This is a general definition which covers all the various types of American whiskey. Therefore you will never find it on any bottles because these would automatically carry the description of the individual type of whiskey they hold.

Bourbon whiskey: Whiskey that has been distilled at not exceeding 160° proof from a fermented mash of at least 51 percent corn (maize) and aged not less than two years in new charred oak barrels.

Corn whiskey: Whiskey that must be made from a mash of at least 80 percent corn but may be matured in used or uncharred barrels.

Rye whiskey: Whiskey distilled from a fermented mash containing at least 51 percent rye and distilled at less than 160° proof. Like bourbon, it must be aged in new charred oak barrels.

Straight whiskey: Whiskey distilled at not more than 160° proof and aged for at least two years in new charred oak barrels. Straight corn whiskey fulfils the proof requirement but can be aged in used or uncharred barrels. Most straight whiskeys are, in fact, straight bourbons or ryes and together they make up about a quarter of all whiskey sales.

Blended straight whiskey: A blend of two or more straight whiskeys. Only a tiny proportion of blended straight whiskey distilled is sold as such; the vast majority of it goes to make blended whiskey.

Blended whiskey: A blend of at least 20°–100° proof straight whiskey, in combinations either with other whiskey or neutral spirit, or a mixture of both. About a quarter of all whiskey sold is blended whiskey of this type. A small amount of blending agent—up to 2·5 percent, usually sherry, is allowed to be added.

The fact that the blender has 80° of neutral spirit and other lighter whiskies to juggle with means that it is much easier to produce a consistent whiskey year after year. Often the blender will need as many as 40 separate and distinct whiskeys to achieve the precise balance he is looking for and although the relative proportions of these to each other may vary slightly from blending to blending, the consumer can be confident that his favourite and familiar whiskey will always taste exactly as he likes and remembers it.

This Jack Daniel's label from 1907 comes from a classic whiskey which is as popular now as it was then.

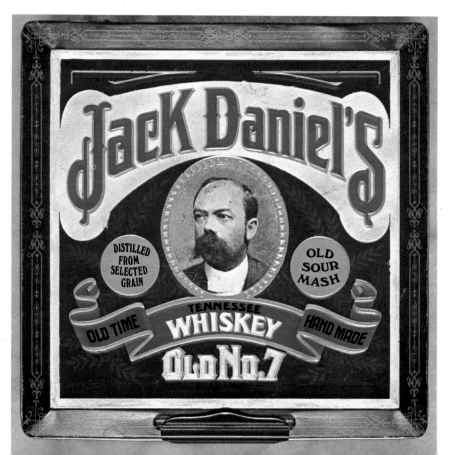

It is also true, unfortunately, that an unscrupulous manufacturer could allow the leeway given him to use a very high proportion of cheap neutral spirit in his blend. Such a blended whiskey is traditionally known as a spirit blend and would not satisfy any but the most scorched and blunted palates. Such do exist.

Grain neutral spirit: Spirits distilled from any material at over 190° proof, whether or not the proof is subsequently reduced. Spirits distilled at such extremely high proof are very nearly pure ethyl alcohol or industrial alcohol and, accordingly, have no flavour at all. All the congeners which give whiskeys their character and uniqueness—the various proportions of oil, aldehydes, fusel oil, and so on—would have been discarded earlier in the distilling process.

Grain spirits: Grain neutral spirits are so characterless that it would seem to matter little whether they were stored in steel drums or glass-lined tanks. But some distillers continued to cask them in oak containers. Such neutral spirits could not help acquiring a certain character under the circumstances and it seemed a pity to penalize distillers who were introducing an element of quality into their product. So in June, 1968, a new standard of grain spirit was introduced to become effective on July 1, 1972. It said: 'Grain spirits are neutral spirits distilled from a fermented mash of grain stored in oak containers and bottled at not less than 80° proof'. The period of ageing in oak barrels may be stated as: 'stored x (years or months) in oak containers'.

Light whiskey: Whiskey distilled at more than 160° proof and less than 190° proof and stored in used or uncharred new oak containers.

Blended light whiskey: Light whiskey mixed with less than 20 percent by volume of 100° proof straight whiskey. As with grain spirits, this definition was adjusted on January 26, 1968, and came into effect on July 1, 1972.

Bottled in bond: This term is usually misunderstood as one that gives a governmental seal of approval to the quality of certain whiskies. Although it is true that most really good American whiskeys are, in fact, bottled in bond, this is for technical, financial and taxation reasons and has nothing to do with quality as such. The

designation is given to straight whiskeys of at least four years old, bottled at 100° proof, and the product of one single distillation at a single distillery in a single season. This whiskey is then matured in government controlled warehouses and the tax need only be paid on withdrawal from stock.

Sour mash whiskey: This is another much misunderstood term. In fact, it is the process in which a proportion of the de-alcoholized ferment from a previous distillation is added to the fermenter—the yeast—of the next. This gives the new yeast a headstart and also ensures a continuity of taste and quality. Conversely, 'sweet mash' is the addition of a pure new yeast culture to the mash. The sour mash process is most often used in the making of bourbon whiskey.

The obsession with proof: It may seem that the American excisemen make a lot of fuss about whether distillation takes place at 160° or 190° proof. The answer is simple. The lower the proof percentage on distillation, the more interesting congeners are carried over into the final distillate. These congeners are the minute quantities of organic compounds which give whiskey its individual character. The higher the proof percentage and distillations, the more of them disappear as they are effectively siphoned off. So good distillers prefer to distil their whiskey off at much lower percentage proofs than those officially allowed them by legislators. The best bourbons, for example, are distilled off at proofs around 125°. The general rule is, the lower the percentage proof, the less 'cutting' with water the finished whiskey will need, and the better will be the end result.

Four Roses bourbon is one of the many light American whiskeys available throughout the world.

Although Calvert is an American bourbon, it is distilled by a Canadian company—an example of how distilling can cross international frontiers.

The noble experiment

By the 1890s, anti-drink laws were in force in many parts of the United States, but even where alcohol was banned, much illicit distilling was being done. Such was the feeling against drink, particularly amongst women, that the police were given many tip-offs on the whereabouts of illicit stills. Here police are seen raiding one such still. But despite their vigilance alcohol continued to be made on a large scale to supply the growing number of speakeasies in the major cities.

By the turn of the century, the American whiskey industry was big business, most of it concentrated in a few powerful hands. The codification of 1909 finally defined what the various types of whiskey should be and government interest in the rich revenues to be harvested meant that production was regularized and controlled. True, some smaller operators still managed to make a living on the fringes of the business but effectively the American whiskey trade had become respectable.

Things were by no means so simple at the consumption end. A number of forces were slowly finding a common interest that was eventually to change the face of American society for 13 years. This interest was not dedicated to regulating the production and sale of whiskey and other beverages. It was hell-bent on prohibiting it entirely. As whiskey grew and flourished, its most adamant enemies grew and flourished with it.

There were several disparate groups to be found in this prohibitionist camp. First, there were the non-conformist churches, led by the Methodists—and Methodists of a mainly rural and fundamentalist nature. Secondly, there were the women influenced both by religious and political considerations. The developing suffragette movement had taken up prohibition with a vengeance and the women's lobby was a powerful and united one. Third, there was the American medical profession which saw whiskey and other spirits as a direct threat to its livelihood. This was because, for generations, whiskey had been literally the only medicine the frontiersman had available. It purified his water, sterilized his wounds and restored his morale in times of stress and danger. The doctors saw this as dangerous competition and their pressure culminated in a resolution passed by the American Medical Association in 1917. It simply said:

'WHEREAS, we believe that the use of alcohol as a beverage is detrimental to the human economy and WHEREAS, its use in therapeutics, as a tonic or a stimulant, or as a food has no scientific basis, therefore be it RESOLVED, that the American Medical Association opposes the use of alcohol as a beverage; and be it further RESOLVED that the use of alcohol as a therapeutic agent should be discouraged.'

But other and even more powerful forces had long been gathering. The sophisticated society of the big cities, with their imported European luxuries, their books, their theatres and opera houses, were blind to what was happening 'out in the sticks'. Yet this was where real political power lay. The American Constitution, formulated when the United States was almost totally rural, had made sure of that. The sparsely-populated states of the middle and far west were grossly over-represented in Congress, especially in their domination of the Senate.

In 1880 the state of Kansas officially went dry. The production and consumption of alcohol within the boundaries of the state were forbidden. In 1907 Georgia followed suit and by 1920, when nationwide prohibition came into force, no less than 33 of the 48 states had opted to ban alcohol altogether.

To be fair, the whiskey distillers and other alcoholic drink manufacturers had been less than sensible. All too often, individual manufacturers and groups of manufacturers had backed various prohibitionist interests as allies in internal trade wars. So, all too often, the whiskey distillers concentrated their fire on gin, wine and beer while ignoring the massive and growing power of the prohibitionist lobby.

The end of an era. At the beginning of Prohibition millions of dazed Americans found that their favourite bars were suddenly out of business. But illegal speakeasies soon sprang up in their place.

'......is hereby prohibited'

But the major mistake was a quite unforeseeable one. It happened that by historical accident a very large proportion of people involved in brewing and other trades connected with the production of alcohol were either German or of German extraction. Cities like Milwaukee, the heart of the American beer industry, were very largely German. So in the American public mind Germany and alcohol went very closely together. To counter this prejudice, a national German-American alliance was formed in 1901, heavily subsidized by the American alcohol producers. Its stated intention was to make American-Germans, and Germany itself, more popular with the majority of the American public. The alcohol producers saw it as a useful front against the prohibitionists and supported the movement in every way they could. It was a policy which backfired disastrously in 1917 when the United States went to war with Germany.

By the time the war started, the whole question of drink and the American people was in a highly volatile and, indeed, explosive state. Those politicians who favoured a liberal policy about alcohol were afraid to speak out on account of the powerful and vociferous prohibitionist lobby, while those who were on the 'dry' bandwagon had no compunction in attacking alcohol in every possible way. Alcohol was spoiling the aim of American riflemen; American boys, drugged by whiskey, were catching unspeakable diseases off predatory French harlots; the grain used for American whiskey could feed America's starving allies; the distillers themselves were a bunch of pro-German traitors—it was a brave man indeed who spoke up in favour of being allowed to enjoy a quiet glass of bourbon in his own sitting room. Ironically, all the evidence now available shows very clearly that at the height of the uproar only about one in five Americans actually approved of prohibition. Certainly, few of the doughboys in the trenches in France, whom the prohibitionists were so anxious to protect from the perils of the demon drink, would have welcomed their protection. Nevertheless, the sheer self-confidence of the 'dries' and their complete belief in the certainty of their victory seems to have paralysed the will of the majority of the people, who found few champions to speak on

their behalf. There were no songs to counter:

'Whiskey spiders, great and greedy
Weave their webs from sea to sea;
They grow fat, and men grow needy
Shall our robbers rulers be?'

Even the leaders of the labour movement, most of whose members had always assumed a natural right to a glass of beer or a slug of rye, spoke with uncertain voice. We read in the *Seaman's Journal*: 'Whiskey is a most valuable friend of capitalism'. Indeed, if workers did not remember the scandals of the Whiskey Ring under President Grant and the Whiskey Trust of 1887, there were now plenty of people to remind them.

The first practical blow fell in 1913, when the Webb-Kenyon Law was passed by 63 to 21 votes in the Senate and by 246 to 95 votes in the House of Representatives. This law controlled inter-state traffic in liquor, especially between 'wet' and 'dry' states. Then, in 1914, Representative Hobson introduced a bill into Congress to establish national prohibition. Although it was narrowly defeated, it was a formidable show of strength by the 'dry' lobby. Voices of reason were still to be heard, however, and Representative Kahn, of California, said: 'We are trying to regulate all forms of human conduct by laws, laws, laws. Efforts of that character are as old as the world. And they have inevitably resulted in failure.' His words were ignored.

On July 30, 1917, the Senate passed the 18th Amendment to the Constitution, which stated that national prohibition would be imposed after ratification by 36 states. The vote was 65 to 20.

On December 17, 1917, Congress passed the same act by 287 votes to 100. America was now committed to the national prohibition of alcohol in any form. The Amendment read:

'Section 1: After one year from the ratification of this article the manufacture, sale, or transportation of intoxicating liquors within, the importation thereof into, or the exportation thereof from, the United States and all territory subject to the jurisdiction thereof for beverage purposes is hereby prohibited.

'Section 2: The Congress and the several states shall have concurrent power

The origins of prohibition. Whiskey-hating women pray outside a saloon in the late 19th century. The move towards prohibition while relentless was gradual so that by the time the whiskey producers and consumers had wakened up to the threat it was too late; the bandwagon had rolled to such an extent that it was impossible to stop.

to enforce this article by appropriate legislation.

'Section 3: This article shall be inoperative unless it shall have been ratified as an amendment to the Constitution by the legislatives of the several states, as provided in the Constitution, within seven years from the date of the submissions hereof to the states of the Congress.'

The rather general nature of these terms were made particular in 1919 when the Volstead Act was passed. This gave teeth to the prohibitionists by spelling out in detail the penalties for producing, distributing, selling and drinking alcohol. It signalled the beginning of 13 years of the silliest, funniest and bloodthirstiest times in American domestic history.

On January 16, 1920, prohibition became the policy of the United States government under the terms of the 18th Amendment to the Constitution. America was dry.

The dry years

In the early hours of the day after America officially went dry, six masked and armed men overpowered two railway hands at a Chicago railway depot and made off with $100,000 worth of whiskey. It was a sinister omen and one that was to be multiplied a thousandfold over the next 13 years. Even within a few months, the sheer impossibility of enforcing a law with which four out of five people disagreed became apparent. In brutal terms, the people refused to obey the law and the police refused to arrest them for breaking it. Those people who were arrested by the

enforcement officers appointed especially by the government were usually found not guilty by juries, and those that were found guilty were given derisory fines by judges. Worse, the opportunities for corruption on a mind-stunning scale were quickly seen and taken advantage of.

The first dismissals of prohibition agents for corruption occurred within a few weeks of prohibition coming into effect, and this was the signal for shrewd 'businessmen' like Al Capone who saw where opportunities for speedy and substantial profits lay. For instance, an enterprising taxi

State police net a haul of illicit whiskey. The risks involved in making hooch were high but the profits were astronomical.

driver found that a case of whiskey that cost $10 in Canada could be sold for $80 in New York. It did not take him long to become a millionaire. But even tougher businessmen worked out that if you made the whiskey yourself and 'persuaded' barmen to sell it in the illegal speakeasies and 'blind pigs' that soon sprang up in their thousands, you could become very much richer very much more quickly. 'Persuasion' in these cases could often be permanent and most barmen and saloon owners preferred to do business with them.

The 'whiskey' they produced was often of a curious nature. One recipe was:

'Fusel oil	64 ounces
Potassium acetate	4 ounces
Sulphuric acid	4 ounces
Copper sulphate	$\frac{1}{2}$ ounce
Ammonium oxelate	$\frac{1}{2}$ ounce
Black oxide of manganese	1 ounce
Water	8 ounces

Place them all in a glass percolator and let them rest for 12 hours. Then percolate and put into a glass still, and then distil half a gallon of the Bourbon Oil.'

This was added to crude industrial alcohol, all too cheaply and easily diverted from its official destination, to make a very acceptable bourbon whiskey. Similarly, 'Scotch' was made by adding caramel, prune juice and creosote to industrial alcohol.

The prohibition agents appointed by the government to enforce the new law became the most hated men in America; much more so than the gangsters who were making millions of dollars from extortion, bootlegging and murder. The trouble was that the agents were armed and encouraged to use their guns to discover the whereabouts of stills and illicit liquor stores. They were not backward in using them. Several innocent people were soon shot down, including a girl of eleven and a boy of eight. This added immediate fuel to the people's hatred of these snoopers. Not that the agents themselves went unscathed. Nearly 300 of them were killed as against the thousand or so civilians they themselves shot by accident or design.

Two prohibition agents made a small niche in history through the incredible lengths they would go to make an arrest. They were called Isadore Einstein and Moe Smith, or, more familiarly, Izzy and

Moe. They soon became national figures and their exploits, lovingly recorded in newspapers the length and breadth of the country, were followed by millions of Americans.

The American journalist Herbert Asbury records: 'Izzy's first assignment was to clean up a place in Brooklyn which the enforcement authorities shrewdly suspected housed a speakeasy, since drunken men had been seen staggering from the building, and the air for half a block around was redolent with the fumes of beer and whiskey. Several agents had snooped and slunk round the house; one had watched all afternoon from a roof across the street and another had hidden for hours in an adjoining doorway, obtaining an accurate account of the number of men who entered and left. But none had been able to get inside. Izzy knew nothing of sleuthing procedures; he simply walked up to the joint and knocked on the door. A peephole was opened, and a hoarse voice demanded to know who was there, and why.

The Big Fellow! When Prohibition was introduced, Al Capone was a smalltime hoodlum and bodyguard. Within a few years he had become a multimillionaire and one of the most feared men in America. His rise to power was ruthless; competitors were gunned down, leaving Capone the dominant figure in illicit whiskey. His power reached into the politics of the day and, because no one would testify against him, his reign of terror became bloodier and bloodier. Eventually, he was imprisoned in 1931, not for murder, coercion or breaking the Prohibition laws—but for tax evasion.

'"Izzy Einstein," said Izzy, "I want a drink."

"Oh, yeah? Who sent you here, bud? What's your business?"

"My boss sent me," Izzy explained, "I'm a prohibition agent. I just got appointed."

'The door swung open and the doorman slapped Izzy jovially on the back.

"Ho! Ho!" he cried. "Come right in, bud. That's the best gag I've heard yet."

'Izzy stepped into a room where half a dozen men were drinking at a small makeshift bar.

"Hey, boss," the doorman yelled. "Here's a prohibition agent wants a drink. You got a badge too, bud?"

"Sure I have," said Izzy, and produced it.

"Well I'll be damned," said the man behind the bar, "looks just like the real thing."

'He poured a slug of whiskey and Izzy downed it. That was a mistake, for when the time came to make the pinch Izzy had no evidence. He tried to grab the bottle but the bartender ran out of the back door with it.

"I learned right there," said Izzy, "that a slug of hooch in an agent's belly might feel good, but it ain't evidence." '

Herbert Ashbury continued the story: 'The trail of illegal liquor led Izzy and Moe into some mighty queer places, but they followed wherever it led, and were always ready with the appropriate disguise. Dressed as a longshoreman, Izzy captured an Italian who used his cash register as a cellarette; its drawers were filled with little bottles of booze. In the guise of a mendicant, Izzy pawned an old pair of pants for $2 in Brooklyn, and snooping about the pawnshops a bit he found $10,000 worth of good liquor that had been wrapt in clothing and left as pledges. He got into the Half Past Nine Club, on Eighth Avenue, as a prosperous poultry salesman, playing tipsy and carrying a sample, and found a large stock of liquor in a stuffed grizzly bear.

'On another occasion an angry bartender shoved a revolver against Izzy's stomach. But Izzy didn't bat an eyelid; he calmly shoved the gun aside.

"Put that up son," he said soothingly. "Murdering me won't help your family."

'Fortunately the bartender had a family,

and Izzy's warning brought to his mind a vision of his fatherless children weeping at the knee of their widowed mother, who was also weeping. He stopped to think. While he was thinking, Moe knocked him cold.'

But although prohibition had its lighter side, there is no doubt that it was a political error of monumental proportions. It is always difficult to legislate for people's morals and, in a freewheeling society like America's, this is especially so. The law was treated with increasing contempt and more and more openly defied.

The scale of lawbreaking was staggering. In 1921, a year after the law came into effect, 95,933 illicit distilleries and stills were discovered. By 1925, this total had risen to 172,537 and, by 1930, to 282,122. Tens of millions of gallons of hooch poured from hundreds of thousands of stills, ranging from the fully sized industrial to the crude buckets and tubs of the

Ingenious drinkers went to extraordinary lengths to conceal their favourite tipple. But prohibition agents found equally devious stratagems to discover it. In various restaurants and cafes, hooch was served in a tea or coffee pot and drunk from cups!

amateur bathroom distiller. From these stills it poured into bottles whose labels made claims that would have made Dr Goebbels blush and, from there, down tens of millions of thirsty and insistent throats. On top of this, there was the inflow of whiskies from abroad, across the Canadian and Mexican borders and from outside the coastal limit into the countless bays and inlets the length of the east and west coasts It is impossible to estimate the quantity of booze that flowed into America from outside its borders but it certainly ran into millions of gallons a year. One small indicator is the amount of liquor imported into small offshore islands like the Bahamas: during prohibition they imported enough to keep the entire population drunk for centuries.

Another measure was the rise of the hangover. The trouble with home-distilled whiskey is that the amateur distiller has not got the skill to take only the middle cut of the distillation. All the undesirable aldehydes which come off at the beginning of distillation and the heavy fusel oils which come off at the end were included in the distillate—and these unwanted congeners are the ones which give you a hangover. A hangover from too much good whiskey is bad enough: a hangover from home-made hooch must have been a fearful experience. Still, the hangover was the fashionable disease: a sign of virility for men and emancipation for women.

Another bizarre effect of prohibition was to make the saloon respectable again. The pre-war campaign against the saloon by the churches had been remarkably successful and saloons were closing down by the thousand. But prohibition made the illegal saloon—the speakeasy—fashionable and exciting and saloons mushroomed again all over the country—there were 30,000 in New York alone.

Towards the end of the Twenties the popular clamour for the repeal of the 18th Amendment became louder and louder but the matter remained a hot potato for the politicians. Most of them were content to make pious noises about the duty of the citizen to obey the law before going home to their own private store of first-class Scotch or bourbon: they could usually afford high-class bootleggers.

More and more Americans began to enjoy the benefits of foreign travel where moderate drinking was seen as one of the pleasures of civilized life. For obvious reasons, Canada was popular:

'Four and twenty Yankees
Feeling mighty dry
Took a trip to Canada
And bought a case of rye.
When the case was opened
The Yanks began to sing
"To hell with the President
God Save the King!"'

But one or two shrewd politicians realized that a firm stand on the issue of prohibition was a positive vote catcher. The 'dry' case was now hopeless and those politicians who were supporting it were being defeated in election after election. Franklin Delano Roosevelt, contender for the leadership of the Democratic party and thus for the presidency, supported repeal and the Democratic Convention of 1932 also came out strongly in favour of a return to civilized drinking. To be fair, the Republican party had also seen the dangers of appearing to support the continuation of prohibition but they came later in the field and their voice in favour of repeal was more faltering than that of their Democratic opponents.

On November 8, 1932, Roosevelt was swept into power and on February 16, 1937, the Senate passed the 21st Amendment which repealed the 18th Amendment by 63 votes to 23. Four days later, Congress confirmed this by 289 votes to 121 and America's 13-year nightmare was finally over. Whiskey was respectable again.

I have never come across a complete list of American whiskeys and I suspect that such a thing does not exist. Nevertheless, there are a number of world-famous brands that every whiskey drinker knows and some others that have been personally recommended by people whose judgment I respect. Among these are:

Ancient Age Kentucky Bourbon, Makers Mark, Four Roses, Bellons Partners Choice, County Fair, Cream of Kentucky, Dobbs, Early Times, Embassy Club, Golden Wedding, Hill and Hill, J. W. Dant, Kentucky Gentlemen, Kentucky Tavern, Kinsey Gold Label, Old Kentucky Tavern, Old Overhold, Old Stag, Old Sunnybrook, James E. Pepper, Rittenhouse, Schenley Reserve, Three Feathers, Very Old Barton and, of course, Jack Daniels, the 'daddy of them all'.

Making American whiskey

The processes of distilling American whiskey—rye or grain—are almost exactly analogous to those of distilling Scottish grain whisky. The stills used are very large continuous process stills and, although the materials used and their relative proportions can and do differ substantially, a skilled Scottish grain distiller would soon find himself completely at home in an American distillery—and vice versa.

Selecting and storing grain: The finished whiskey can only be as good as the mash it started from, so distillers in the United States take a lot of time and trouble to choose the corn, rye or barley malt that exactly suits their purposes. Almost no distiller in America malts his own barley but obtains it from specialized companies, as is rapidly becoming the custom in Scotland. The selected grain is screened, cleaned and piped into storage bins until needed.

Milling: As and when a batch of grain is needed, it is fed, normally by gravity, to mills which reduce it to a usable grist. This is usually done by hammer mills, but these have always presented a problem because they produce a certain amount of heat. This is undesirable because, if the grist is allowed to get too warm, this can produce a rancid reaction later in the distilling process. Moreover, hammer mills also produce flour as well as the required coarse grist and this interferes with efficient distilling. Nevertheless, hammer mills continue to be used satisfactorily in a number of distilleries. But distillers are tending to move to a three-high roller mill. This is by no means a new invention, since the principle has been in use for more than 50 years, but such mills are, however, considerably more expensive than conventional mills. Even so, more and more distillers consider that the advantages outweigh the disadvantages.

Cooking: Cooking makes the starch in the grain soluble. It also sterilizes it. This is necessary because natural grain carries on it a variety of wild yeasts, moulds, bacteria and fungi. Cooking eliminates all these.

There are three basic types of cooking which are used in the production of whiskey. The first is by using an 'atmospheric' cooker. This is simply a large tank equipped with mechanical agitators, a steam inlet called a 'sparge' and some method of cooling the finished mash, usually a system of coils inside the tank.

Into the tank is pumped a measured amount of limestone-bearing water, followed by a quantity of milled grain weighed automatically. Then, simultaneously, steam is blown in and the mechanical agitators are started. The temperature soon begins to rise until eventually the boiling point of water is reached. This is maintained until the distiller is convinced that the cooking process is complete. He then uses his cooling coils to reduce the temperature of the mash to about 140°F (60°C).

It is at this temperature that malted barley can be added to start the enzyme actions. Significantly higher temperatures destroy the enzymes of the malt, which is sometimes added in the form of milled grain and, at other times, as a slurry of water and milled grain. The precise form of the malt makes no difference to the finished whiskey. When the enzymes' action is complete the mash goes on to storage tanks, there to cool and await the next process—fermentation.

A second type of cooking uses the principle of the pressure cooker. Here, higher cooking temperatures can be used and these are both quicker and more effective. The 'enclosed batch pressure cooker' can also be used as an ordinary atmospheric cooker, which makes it very versatile.

This is useful for the distiller because, although corn responds extremely well to very high temperatures and pressures, rye does not and no distiller would ever try to cook them together. Rye is very easy to cook and if anyone tried to cook the two together he would have to make one of two bad choices: perfectly cooked rye and undercooked corn, or perfectly cooked corn and overcooked rye. In practice, therefore, they are cooked separately and combined later in the fermenter.

The third type of cooker is known as the continuous unit. The grain to be cooked is made into a slurry by the addition of water and this is then injected into a long metal tube. At the same time, steam is blown in. By the time the mash reaches the far end of the tube it is perfectly cooked. This system can operate either atmospherically or under pressure. Most distillers think it particularly suitable if

Huge areas of the United States are ideal for growing cereal, much of which finds its way to the whiskey distillers of the Bourbon States. The grain being sown, grown and threshed here would eventually go to the mill where it is reduced to a usable grist. It is then mixed with water and cooked and cooled before fermentation begins.

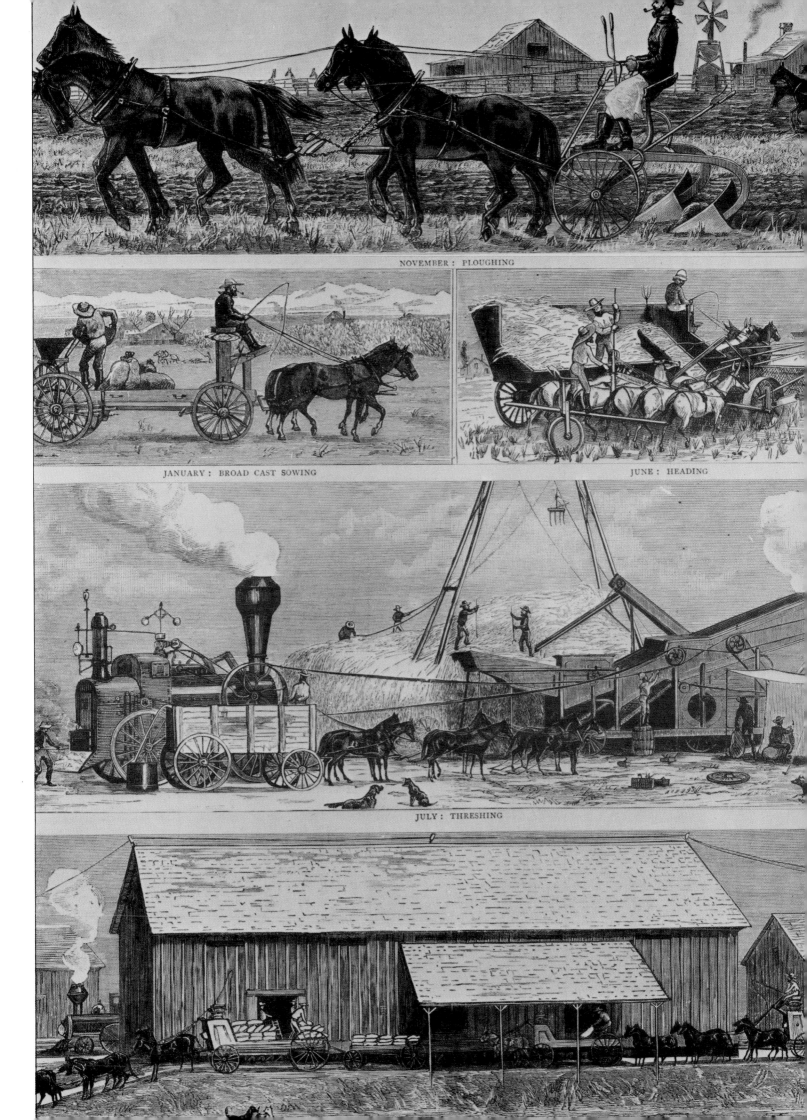

NOVEMBER : PLOUGHING

JANUARY : BROAD CAST SOWING

JUNE : HEADING

JULY : THRESHING

the end product is to be neutral grain spirit, but prefer more traditional methods if they are making bourbon or rye whiskey.

Cooling: Fully cooled mash is still hot—about 140°F (60°C)—and needs to be cooled to about 70°F (21°C)–75°F (24°C) before the yeast can be added. Cooling is usually accomplished by metal coils within the cooling tank through which cold water circulates. If the distiller is lucky enough to draw his water from springs or deep wells, the water will be cold enough for him to operate all the year round. But if he draws his water from the surface—rivers, pools or lakes—he may find that the water in summer is just not cold enough and he may be forced to close until the weather changes and his water is cool enough to use. More logically, many distillers now refrigerate their water.

Another and newer cooling process is to reduce the pressure above the mash so that it boils at a lower temperature. Then, automatically, the time taken to bring the temperature down to the required level is greatly reduced.

Fermentation: Traditionally, the fermenting tanks in the American whiskey business were made of wood but today stainless steel is more common. Wood is much more difficult to sterilize and is far more susceptible to structural damage so, although sentiment and tradition take a knock, efficiency and quality control usually are decisive.

The cooled mash slurry is piped to the fermenter where yeast is added from the distiller's scrupulously sterile yeast culture. A common practice is to inoculate a small amount of grain mash with yeast in the yeast room itself and leave it for a couple of days. At the end of this time the yeast population has multiplied so vigorously that the yeasty mash can be added to the main body of mash. At this point the yeast will be at its optimum level, that is about 150 million cells per teaspoonful. If the distiller has got his mix right, fermentation now rapidly begins. Fermentation produces heat and this must be carefully controlled: below 80°F (27°C) yeast reproduces itself; above this yeast produces alcohol and carbon dioxide. This, after all, is what the exercise is all about and so the distiller controls the temperature in his fermenters carefully.

He is well aware that 100,000 gallons

of mash produce as much heat as a ton of coal and so controlled cooling is very important to him.

Some distillers cool their ferment by simply diluting it with cold water. Even more use the ubiquitous cooling coils, now often thermostatically controlled, so that the distiller can simply set the temperature level he desires and leave the rest to science.

After three or four days, fermentation is complete, which means that nearly all the convertible sugar is now alcohol and nearly all the yeast cells are dead. The proof content is now about 14° or 15°, depending on a number of variable factors such as climate, type of cereal, yeast culture, and so on.

Distillation: The 'distiller's beer' is now ready for the final process of distillation. This is accomplished by feeding the alcoholic 'beer' into a series of tall, copper distilling columns heated by steam, when the alcohol and its various congenerics are floated off. The distiller now has a very

Mash is always sampled before being added to the fermenter. It is little checks such as these which ensure that what is eventually bottled is perfect.

After sampling, the mash is poured into the fermenter. Stainless steel has superseded wood as the material from which fermenting tanks are made.

sensitive—if physically very large—apparatus at his command and he can control the quality and character of the whiskey he pulls off to very fine limits. The principle by which the distilling columns operate is exactly the same as the patent or Coffey still, although a number of refinements have been introduced.

The strong, pure, spirit produced is now reduced in strength to about 100° to 125° by adding distilled or deionized water. It is then barrelled in charred white oak casks or whatever containers the federal regulations specify.

Maturation: Traditionally, the barrels now go to the rackhouses for their long, quiet sleep to maturity. Until comparatively recently this was done literally on racks, with the casks on their sides. But the introduction of pallets and fork-lift trucks—plus the inevitably increasing costs of human labour—are now replacing this method by another, which stands the casks on their ends for easier mechanical handling. This makes no discernible difference to the quality of the fully matured whiskey.

During maturation a series of complex chemical processes take place that nobody fully understands but which have a profound effect on the character of the casked spirit. There is some kind of interchange between spirit, cask and ambient air, with the whiskey losing its sharp and fiery components out through the wooden skin of the barrel. We know this must be so because the amount of whiskey in the barrel diminishes quite substantially over the years. We also know that the wooden cask itself gives something back to the

whiskey it contains because, if one leaves the whiskey to mature for too long, it begins to acquire unpleasantly woody characteristics. But a perfect balance can be, and usually is, obtained and the perfected whiskey is then ready for bottling or blending.

In the former case it will merely be reduced to bottling strength and then bottled—no colour is allowed to be added. This is for straight bourbon and rye whiskey. In the case of blending, all the skills of the blender are called into play to produce a whiskey of consistent quality. Along with the miniscule quantity of blending agent, the blender is allowed to use a little carmel to standardize the colour.

Bottling: This is almost totally automated, using highly sophisticated and electronically controlled machinery. The marketing and distribution of American whiskey is also a highly complex and expensive operation, too, with many hundreds of millions of dollars being spent on advertising and promotion.

American whiskeys are carefully aged in large maturing sheds or warehouses. Every stage of whiskey production is carefully monitored by the U.S. Government.

When one considers the population of the United States, it is not surprising that bottling is carried out on a very substantial scale.

7 IRISH WHISKEY

Some brands of Irish whiskey are among the greatest. Certainly it is the oldest, although, like the Irish themselves, the history of Irish whiskey is a little hard to pin down. Irish whiskey historians speak with an assurance I wish I could share about missionary monks bringing the secret of distillation to Ireland between AD500 and AD600 but they are decidedly reticent about where it came from. They also talk with great confidence about the soldiers of Henry II invading their country in the 12th century, although there is some confusion about precise dates. One authority says that these English soldiers 'were greatly taken by the native "uisca beatha" and quickly anglicized "uisca" into "whiskey"'. This seems to me to be extremely dubious on both historical and etymological grounds and is scarcely supported by the *Oxford English Dictionary*. Another more modest source says, 'What we do know almost [!] for sure is that, so far as whiskey distilling is concerned, Ireland invented it a bare minimum of seven centuries ago'. The first real reference to Irish whiskey that I have seen recorded is in *The Annals of the Four Masters* in 1406, so perhaps we can leave its actual date of origin somewhere in early medieval times.

Richard Stanihurst, an Elizabethan chronicler who was at Oxford in 1563, mentions the virtues of whiskey and John Marston's play *The Malcontent*, which was seen in London in 1604, has the following lines:

> 'The Dutchman for a drunkard
> The Dane for golden locks
> The Irishman for uisca beatha
> The Frenchman for the pox.'

Sir Walter Raleigh, on his last visit to the West Indies in 1617, called on his friend the Earl of Cork and records with delight in his diary that he was given 'a supreme present of a 32 gallon keg of home-distilled "uisca beatha"'. Queen Elizabeth I was reputedly fond of a tot of Irish whiskey and this, of course, at a time when anyone with any taste would have turned their noses up at the barbarous spirit distilled north of the English border.

But it was in the reign of her successor, James VI and I, that Irish whiskey really came into its own. For in 1608 Sir Thomas Phillips, the King's Deputy in Ulster, was given the authority to grant licences to distil. Being no fool, the first one he granted was to himself and he set up the world's very first whiskey distillery at Bushmills on the banks of the River Bush on the road between Tara, ancient capital of Ireland, and Dunseverick Castle. The Giant's Causeway is not very far to the north. There is also a ford nearby, so perhaps, like Macallan on Speyside, this was a contributory reason for choosing the site. In any case, this distillery can certainly claim precedence over all others, and does so.

Distilling flourished in Ireland in the 17th century although, as in Scotland, the stills tended to be small and domestic. The type of spirit, again, must have been crude and harsh and heavily loaded with congenerics. There is, however, no evidence of any complaint.

As in Scotland too, there were frequent and complicated attempts to regulate the production of Irish whiskey by legislation. These well intentioned though muddle-headed forays into law inevitably failed. E. B. Maguire in his book *Irish Whiskey* records:

'On 15 October 1695, seven Dublin distillers complained that the licensing commissioners had summoned them as retailers, requiring them to take out a licence despite a judgement in 1657 that a distiller selling only in his own shop was not a retailer. They added that, if licensed, they could have soldiers quartered on them.'

When Sir Walter Raleigh went on his various journeys he took a barrel of finest Irish whiskey with him.

There is an old Irish saying: 'If his mother had raised him on whiskey, he'd have been a suckling babe to the day of his death'. Perhaps this illustration of the 1840s could be described as depicting a product of mother love.

Maguire adds dryly, 'The result of quartering soldiers on a distillery can well be imagined'.

The perpetual problem was enforcement. As one loophole was blocked—another was found. In 1731 an act was passed to gain control by forbidding distilleries to be operated where the exciseman could not penetrate, a highly optimistic piece of legislation. It stated 'whereas distillers of aqua vitae and other strong waters for sale frequently fixed their stills and alimbecks and black pots in mountainous parts of the kingdom remote from any market town with intent to avoid the payment of excise . . .'

The beginning of the 18th century saw a new trade emerge in Ireland. Its operatives were known as 'sugar bakers' and their task was to make fermented wash to sell to distillers. It stands to reason that however fast the process of distillation—and it was getting faster all the time—fermentation will always take three or four days. The sugar bakers acted as a useful reserve or, in some instances, allowed small-scale distillers to operate with stills only and without having to capitalize washbacks and the whole brewing process.

Peter the Great of Russia declared that 'Of all wines the Irish wine is best', and although Samuel Johnson's dictionary, published in 1755, does not contain the word 'whiskey' as such, he speaks of 'usquabaugh' as 'a compounded distilled spirit . . . the Irish sort is particularly distinguished for its pleasant and mild flavour'.

Early in the 19th century, Thomas Moore wrote:

'Never was philtre found with such power
To charm and bewilder, as this we are
* quaffing,*
The magic began, when in Autumn's
* rich hour,*
As a harvest of gold in the fields it stood
* laughing.*
There, having by nature's enchantment
* been filled with the balm and the*
* bloom of the kindliest weather,*
This wonderful juice from its core was
* distilled*
To enliven such hearts as are here
* brought together.'*

The wine and spirit company which supplied Charles Dickens with Irish whiskey direct from Dublin is still in business. Dr W. G. Grace, the great English cricketer, liked an Irish whiskey and soda between innings and at close of play. A famous journalist contemporary of Grace, George Augustus Sala, was also very fond of his tot of Irish: 'Whiskey is essentially an Irish question . . . the mellowness, the generosity and the wholesomeness of that Irish speciality. . . . Irish whiskey owes its incomparable flavour to the more delicate and ethereal essences evolved from the best barley procurable by the distiller skilled in the management of the pot-still . . . its purity, wholesomeness and suitability have enabled it not alone to hold its own but to a constantly growing extent supersede most other stimulants.' I couldn't have put it better myself. Finally, Arthur Barnard in his book *The Whisky Distilleries of the United Kingdom*, published in 1887, lists 28 distilleries in Ireland at that time.

These literary references show that Irish whiskey has indeed a long and distinguished lineage but I think that it would be generally agreed that the real beginnings of the modern Irish whiskey business took place in Dublin and Cork in the late 18th century.

It was in 1779 that Thomas and Francis Wise built the North Mall distillery on the site of an old Dominican friary by the banks of the River Lee in Cork. A year later John Jameson opened his distillery at Bow Street in Dublin. The next four decades saw an unprecedented burst of distillery building. In 1791 John Power opened another Dublin distillery in John's Lane near what was then the Western Gate of the Old City. Cork saw the building of the Watercouse distillery by Thomas Hewitt in 1793, which was shortly followed by George Waters' distillery in the Green in 1796. In 1807, Daly added the fourth Cork distillery in John's Street. Midleton distillery, some 13 miles east of Cork, had started life as a worsted mill but it was converted by James Murphy and his brother in 1825. Here they installed the world's largest pot still—33,000 gallons—which remained in use until July 1975. In 1829, Daly built himself yet another distillery at Tullamore, almost at the geographical centre of Ireland.

So the production of Irish whiskey multiplied many times in comparatively few years. A taste for it developed in Victorian Britain and there was a growing export trade to the United States and other parts of the world. The quality of the whiskey produced quickly put the legendary illicit stills effectively out of business and Irish whiskey attained a reputation it has never lost.

In 1867, the five Cork distilleries amalgamated to form the Cork Distilleries Company and, almost exactly a century later, all the distilleries in Ireland merged to form one large all-Irish distilling company—Irish Distillers Limited.

Towards the end of the 1960s it became obvious that no programme of expansion and rebuilding could possibly meet the planned growth of Irish whiskey production. Too many of the old distilleries were in city centres and there were growing problems of water supply. So Irish Distillers Limited decided to build themselves a totally new distillery which would offer them all the advantages of modern technology while preserving all the traditions which give Irish whiskey its unique character. After much thought and exploration, the site at Midleton was found to be the most suitable from every point of view—including possible future expansion—and building began in April 1973. It was completed in July 1975 at a cost of over £9,000,000. Part of this enormous cost was caused by the insistence of the directors that their new distillery should 'be capable of producing all the famous whiskies—Jameson, Power, Paddy, Tullamore Dew—in exactly the way they have always been made and to ensure their unique flavours and characteristics are preserved'.

So the New Midleton is best viewed as a complex of distilleries rather than one large unitary distillery. The fact that it is planned to produce over five million gallons of whiskey a year makes this point very clearly.

Much thought went into the physical planning of New Midleton: it uses enormous quantities of water without the slightest hint of pollution or harm to natural life and the atmosphere is also kept perfectly clean and smoke free. Landscaping with trees and shrubs has helped the new distillery blend with its surrounding rural scenery.

Just as in Scotland, the production of whiskey depends on cold clear plentiful water. This stream in Connemara is typical of the many Irish rivers and streams which are ideal for the basis of a whiskey industry.

The making of Irish whiskey

Like Scotch malt whisky, Irish whiskey is pot-still produced but there are important differences in manufacture. In the first instance, Scottish malt is dried over peat which gives it a distinctive flavour: ironically, the whiskey of Ireland, above all others the land of peat, kilns its malt over coal, which gives no discernible flavour. Also Scottish malt whisky is made from 100 percent malted barley, while Irish whiskey is made either from a mixture of malted and unmalted barley or a proportion of malted barley (25 to 50 percent) and other unmalted cereals—barley, oats, wheat and, very occasionally, rye.

As with Scotch, the cereal is ground and mashed in a mash tun, often called a 'kieve'. As with Scotch, too, the water used must be pure and soft and with a very low mineral content. Wort is produced in the conventional manner which is then fermented in a washback or fermenting vessel. After some three days, fermentation ceases and the wash is ready for distillation. Here, perhaps, the greatest differences can be seen. First, Irish pot stills are vastly bigger, holding up to 33,000 gallons. Secondly, three of them are used rather than two. The still heads are quite differently shaped, being very high, often with their horizontal or 'lyne' arms (between the still head and the condenser) running through a water-filled channel. Sometimes reflux (see p. 57) is used to the distiller's advantage by having a return pipe from the lyne arm to the body of the still itself. This is sometimes called the 'foul pipe'.

The three stills can be regarded as two low-wines stills and one spirit still, although, in fact, the processes of distillation are a little more complicated than that. The first distillation sends forward 'low wines' which are then distilled into 'strong low wines' and 'weak low wines'. The 'weak low wines' go back for redistillation while the 'strong low wines' are distilled for the third still in a second distillation. Here, again, the 'cut' that the distiller wants goes on to the spirit receiver while the foreshots and feints go back for redistillation. Not surprisingly, a higher degree of rectification is brought about than in Scottish malt whisky and the resultant spirit is both stronger and purer. A typical first distillation would convert 33,000 gallons of wash to 11,000 gallons and

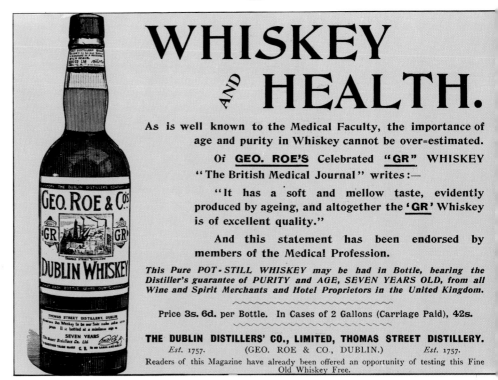

this would in turn produce 5,000 gallons. The final distillation could result in some 3,000 gallons of spirit, an 11:1 reduction of the original wash.

Irish whiskey is matured in casks which previously held sherry, bourbon or rum; sometimes new American oak casks are used. These impart subtly differing flavours to the whiskey they contain and one of the blender's arts is to get the balance between them exactly right. The minimum age in the wood for Irish domestic consumption is three years but it is usual to mature the whiskey for much longer than this. Ten or twelve years is standard for some brands. During maturation, up to a third of the spirit escapes in evaporation.

When the whiskey is judged mature enough for bottling, it is blended with the whiskey from at least 700 other barrels to maintain the standard and quality the blender requires. Put another (and suitably Irish) way, every bottle of Irish whiskey contains 700 casks!

Until comparatively recently, Irish whiskey was marketed as a straight pot still whiskey and almost nothing else. Blended pot still and grain whiskey was almost unknown. Over the last few years the practice of blending Irish and grain has developed and now Irish whiskey brands range from the very full-bodied to the lightest of the light.

In 1877, two gallons of Irish whiskey cost less than a bottle does today.

145

The qualities of Irish whiskey

When the Shah of Persia visited London in 1899 he was offered a glass of Bushmill's Irish whiskey. From the size of his glass, he must have developed a taste for it.

In an American advertising campaign some years ago Irish whiskey was described as 'smooth, burnished' and that is probably as convenient a point of departure as any other. 'Smooth' is certainly true of older, well-matured whiskey, although over-young Irish whiskey can have a ferocious bite not encountered in any Scotch.

'Burnished' implies glowing and rounded; these are certainly two qualities to be found in all good Irish brands. They have a fullness on the palate and a richness of aftertaste that can only be compared with that given by the heaviest of Scottish malts. It is not so easy to be sure about 'nose'. Compared to the nose of a good malt, the nose of even the finest Irish whiskeys is a little coarse. The addition of even a little water often helps, although one should respect the taste of those who prefer a fine old Irish whiskey as an after-dinner liqueur.

In recent years Irish distillers have made a successful effort to increase their share of the worldwide spirits market.

The five major brands of Irish whiskey are Jameson, Power, Paddy, Tullamore Dew (my own preference) and Old Bushmills. Amongst the other better known brands are Ballagary, Burke's Three Star, Coleraine, Daly's Special, Dublin Cream, Four Leafed Clover, Green Label, Old Kenko, President, O'Sullivan, Slainte and Vat 36.

Potheen

Whenever Irish whiskey is mentioned, someone usually talks of potheen, or illicitly distilled spirit. There is no evidence that illicit distillation was more frequent in Ireland than in Scotland or North America but nevertheless this legendary liquor has caught the imagination of generations. Perhaps it is no surprise that the land that produced the leprechauns and the Blarney Stone should also produce the fabled dew of the mountains.

But having said that, potheen certainly existed and may still exist. I myself have never tasted it and this is certainly not for the lack of trying.

For centuries the British government was bedevilled by the enormous amounts of illicit Irish whiskey being produced and, what hurt more, by the great loss of revenue that accompanied it. They made continuing and determined—if unsuccessful—attempts to prevent earlier generations of people like myself getting hold of it. The history of illicit distilling is the history of these attempts.

It is almost certain that the processes of making potheen did not vary much through the centuries. It was a folk skill that would be resistant to change once it was established, almost certainly, by trial and error.

The distilling of potheen was both hazardous and difficult, but even in 1871, when this picture was drawn it was still widespread in the remoter parts of Ireland.

Even the army was sent in

A certain Professor Donovan, a chemist by profession and thus well acquainted with the process of distillation, visited an illicit still in 1830 and describes it thus, '. . . the distillery was a small thatched cabin. At one end was a large turf fire kindled on the ground and confined by a semi-circle of large stones. Resting on these stones, and over the fire, was a forty gallon tin vessel, which answered both for heating the water and the body of the still. The mash tun was a cask hooped with wood, at the bottom of which, next the chimb, was a hole plugged with tow. This vessel had no false bottom: in place of it the bottom was strewed with young heath; and over this a stratum of oat husks. Here the mash of hot water and ground malt was occasionally mixed for two hours; after which time the vent at the bottom was opened and the worts were allowed to filter through the stratum of oat husks and heath. The mashing with hot water on the grains was then repeated and the worts were again withdrawn. The two worts being mixed in another cask, some yeast added and the fermentation allowed to proceed until it fell spontaneously, which happened in about three days.

'It was now ready for distillation and was transferred into the body, which was capable of distilling a charge of forty gallons. A piece of soap weighing about two ounces was then thrown in to prevent its running foul: and the head, apparently a large tin pot with a tube at its side, was inserted into the rim of the body and luted with paste made of oatmeal and water. A lateral tube was then luted into the worm, which was a copper tube of an inch and a half bore, coiled in a barrel for a flakestand [a worm tub]. The tail of the worm where it emerged from the barrel was caulked with tow. The wash speedily came to the boil and water was thrown on the fire: for at this period is the chief danger of boiling over. The spirit almost immediately came over: it was perfectly clear; and by its bead, this first running inferred to be proof.' Donovan thought the flavour excellent and said that in his opinion it would have passed for whiskey three months old, which tells us a great deal more about the quality of early 19th century Irish whiskey than the good professor intended.

The potheen maker used whatever cereals he had to hand but always, of course, with a proportion of malted barley to get the saccharifying process started. He would make his malt by steeping a sack of barley in bog water and spreading it on the floor of his hut to allow it to germinate. When this process was complete he would bag it and take it to a properly licensed kiln along with a sack of raw corn. Donovan goes on to say what occurred:

'The raw corn was spread out on the kiln; but during the night when the kiln owner had retired to rest, the raw corn was removed, and malt spread on, dried, and replaced by the raw grain before day. The owner of corn drying on a kiln sits up all night to watch it. In this way the discovery was eluded, and the malting completed.'

Although most illicit stills were small and primitive, this was not always the case. A generation earlier than Donovan often saw pitched battles between potheen makers and excisemen and, on some occasions even artillery was brought in. A report of 1788 makes exciting reading:

'Limerick, February 25th. On the 20th instant, John Downes, esquire, inspector of excise, accompanied by other civil officers and a detachment of the 27th regiment, with two field pieces, proceeded to attack the Castle of Ognolly, in which has been carried on for some years an immense distillery in open defiance of the laws; but on the first appearance of the military force the castle surrendered without the least resistance. In it was found one of the most complete distilleries in the kingdom, which was totally destroyed.' The report does not disclose, alas, what the soldiers did with the whiskey but the use of soldiers to attack a distillery can be regarded as a military operation with hazards quite outside those to be found in most field manuals.

Coffey, who was later to invent the patent still that still bears his name, records another hazard of dealing with illicit distillers. He says the trade was '. . . chiefly, if not entirely, carried on by persons of a very low rank in life, who generally fermented not more than one sack of grain at a time; they made weak mash of it, fermenting it in a short time and distilling it off rapidly, making about ten or twelve gallons of illicit spirit with it, and before the individual made any more he generally

148

brought it to market; perhaps half a dozen or at times a dozen men would come to market, armed with heavy cudgels riding together; so that no officer would attack them, unless he had a military party and he could hardly ever come up with them, unless his party were cavalry.'

The reasons for the decline in illicit distilling are many. The growing certainty of detection, the heaviness of fines and sheer expense were all partly responsible, although perhaps the quality of legally distilled Irish whiskey probably had most to do with it. Romance apart, who would want to drink a crude and reeking spirit when a well-matured John Jameson was available at a reasonable price? The number of detections over the years makes the point very clearly:

1860	2396	1900	1828
1870	2215	1910	1139
1880	685	1920	947
1890	1819	1922	172

Three reservations must be made about these figures. First, these are detections only, and not the number of stills operating, which would invariably be greater. Second, they give no indication of size—from an illicit bottle to an illicit still. Thirdly, the detections were mainly very small fry. Nevertheless they are evidence of a steep decline.

The last instance of an illegal still being discovered, I have found, was in December 1957. In that year a Mr D. Finch of Ranyar, a jeweller by trade, was caught making potheen in his flat. He had left his still unattended for a short while and it overflowed while he was away—into a newspaper office below.

Let another Irish writer, Maguire, say the final word on potheen:

'Illicit distilling is likely to persist as long as there is duty on spirit. It is poor stuff compared to the legal article, but it is cheap and will always have its advocates who will praise it with the zeal of eccentrics.'

Barley is ideal for making potheen, but the illicit distillers in Ireland used whatever cereals were available. Some barley was always used, however, to get the process started. The more malted barley used, the better the end result.

8 CANADIAN WHISKY

No one has officially recorded when whisky was first distilled in Canada but there is no reason to suppose that they were much behind their American neighbours. In fact, the conditions that produced the first American whiskies were there in Canada too—only more so. The climate was harsher, the winters longer and colder and the privations facing the early pioneers more severe. So it would be astonishing if early Scots and Irish settlers had not used the distilling skills they had taken with them. Of course, we know they did. One Canadian distilling company has been established for nearly 150 years and four others are well past their centenary.

Just as in the United States, and for similar reasons, there has always been a strong temperance movement in Canada, and there have been in the past dry provinces which have totally forbidden the manufacture or import of alcohol. But this has never been Canadian federal policy and so it has proved difficult, if not impossible, to enforce. Even so, the government regulates the sale of all alcoholic beverages very carefully, not least native Canadian whisky.

At the beginning of the century, Thomas Dewar, the famous Scotch distiller, came to Quebec on business and was disconcerted to find a commission sitting discussing the possibility of applying prohibition across the whole of Canada. His prompt refutation of the prohibitionists' case was not well received, but he found the bright side of Canadian prohibitions a little later when he arrived in a dry province. He found he could not get a drink on the train and asked the conductor's advice. He was told to try a local store at the next stopping place and did so, requesting a bottle of whisky. Asked if he had a medical certificate, he ruefully admitted he had not. The storekeeper told him, in that case, he could not sell him whisky but that he might find the local cholera mixture to his liking. He was handed a familiar shaped bottle full of a familiar coloured liquid. It was a bottle of Dewar's, his own Scotch whisky.

In February 1919, the Canadian government issued the Canadian Consolidated Prohibition Order, incorporating an earlier order of 1917. This earlier order prohibited the importation of liquor into any part of

Although the original pioneers in Canada had a backbreaking task in conquering the virgin soil, by the 1890s vast areas of that country had been opened up and given over to grain production. This is the basis of the Canadian whisky industry which now produces some of the most popular whiskies in the world.

150

'A flood of whisky'

Canada after April 1919, and the manufacture of intoxicating liquor at a date to be fixed later. This order officially expired on 1st January 1920, but was never remotely operational because, almost simultaneously, prohibition was imposed in the United States and the economic opportunities offered by their mighty and thirsty southern neighbour were too good to be missed. A flood of Canadian whisky began to flow across the 49th parallel and the Canadian whisky business was given an enormous boost.

However, the prohibitionists did not give up. At the beginning of 1923, the British government was sent a formal note on new alcoholic regulations in Canada. These included the abolition of bar sales throughout Canada, the imposing of pro-

hibition in seven of the nine provinces and the imposition of strict government control in the remaining two. Once again, like all sumptuary laws, these restrictions proved impossible to apply and Canadian distillers continued to produce and market and, increasingly, to export their whisky. In comparison with the bootleg and the often semi-poisonous whiskies made in the United States during prohibition, Canadian whisky soon gained a high reputation in the United States, and one which it has successfully maintained. Today it has also made substantial inroads into other world markets and there can be few places where it is impossible to buy Hiram Walker's excellent Canadian Club or Seagram's whisky. At the last count Canadian whisky could be found in 154 countries.

Seagram's V.O. is one of the classic Canadian whiskies. Along with Canadian Club there are few places in the world where it cannot be found.

Making Canadian whisky

"CANADIAN CLUB" WHISKY.

The age and genuineness of this Whisky are guaranteed by the Excise Department of the Canadian Government by Certificate over the capsule of every bottle.

Obtainable throughout the World.

This advert for Canadian Club appeared in an English magazine in 1902. Even then, it was obtainable throughout the world and is today one of the market leaders in the Canadian industry. Their most recent advertising campaign has been very cleverly aimed at younger whisky drinkers making the brand extremely popular with all those who identify with youth.

The basic process in making Canadian whisky is very similar to that used in making bourbon or rye. Maize and malted barley, selected for their convertible starch and moisture content and cleaned and screened, arrive at the distillery for storage. When they are needed for distillation they are weighed and ground separately and conveyed to grain meal bins and malt meal bins, having been frequently tested to ensure that the correct and uniform grind size has been maintained.

The malt meal goes from the storage bin to a malt slurry tank where water is added to form malt slurry. The grain meal goes to a cooker where it is mixed with a predetermined amount of water, this mixture being known as mash. This mash is then cooked under pressure so that the starch is softened and gelatinized in order that it can be broken down by enzyme conversion. Malt slurry is now added to the grain mash and the mixture dropped into a conversion tank at a temperature of 140–148°F (60–64°C). The malt enzymes get to work, transforming the starch in the grain mash into fermentable sugar and, when this has been accomplished, the mixture is pumped through cooling condensers, where the temperature is reduced to 85°F (29°C).

While this is going on, another essential process is taking place in the yeast laboratory. The pure yeast culture is taken from its special refrigerator and a few cells extracted. These are now placed in a small flask containing sterile malt syrup wort and the flask placed in an incubator. The yeast cells immediately begin to multiply. After 24 hours of incubation the small flask is poured into a larger one, also containing sterile malt wort as a medium. When this again has been incubated for 24 hours it is conveyed to a 200-gallon tank. After yet another 24 hours it goes to an even larger tank. In this way a few healthy yeast cells can produce 6000 gallons of active yeast in no more than a few days.

The grain mash, incorporating all its fermentable sugars, is now pumped to the fermenters, and the yeast, in its turn, pumped into the mash. Rapid fermentation now takes place. When this is complete, the fermented mash (called 'distiller's beer') is pumped into a beer still (sometimes confusingly called a 'whisky still'), where it flows down in a zigzag fashion over horizontal plates evenly spaced throughout the length of the still, just as in a Coffey still. Steam is injected at the base of the still and, as it rises through small holes in the horizontal plates, it evaporates off alcohol in the descending mash on each plate. The gaseous alcohol rises to the top of the still, where it is led off and condensed into what is called 'new whisky'. This raw liquid is run through further stills (an extraction column, a rectifying column and a barbet unit) to remove undesirable congeners such as fusel oil. This redistillation produces a whisky with almost none of the heavier congeners. Canadian whisky is well-known as being the lightest whisky in the world.

The alcohol-free grain mash, known as 'stillage', falls to the bottom of the still from where it is pumped to a plant which centrifuges it, evaporates it and finally flash-dries it to produce the familiar 'distillers dried grains'. This, mixed with other nutrients, makes an excellent cattle food.

The unmatured whisky is now filled into wooden casks which may or may not be charred on the inside, and left for four, six, eight or 12 years in temperature-controlled warehouses. When the desired state of maturity has been reached, individual whiskies are 'married' or blended. They are then filtered, tested and bottled in the normal way.

Historically, Canadian whisky has always been of great interest to the government and this tradition continues. The Canadian distiller is more closely watched and controlled than any other manufacturer in the country, and a large number of excisemen oversee every stage of the process from the arrival of the cereal at the distillery to the final shipment of the mature spirit. There is, though, and very sensibly, no interference with the actual process of distillation itself. Each distiller makes his own whisky in exactly the way *he* wants.

The man who made Chivas Regal

In 1926 Seagrams was a small, old-fashioned company founded in 1857 (ten years before Canada was granted Independence) with a distillery at Waterloo, Ontario. The unquenchable thirst of the

Americans, with whom prohibition was in full cry, meant that it was kept busy enough but very little of its product was drunk in Canada or anywhere else but south of the 49th parallel. In fact, far more Scotch than Canadian whisky was drunk in Canada because nobody thought much of the native product and there was not much of it about.

By 1970, Seagrams, or rather the Distillers Corporation-Seagrams Limited, was the largest distilling organization in the world, with distilleries in 14 countries. And more Seagrams' VO Canadian whisky is sold than any other whisky exported from any country—and that includes Scotland and the United States.

This astonishing transformation was the personal achievement of one man, Samuel Bronfman, who changed the face of the world whisky business. How he did it is the story of a dedication amounting to an obsession and an appetite for work amounting to a mania.

Bronfman started his working life in the liquor mail order business in Canada before the First World War. With his brother, he was soon moderately prosperous, with warehouses and mail order offices in every province. But in the early 1920s things began to go wrong. Bronfman later wrote,

'Early in the 1920s, the Provincial Governments, one by one, took over the control and sale of liquor in their respective Provinces. This eliminated us from the mail order business and I therefore decided to build a distillery to supply consumers through the newly created Government Liquor Control Commissions and Boards.

'I had moved my house to Montreal by that time and the site I selected for our distillery was in Lasalle, a suburb of Montreal. The name of our new firm was Distillers Corporation Limited.'

He goes on to describe the early years of his new company.

'There was really little Canadian whisky in Canada in the early 1920s because Canadian distilleries had been shut down by Government edict all through World War I, and on to 1920 when the final peace treaty was signed. Far more Scotch than Canadian whisky was consumed in Canada at that time because in Scotland, distilleries had continued to operate all

through this period. Our first job, then, was to build inventories of Canadian whiskies to mature for the future.

'In 1926, with a view to enlarging our business in Canada, we invited the Distillers Company Limited of Great Britain, then the world's largest distilling firm, to join our venture. This arrangement gave us additional knowledge of the Scotch whisky business as well as the right, in Canada, to several well-known brand names . . .

'. . . In the same year we acquired the shares of Joseph E. Seagrams and Sons Limited, of Waterloo, Ontario.'

Bronfman's company has been familiarly known as 'Seagrams' ever since.

He continued in his obsessional endeavours to improve the quality, and to increase the quantity, of Canadian whisky by installing new stills and new equipment at both his Lasalle and Waterloo distilleries.

'I paid personal attention to every aspect of the production process: to grains, water and yeasts, to milling, to cooking procedures and temperatures, to fermenters, to stilling and distilling techniques, to barrels used for maturing whisky, to packaging and bottling.'

Like every other whisky blender in the world, this Canadian blender uses his nose, not his palate, to judge the excellence of the whiskies he intends to use in the blend.

Bronfman decided very early on that Seagrams VO Canadian whisky was going to be the big money-spinner and he devoted much time and thought to developing and promoting the brand. One especially imaginative touch was the use of the Seagrams racing colours in a ribbon round the neck and shoulders of the bottle. This practice was successful and has continued to this day: nowadays Seagrams uses more than 10,000 miles of this ribbon every year.

Shrewdly, Bronfman was always very interested in the presentation of his whiskies.

'I have always been very conscious of the importance of packaging and have spent hundreds, perhaps thousands of hours on this fascinating subject. I well remember, for example, the Saturday mornings I used to spend in my office with Frank Lafleche of the Dominion Glass Company and we discussed the pros and cons of this type of glass and that type of design.'

By 1928, far-sighted businessmen could see that prohibition in the United States was doomed to failure and Bronfman was never less than far-sighted.

'. . . I became convinced that the Prohibition in the United States would soon come to an end and I started to make plans for that day, having in mind that we would enter the American market when this occurred. Accordingly we enlarged production in our Lasalle and Waterloo plants, built warehouses and began to fill them with maturing whiskies.

'When it looked as though Repeal was definitely on the way, we began to discuss how we would enter the American market. Our partners, the Distillers Company Limited, came to Montreal to join the discussions. They indicated that they preferred not to become American distillers, and wished to concentrate instead on their world-wide interests in Scotch whisky. They offered to sell us their shares and we accepted.

'Our association with the Distillers Company was and is a happy one. We have a continuous business relationship and have remained good friends all through the years.'

The incident that Bronfman recalls raises several interesting points. First, it shows very clearly the interlocking nature of the international whisky business with a number of very large multinational companies operating highly complex bilateral and multilateral manufacturing and marketing arrangements. In the 1920s it was complicated but the outsider stood some chance of understanding it. But today, with Seagrams, D.C.L., Hiram Walker and Suntory—to name but four monsters—all competing and co-operating with hundreds of brands in more than a hundred markets, the necessary web of interrelationships defies description. Second, there is the curious decision of D.C.L. to pull out of the partnership just when the American market was about to expand explosively. I can understand their need to concentrate on the profitable production of Scotch at this particular time but I am surprised that the two activities seemed to them to be mutually exclusive. Natural caution—ca' canny—is an admirable Scots quality but on this occasion it seems, to say the least, excessive. Lastly, there is the extraordinary vision of the man. As Bronfman tells it, the coming repeal of prohibition was quite obvious. In fact, in 1928, it was by no means so obvious and it had five full years to go. Only a superb judge of probabilities and a brave man would have taken the very substantial business risk that Bronfman took at that time.

Luckily his gamble paid off handsomely. Immediately after the repeal he opened up in the United States, taking offices in the Chrysler Building in New York. The first practical step was to acquire a distillery, which he soon did by

Samuel Bronfman, the founder of the Seagram empire. Even today the empire is still growing and is trying to gain control of a larger share of the Scotch malt whisky market. In 1977 it purchased The Glenlivet.

The Seagram Building in New York is considered by many to be one of the finest examples of modern architecture anywhere in the world.

buying the Lawrenceburg distillery in Indiana. This gave him a base in the Midwest. Next he bought the Calvert distillery in Relay, which is in Maryland. He immediately set about enlarging and modernizing these distilleries and building up stocks of American whiskeys. At the same time Bronfman was taking a cool and critical look at the traditional way in which the American whiskey business operated. Rye whiskey was made in the east and bourbon in the Midwest. These whiskeys were then sold, in barrels, to rectifiers who bottled them and sold them to retailers who, in turn, sold them to the public. This inevitably meant that the producers of American whiskeys had no control over them after they left the distillery, with all that this implies in, for instance, strength, age and quality control.

Bronfman decided that this just wasn't good enough for his whiskeys. Like the Scotch whisky distillers, he wanted complete control of the whole process from distilling to bottling. He also saw that the majority of American distillers, newly operational after the repeal, were distilling straight bourbon and rye and selling it as straight whiskey, that is, not blended. His experience told him that, as in Scotland, blended Canadian whiskies sold best, and blending meant that it was much easier to maintain standards of quality year in, year out. He therefore made the profoundly significant business decision to go for blended whiskeys in the United States. This decision was to have far-reaching consequences.

Another problem—though hardly an unhappy one—was the large stock of top-quality, fully matured Canadian whisky which had been built up in the years preceeding the repeal. These had to compete with raw straight American whiskey sold almost straight from the still. Bronfman knew exactly what to do.

'We shipped four, five and six-year-old whiskies from Canada to Lawrenceburg and Relay, and there blended them with neutral spirits distilled in our U.S. plants.

155

'An immeasurable contribution'

At the same time we were, of course, producing whiskeys in the United States and maturing them to coincide with the inevitable depletion of our Canadian stocks. In this way, we were eventually to have whiskeys of similar ages—four, five, and six-year-olds—all produced in the United States.'

Even under extreme competitive pressure Bronfman was not prepared to compromise the quality of the whisky he made. He goes on to say,

'I have never been accustomed to blending white (unaged) spirits in our whiskies. I therefore delayed blending to give our U.S. produced spirits at least some development in wood.

'I insisted on this delay even though some shareholders called on me to protest that we were doing nothing while other distillers were busy marketing and making lots of money. This was true. During this period other distillers were enjoying a bonanza in sales. No matter, I waited. Quality in the bottle, and our reputation for quality, were much more important to me than immediate profits.'

Again, Bronfman's obsession with quality brought its deserved reward.

'The rewards of patience and the proof of craftsmanship came in the fall of 1934. In August we introduced our Seagrams Five Crown and Seagrams Seven Crown brands.

'The entire Industry well remembers what happened. In just 60 days we were able to tell the public that these blended whiskeys were outselling all others through the country . . . Not only had we become Number One in America but we have remained Number One ever since.'

This triumph of foresight and insistence on good whiskey was followed by the introduction of other successful brands such as Calvert Special and Calvert Reserve. Fortune smiled on Samuel Bronfman and it seemed that he could not put a foot wrong. In 1936 he built a brand new distillery at Louisville in Kentucky, which remained the apple of his eye.

It was shortly before this that Bronfman also bought heavily into Scotch whisky. He acquired the Robert Brown Company (founded in 1861) and immediately began to lay down stocks of Scotch whisky. A little later he bought the Strathisla-Glenlivet malt whisky distillery at Keith (incidentally the oldest distillery in Scotland).

He then bought Chivas Brothers of Aberdeen. Among other brands that this company blended was a de luxe 12-year-old whisky called Chivas Regal. Bronfman fell in love with this splendid blend and decided not only that he would improve it but that he would expand it so that the whole world would be able to experience the pleasures of a premium Scotch blended whisky—at a price. He mothered and fussed over Chivas Regal, paying close attention to its packaging and marketing until he finally turned it into the best-selling de luxe Scotch in the world. In fact, he did even more. He insisted that they matured some Chivas Regal for 21 years. This he called Chivas Regal Royal Salute, an unsurpassable blended Scotch whisky.

Seagrams continued to expand in North America. In May 1939 the visit to Canada of King George VI and Queen Elizabeth saw the introduction of Seagrams Crown Royal. September saw the outbreak of the Second World War and once more, with other industries, the whole of the international whisky business was thrown into turmoil. Alcohol is an essential ingredient in the manufacture of much essential war material (such as synthetic rubber) and so the production of whisky ceased abruptly both in Canada and the United States. This meant that stocks of North American whiskies began to run down because they

Seagram's Crown Royal was introduced in 1939 on the occasion of the visit of King George VI and Queen Elizabeth to Canada.

The Seagram distillery at Waterloo retains the original entrance which proudly proclaims that the firm was established in 1857.

that the war was over, we had an opportunity to build up very large stocks of spirits in wood. We built many new warehouses and eventually we had over 125 million gallons of spirits in wood, sufficient for a four to five year supply.

'Thus we were able to blend with *aged* spirits which had been in oak barrels for a minimum of four years. Even though the U.S. Government regulations would not permit distillers to claim or mention in advertising, or on labels, the length of time spirits are matured in wood, I knew the quality was there and, obviously, so did the public.

'Up to this time, through all the years since Repeal, we have refused to join in the straight whiskey business because, to have done so, we would have had to sell young, immature whiskeys.

'Now, however, with sufficient stocks built up, we would put fully matured straight whiskey into our bottles. We therefore set up a straight whiskey company under Frankfort Distillers which today sells straight bourbon whiskeys from five to ten years old.'

During the war years, Bronfman had also acquired the British Columbia Distilling Company Limited, because he felt he needed a distillery in British Columbia. This acquisition also brought him a second distillery in Ontario, at Amherstburg. In the early 1950s he acquired a second distillery in British Columbia, following this up with another in Quebec.

It was during this period that Mies van der Rohe built the Seagram Building on Park Avenue, New York, an architectural masterpiece of 38 bronze-clad storeys and a half-acre of pools, fountains and trees. Many claim that it is the most beautiful building in New York.

The Bronfman empire continued to expand through the 1960s. By 1970 they had plants not only in Canada, the United States and Scotland, but in Jamaica, England, France, Germany, Italy, Israel, Mexico, Costa Rica, Venezuela, Brazil and Argentina. Those countries that were not making whisky for Seagrams were importing it.

Samuel Bronfman, still very much in charge, celebrated his 80th birthday in 1970, but in 1971 the man who had done more than anyone else to shape the world whisky business in modern times died.

were simply not being replaced. Bronfman found two answers for this. Sadly, he had to introduce a form of rationing so that everyone had a fair share. Secondly, he bought the Frankfort Distillering Company in Kentucky with its big inventory of Four Roses whiskey which not only gave him more whiskey to distribute but a new distillery to operate when better times arrived. Which they inevitably did:

'At the end of World War II our inventories were very low. We began at once to rebuild them, but it was a process of several years, and during that time we had to continue rationing. We also had to consider developments in production.

'As mentioned earlier, I do not approve of blending with white (unaged) spirits. I had hoped, as time went on, to build a sufficient inventory of spirits in wood [oak barrels] so that we could carry on our blending on the same basis as we did in Canada and Scotland.

'Fortunately, I had built a sizeable inventory of spirits in wood in America before the war. This inventory did much to keep our quality high and uniform through all the years of shortages. Now

9 JAPANESE WHISKY

Japan is the second largest consumer of whisky in the world. Only in the United States do they drink more. It will come as no surprise that the Japanese have created a sophisticated and highly efficient whisky industry that produces a first-class range of whiskies to meet this demand.

The history of whisky in Japan is, like D.C.L. in Scotland, largely the history of one man and one company. In 1899, Shinjiro Torii, a young man of 20, set himself up as a wine merchant. In 1907 he produced Japan's first domestic sweet wine. He prospered mightily and, by 1919, had opened a big plant in Osaka.

In 1923 he built Japan's first whisky distillery in the Vale of Yamazaki, near Kyoto. At the time this was seen as an extremely bold, even quixotic, act. To make whisky of the type he wanted to make outside Scotland was seen as presumptuous, if not absurd. But he persevered and, seven years later, he came up with the first genuine whisky ever produced in Japan. He called it Suntory Whisky White Label. By the time it had gained any kind of widespread recognition, the Second World War had broken out and Shinjiro Torii ended up with his head offices and the Osaka plant in ruins. But

the Yamazaki distillery and its large stocks of mature whisky were not touched and so Suntory was perfectly poised to take advantage of the post-war whisky boom in Japan. In 1946, government price control of alcoholic drinks was abolished and Torii's whisky came onto the market again. 1950 saw the re-introduction of Old Suntory whisky, introduced shortly before the war.

In 1957, Suntory was forced to enlarge the distillery at Yamazaki and a new bottling plant at Tamagawa was built. Japan's new surge of prosperity brought a demand for high quality products and Suntory responded to it with a series of popular whiskies. Suntory Whisky Red appeared in 1964, Suntory Whisky Gold in 1965 and Suntory Whisky Custom in 1967. These were all 'light' whiskies in line with the general world trend towards lighter whiskies. Alongside these, the company also marketed a number of premium brands, blended for the top end of the market, where buyers were not particularly worried about what they paid so long as they got what they wanted. Suntory Whisky Royal came first in 1960, Suntory Whisky Imperial in 1964, Suntory Whisky Special Reserve in 1969

The vast complex at Yamazaki has little in common with the original plant which was built in 1923. It is interesting that the slogan is in English, not Japanese.

Two blended whiskies produced by Nikka (top) and Suntory (bottom).

Far right: These barrels, with their English titles, proudly announce that they are from the original distillery at Yamazaki.

The whisky stills at Suntory's new distillery are Irish in appearance but the spirit produced is more like Scotch.

and Suntory Whisky Excellence in 1971.

These blends were part of an expansion in demand for whisky that was explosive. In 1973 Suntory responded to this by building a second distillery in Hakushu, just below the Southern Alps of Japan. This was the largest malt distillery under one roof in the world and, indeed, Suntory make whisky here on the grand scale. The site is over 6,000,000 square feet, which is more than 50 full size football pitches, and the distillery itself covers close on 300,000 square feet. Twenty-four enormous copper pot stills produce nearly 10 million gallons of

whisky a year. Suntory are now also producing whisky locally in Mexico, Brazil and Thailand. The story of Suntory whisky is a spectacular one.

Nikka is the only other widely-known whisky from Japan. Its founder, Masataka Taketsuru, was born in 1894 and spent three years from 1918 in Glasgow studying how whisky is made. For good measure he married a Scots lass. He originally worked for Suntory but founded his own firm at Yoichi Hokkaido in 1934, first distilling whisky in 1940. In 1952 he changed the whisky's name to Nikka. It is not exported to Britain, but some goes to the United States.

But how about the whisky itself? I must admit immediately that I have tasted only the top range of Suntory whiskies (understandably they do not export their standard brands) and I have found these very good. To be fair, it is unwise to approach them expecting them to taste like Scotch. They do not. This is just as it should be because they do not imitate Scotch but are whiskies very much in their own right. Drunk in this way, you will discover their true excellence. Alas, they are not cheap.

10 AUSTRALIAN WHISKY

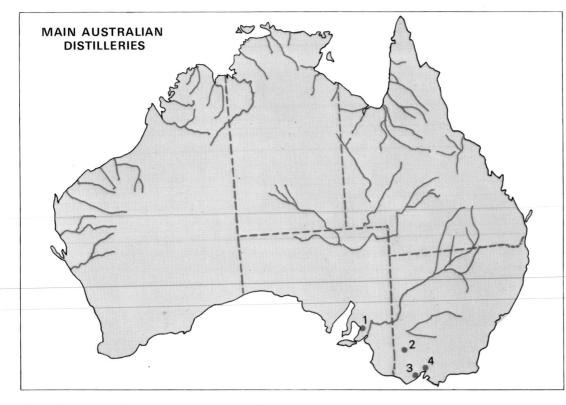

MAIN AUSTRALIAN DISTILLERIES

1 Adelaide
2 Ballarat
3 Geelong
4 Melbourne

It is very interesting, and obvious from this map, that whisky production in Australia is concentrated in the south-east of the continent. The reasons for this are both historic and climatic. The southeast is where the first settlers established themselves and where today the main industries are found. Also, the major centres of population have always been in this part, so it was sensible that where there was a demand for whisky and where conditions were ideal for distilling, the distillers would establish their plants.

The climate of large parts of Australia has naturally led to the development of viticulture, and brandy is unquestionably the most important spirit distilled in Australia. Nevertheless, Australia also has a substantial and growing whisky industry, and one which is recognized as being a 'proper' whisky producer, along with Scotland, Ireland, the United States, Canada and Japan.

For many years Australia was seen only as a market for the export of Scotch whisky. As early as 1856 one enterprising company, Thomas H. Slater and Co., were exporting Scotch whisky to Australia and most of the big blending houses had offices or agencies there by the late 19th or early 20th century. John Walker opened an office in 1890, followed a year later by Dewar's. D.C.L. came into Melbourne in 1897 and Sanderson opened up at Perth in 1912. Until the Second World War, in fact, Australia was the biggest single export market for Scotch whisky and, at one time, in 1916, the demand rapidly exceeded supplies, perhaps not surprisingly in the middle of a worldwide war. Nevertheless the Scotch whisky import traders 'viewed with much concern the growing diminution in existing stocks of whisky and the increasing difficulty experienced in obtaining further supplies

from Great Britain'. Some went so far as to 'cable direct to distillers in Scotland seeking exclusive shipments'. Unfortunately the dictates of naval strategy meant that their pleas went largely unanswered and inevitably the cost of a bottle of Scotch soon increased by 50 percent.

However, by the middle of the 1920s, the Australian government had put tariffs on all imported spirits and it made sense to bring in Scottish expertise to produce whisky in Australia where the locally-produced whisky, which had been on a relatively small scale for some years, enjoyed a protective tariff which put nine shillings on every gallon of Scotch. So it was agreed that, in conjunction with the chief whisky merchants of Australia, D.C.L. should build a new Australian whisky distillery in Geelong, Victoria. Ross of D.C.L. put the case thus, 'The object in . . . these cases is to take advantage of the preferential treatment given . . . to the domestic product as compared with the imported whisky. . . . The Directors have strongly impressed upon their associates in this venture that they can never hope to make Scotch whisky in . . . Australia and believe that there will still be a demand for the Scotch made article from those to whom price is no consideration. . . . If there is to be a change over

from a Scotch to a locally made article, then the company must be prepared to meet it.' The distillery was duly built with D.C.L. owning 51 percent of the shares and with the right to appoint the chairman.

Gilbeys also established themselves in Australia and were soon marketing the Australian whiskies—Castle Malt, Gauntlet and Round 7.

The largest whisky distilleries in Australia are at Port Melbourne and Corio Bay (Geelong). There are smaller distilleries at Ballarat (Victoria), Adelaide (South Australia) and Kingsford (New South Wales).

The story of Australian whisky starts in 1866 when Myers Ballarat Distillery was opened on the shores of Lake Wendouree in Victoria. Two years later a spring with water ideally suited for distillation was found at the base of Mount Warrenheip and a new distillery was built there. Over the last century this site has continued to be developed and it has now become Australia's largest distillery.

In 1870 an expatriate English chemist called Henry Brind joined the Myers Company as secretary. He was an able and hard-working man and in the course of time, rather like an antipodean William Ross, he took over the company, eventually renaming it Henry Brind and Co. Until 1886 it was the only whisky distillery in Victoria but by then the population of Melbourne had reached 300,000 and, as in frontier America, there was a demand by the farmers and bushwhackers for a cheap and potent spirit to console them for the backbreaking work involved in opening up a new continent. So in that year two new distilleries were opened, one at Port Melbourne by the Brothers Joshua and the other at Abbotsford by the Brothers Preston. We have no record of what their whiskies tasted like but the distilleries flourished and so their spirits must have pleased the taste of their customers.

In 1896 the Brothers Preston moved their distillery to South Melbourne where new stills were installed. They continued to operate there until 1912 when they were bought out by the Australian Distillery Company. In 1914 a new distillery was built at Warrenheip by Messrs Breheny Bros and Kenna. By this time the Aus-

tralian government had begun to take the usual and obvious interest in this new and flourishing industry and had inevitably introduced regulations to control the quality of the spirit produced.

By 1922, the four distilleries had realized the disadvantages of unrestricted competition, the benefits of rationalization and the need for united policies in the face of increasing government regulation. So, in that year, the four operating distilleries merged to form Federal Distilleries Pty Ltd. This new company decided to go for quality and blended a well matured Australian whisky called Old Court. This was an immediate success.

The growing prosperity of the Australian whisky trade had not escaped the attention of the mighty Distillers Company in far-off Edinburgh. Several of its constituent companies had in fact had agencies in Australia for many years. So, in 1927, they moved massively into the Australian market. On 27 May of that year the Distillers Corporation Proprietary Limited was incorporated, being an amalgamation of D.C.L., the Australian Distillery Company, Brinds Limited, Breheny Brothers and Kenna's Brewery Limited together with a number of Australian wholesale wine and spirit merchants.

With advice from D.C.L. experts, the new company built a modern distillery at Corio, Victoria. In 1931 it took a further step, typical of D.C.L., by merging with Federal Distilleries Pty Ltd to form the United Distilleries Pty Ltd. This new company marketed Corio Special Old Whisky which soon became the best-selling brand of Australian whisky. This popularity lasted until 1956 when the company introduced a superior brand, Corio 5 Star Old Whisky. Four years later another premium brand, Corio Black Gold, was introduced. Other United Distillers' whiskies are Four Seasons and Glencar.

In its whisky, United Distillers Pty Ltd uses a mixture of malt and variations of barley, sorghum and/or maize. It is thus doubtful if it would be possible to market it as 'whisky' in either Great Britain or the United States.

Although Australian whisky is produced in substantial quantities—657,362 litres (absolute alcohol) being sold in the year ending March 1977—it would be giving a

Two of the whiskies produced in Australia. Although the industry is growing, most bars still mainly offer well-known Scotch and American brands.

Government definitions

quite false impression that it is a popular drink in Australia. In fact, a great deal more Australian gin, Australian rum, Australian vodka and, especially, Australian brandy is distilled and consumed. And in whisky drinking circles, Scotch remains the 'in' drink. An Australian correspondent writes:

'To understand Australian whisky you need to know that most people in Australia prefer and drink Scotch. Australian whisky is a developing market but it has never challenged Scotch whisky as a status symbol and if you ask for whisky at a local cocktail party or in a bar you will be given Scotch. Having said this, with the growing nationalism in this country, I suspect that the next ten years may see a change in this position, particularly in view of the fact that Corio 5 Star and one or two other whiskies are of a fairly good quality.'

Australia is, above all, a beer drinking land, and although whisky is growing in popularity, the high temperatures experienced in most of the country probably will ensure that beer, a longer and more refreshing drink, will continue to be more widely drunk.

Australian whiskies must contain a minimum of 25 per cent malt and be aged for a minimum of two years. To carry the word 'Old' they must be aged in wood for five years or more. To be labelled 'Very Old' they must have been aged in wood for at least ten years. Australian whisky must be wholly distilled in Australia and a mixture of—for instance —Australian whisky and Scotch could not be sold as Australian whisky although it could be sold as simple whisky.

The Australian Federal Government has laid down strict definitions for what can properly be called Australian whisky:

1. *Australian Standard Malt Whisky*
   a. It must have been distilled wholly from barley malt by a pot-still or similar process at a strength not exceding 45 per cent over proof.
   b. It must have been matured while subject to the control of the Customs by storage in wood for a period of not less than two years; and
   c. It must have been certified by an officer to be pure whisky containing all the essential elements of pure malt whisky.

2. *Australian Blended Whisky*
   a. It must have been distilled partly from barley malt and partly from grain, and must consist of not less than 25 percent pure malt whisky which has been separately distilled by a pot-still or similar process at a strength not exceeding 45 per cent over proof.
   b. It must have been matured while subject to the control of the Customs by storage in wood for at least two years; and
   c. It must have been certified by an officer to be whisky blended and matured in accordance with this definition.

About 25 Australian whiskies are sold but only a few are widely known, and they are nearly all blends. Among them are Chessboard and Old Cobb, marketed in Victoria; Hyland, marketed in New South Wales; Bond 7 and Gilt Edge, produced and marketed by Gilbeys in Victoria; Hamilton Gold Label and Grand Crest, produced and marketed in South Australia; and Marksman which is produced and marketed throughout New South Wales.

Figures issued by the Australian Wholesale Spirit Merchants Association for the month of March in 1976 and 1977 reflect the increase in the consumption of imported whiskies in Australia. State by state, the number of litres consumed in that month of these two years was:

	1976	1977
New South Wales	218,893	306,266
Victoria	64,782	114,075
Queensland	75,278	65,682
South Australia	32,565	31,441
Western Australia	55,177	21,248
Tasmania	879	726
	447,575	539,438

If the total figure is projected over one year, we can see that the amount of whiskies imported into Australia makes it a valuable export market for the main whisky-producing countries of the world. But the recent awakening of Australian nationalism and the continuing growth of the domestic whisky industry may mean that the increase in imported whisky will gradually tail off.

GOLDEN ARROW
FINEST BLENDED
WHISKY

Whisky
Oy ALKO Ab

Genuine
SCOTCH
WHISKY
Distilled, matured and blended
in Scotland under Government
Supervision
Imported and Bottled by
OY ALKO AB
120

FINLAND
CZECHOSLOVAKIA
NETHERLANDS
YUGOSLAVIA

NIGERIA

Lion Blend
WHISKY
LB
LION BLEND
WHISKY
Skotlantilaisen mallasviskin
ja suomalaisen viljaviinan sekoitus
Blandning av skotsk maltwhisky
och finskt sädesbrännvin
OY ALKO AB
118

OY ALKO AB

WHISKY LB LION BLEND

JUGOSLOVENSKI PROIZVOD
VISKI - WHISKY

NAVIP · BEOGRAD-ZEMUN

RACKE RAUCHZART · RACKE RAUCHZART

RACKE
rauchzart
43 VOL.%
Whisky

Whisky is made in a large number of countries around
the world, and some of their labels are shown here.
On the next six pages we look at the international whisky
manufacturing industry.

It is generally accepted that only six countries in the world make real whisky—Scotland, Ireland, the United States, Canada, Japan and Australia. Nevertheless, a large number of other countries produce spirits which are described as 'whisky' and which are no doubt enjoyed as such by local inhabitants. Nine times out of ten these 'whiskies' are neutral grain spirit variously flavoured, usually though not necessarily with malt whisky, the neutral spirit being distilled from anything fermentable. Practically anything vegetable can be induced to ferment one way or the other, and although most whisky-producing countries do use a cereal base for their spirit, this is not always the case; the Norwegians, for example, at one time used potato spirit. These whiskies, of course, are a great deal cheaper than imported real whisky and it is an interesting reflection that millions of people, who are quite convinced that they have been drinking whisky all their lives, would be astonished if a drop of the real stuff ever passed their lips. I have tasted one or two of these native 'whiskies' and can assert with some confidence that the Scots can sleep easily. One of my most unforgettable experiences was sampling an Indian whisky. It was, to say the least, out of the ordinary and bore little relation to what I think of as whisky.

It is also important to know that not only do such countries produce their own whisky but they often allow its producers to let it masquerade as real whisky, usually Scotch whisky, either by misleading names or labelling or both (or by many other means, including direct misrepresentation). This is quite easy to do with names—Glen Nasty, Highland Swipes, Ben Rubbich—and with labels showing tartans, kilted figures and heather-covered mountains. The Scotch Whisky Association, which brings together all the major and most of the minor whisky distillers and blenders, spends a great deal of time and money on tracking down these spurious Scotches and taking out injunctions against them in their country of origin, although it is reticent about naming the worst offenders.

The less pretentious of these native whiskies are legally unexceptionable, although I am not sure that this could always be said of the spirits themselves.

One of the problems here is, inevitably, the divided mind of Scottish malt whisky distillers themselves. If someone abroad wants to buy their malt in bulk, are they to turn him down or impose unrealistic sale conditions? In any case, blending Scotch malt whisky with local grain is a time-honoured practice—so long as the finished product is not sold as *Scotch* whisky. As long ago as the 1920s, D.C.L. was exporting malt whisky to Canada for this very purpose. William Ross wrote at the time:

'Messrs Bronfman arrived from Montreal with an offer to sell a half interest in a new distillery erected by them near Montreal . . . Messrs Bronfman proposed to import the malt whiskies from Scotland and blend them with the locally made grain spirits, and thereafter to sell the product as a Scotch style of Canadian whisky. A deputation, consisting of the Chairman [Ross himself], Mr Herd and Mr Nicholson, was appointed to visit Montreal and report upon the whole matter. These gentlemen, having carefully considered the situation, agreed to recommend that the company enter into such an arrangement . . .'

The Scotch Whisky Association, again, is rather coy as to how much malt whisky goes abroad for this purpose today but I know that Bunnahabhain, for instance, is exported in bulk to Equador and that several other Latin American countries also import bulk Scottish malt. This leads me to suppose that many other countries import Scottish malts to blend with their own locally-distilled spirits. I am by no means criticizing this—business is business and a country must export or die—but a more open attitude might be healthier. And I would have thought that a pure neutral spirit, whatever it is distilled from, generously spiced with good Scottish malt whisky would make a decent drink. But, of course, most native whiskies are of a much more doubtful provenance.

Today, more and more countries are setting up their own indigenous distilleries to produce their own local spiritous liquors. Since these distilleries invariably use patent stills, they can be adapted to produce anything from vodka to rum. A recent American advertisement, for instance, talks of 'Choice lighter brandies from continuous

The blended whisky market leaders in Brazil. Whisky is an extremely popular drink in that country, usually taken on the rocks, but also often mixed with soft drinks.

stills', which must be interesting news for Martell. So quite naturally many of them produce their own type of cereal-based whisky. Alternatively, they produce neutral spirit which is blended with imported whiskies to produce a whisky-flavoured drink. So long as they do not pretend it is Scotch, bourbon or rye, everyone is happy.

As far as I know, no one has ever compiled a list of all the countries in the world which distil, blend or bottle whisky and, indeed, because new distilleries are being built all the time, this may be impossible. So the tally of countries described here cannot pretend to be more than a personal collection. There is no order of size, quality or preference; my list is decided alphabetically.

Argentina

For many years Argentina produced its own local whisky from local ingredients because imports were prohibited. It must have been an interesting drink. Now the ban has been lifted and Scottish malt is once more arriving in bulk to be blended with local spirit to make Argentine whisky. Seagrams also distil whisky in Argentina.

Austria

Austria produces several whiskies, all of them blends of Scottish malt whisky and locally distilled spirit.

Bolivia

Bolivia has a flourishing whisky industry which came on stream in 1969. It can proudly claim to have the highest distillery in the world at 12,000 feet. It draws its water from ice-cold Andean streams. Bolivian whiskies are, typically, a blend of imported Scotch malt whisky and spirit distilled in the lowlands of Bolivia, which are then redistilled at La Paz. This, they claim, gives them 'an exceptional degree of purity', and they may well be right because these whiskies are not only consumed locally but are exported to the neighbouring states of Ecuador, Peru, Chile and Colombia. They are also exported, oddly enough, to Taiwan. D & B, Special, Tommy Lonsdale, and Cutter are Bolivian whiskies using Scotch malt as a blending base. They also produce a Bellows Club Bourbon.

Brazil

Whisky has always been very popular in Brazil. There has been a thriving whisky industry there since the 1950s, and it is estimated that of the annual consumption of 36 million litres some 85 percent is locally produced, 90 percent of that being a blend of local spirits and imported malt. The market leaders are Drury's and Old Eight. Of the imported whiskies, about half is bottled locally, notably Passport, Bell's and Teachers'. Other popular imported bottled brands are Black & White, Dimple and J.B.

Bulgaria

Bulgaria does not produce her own local whisky but bottles Jockey Club and Suntory Gold under licence, an example of Japanese enterprise if nothing else.

Costa Rica

Seagrams 'bottle whiskies there and plan to produce local whiskies'.

Czechoslovakia

Whisky is made in Czechoslovakia, which is all I am in a position to say.

Denmark

At one time Denmark produced a local whisky under the label Cloc, but this ceased some time ago. Other defunct Danish whiskies are Heather Queen, Red Lion, Special Wonder, Straight Label and The Hamlet.

Ecuador

Ecuador imports Scottish malt whisky (Bunnahabhain is one that I have personal knowledge of) to mix with local spirit to produce an Ecuadorian whisky.

Egypt

With Egyptian whisky we are in somewhat troubled waters. Writing in 1951, Sir Robert Bruce Lockhart says very firmly, 'What is certain is that the Egyptians still make whisky today. It is known as "bolonachi", it was bought eagerly by our troops in the Middle East during the last war and *pace* Field Marshal Montgomery it played its part in the victory of El Alemein'. The official on the North African desk of the British Overseas Trade Board confirmed that he too had heard of Egyptian whisky although he had never seen or tasted it and believed that it had been out of production some years. On the other hand the Egyptian Embassy was equally definite '. . . whisky is not, and never has been, produced in Egypt'. So the mystery remains. I would be grateful if anyone could clear it up for me.

Finland

Finland produces whisky by blending vatted (sic) Scotch malt whisky with locally-distilled grain spirit. It is bottled and sold under the label Lion Blend. In addition to this, the Finns also import 'ready blended Scotch whisky at about 64° proof which is diluted and bottled by us over here'. By 64° proof I assume they mean 64 percent by volume which would make it about 130° British proof. At that strength it would certainly need some diluting.

Guyana

Scotch malt whisky is blended with Guyanan spirit and bottled to produce a local whisky.

Holland

Holland has had a long and successful flirtation with whisky. Bols first started blending it in 1933 under the label Gold Top Whisky, and it is still sold under that name today. It is a blend of vatted Scotch malt whisky and local grain spirit, and is a very drinkable whisky. Over the years Bols has produced a number of similar whiskies. The Dutch grain distillery is at Scheidam and, interestingly, malt whisky is also distilled here from malted barley in a pot still, just as in Scotland. Much of this goes for export, to Japan among other countries, but not, I suspect, to Scotland. Dutch whisky is also exported to Eastern European countries. Just after the war, when whisky was desperately short in Britain, the Dutch, very magnanimously exported their Always Mellow brand to the UK. I remember tasting it but not, alas, what it tasted like. Mr Jouke D. T. Eemka, who very kindly provided this information, tells me that Bols still exports between 800 and 1,000 cases of Dutch whisky to Britain every year. I have never come across it but if I did I would certainly buy a bottle in honour of an ancient friendship. And knowing the Dutch I would expect it to be highly palatable.

India

In spite of the threat of prohibition, there is at least one grain whisky distillery in India because I have tasted its product. A friend records a Mohanz Regal labelled and bottled suspiciously like Chivas Regal.

Iran

Three companies in Iran make whisky, importing vatted Scotch malt whisky and blending it with local grain spirits. The quantity produced is not very large, approximating 50,000 bottles a year, each bottle containing 0·75 litres. Two things about this puzzle me. By definition grain distilleries are very big and three of them must produce an enormous amount of alcohol. Fifty thousand bottles of whisky (which, incidentally, would hardly seem worth the trouble of blending and bottling) would use only a minute fraction of such an ocean. I must assume the rest goes for Arrack and other spirits. The second puzzle is the use of the word 'vatted' which has a very specific meaning in terms of malt whisky, i.e., a blend of malts and malts only. Are we to assume that the Iranians import a blend of malts specially vatted for them or, as I suspect, merely malt whisky in vats, i.e., casks. In this context it must always be remembered that although malt whisky has to be matured before it can be bottled or blended as Scotch whisky, no such restrictions apply to it as an export.

Isle of Man

I read a short item from the *Daily Telegraph* November 1977 '. . . Mr Lucian Landau will start whisky production in the Isle of Man next year after perfecting a secret distillation process said to be faster than that of the Scotch variety. It will have the brand name Glen Kella.' I await its arrival with some impatience but not much hope.

Mexico

Suntory are active in the production of whisky in Mexico. Seagrams too have made a unique Mexican whisky and have high hopes for it.

Nepal

I have heard reports of a locally produced Nepalese whisky. More than that I cannot say, but I would like to taste it.

New Zealand

New Zealand has recently begun to distil its own whisky at Dunedin under the names 45 South and Wilson. These are bourbon-type whiskies.

Norway

Norway at one time produced a local whisky under the label Club Blend which was a mixture of Scotch malt whisky and spirit distilled from Norwegian potatoes. This whisky is no longer produced or sold.

Peru

At least seven whiskies are made in Peru, of which two are bourbon type. This could lead me to suppose that the rest are Scotch types and their names, Mansion House, Cochrane, Black Archer, 21, and Duncan, would seem to confirm this. The TV commercials in Lima talk of it as 'like being in Scotland itself' to the skirl of bagpipes in the background. It all sounds like a big headache to the Scotch Whisky Association. A local trade paper says that, 'One or two of the local whiskies are made here by importing blended Scotch whisky which already has the full alcohol content, obtained from a whisky broker. In this case making the whisky here only involves mixing in the right amount of distilled water', which, in so far as it means anything, sounds highly unlikely. We are also told, 'Most of the local whiskies are made by importing Scotch malt blended with grain alcohol', [equally unlikely] '. . . or alternatively importing malt and using local alcohol, which brings down the price quite heavily'. This latter would seem to me to be the most probable source of Peruvian whisky.

Poland

A Polish journalist Karel Jacubowicz has written a definitive description of how most local whiskies are produced and marketed. This is as follows: 'Walk into a well stocked spirits store in Poland (although it had better be in a big town), and you'll see not one but two Polish made whiskies. One of them has been on the market for at least 15 years. The other one was introduced about three years ago—and the story about the reasons for its introduction are worth telling. The older brand, which is a blend of malt and rye whisky, is not really wholly Polish produced. It is based on a malt concentrate bought from a British company. Poland has developed and patented its own method of making whisky on the basis of that concentrate. The exact formula is a secret. Still, leaks from the spirit industry indicate that the concentrate is combined with rye spirit, and other additives, specially selected to give it its distinctive flavour and bouquet. All the ingredients are rested separately at first, and are then brought together and blended in oak barrels which are fired inside in a special way. There, the whisky is rested again, matured, and finally it goes on the market. All the additives, mind you, are natural. In Poland, they are very fussy about using only nature-grown ingredients in their food—or drink. People in the spirits industry headquarters in Warsaw say they are swamped with offers of synthetic additives and essences from all over the world, but all these offers are turned down. Speaking of genuine Scotch whisky, a Polish businessman attending an international fair once poured Polish whisky into a Johnnie Walker bottle whose contents he put into the Polish bottle. He then asked a Scotsman from a neighbouring stand to say which of the two was more to his liking. The true son of Scotland took a generous draught of each and pointed without any hesitation to the Johnnie Walker bottle containing—unknown to him—Polish whisky. [This anecdote, incidentally, caused some raised eyebrows in Kilmarnock.] Whether Polish whisky can really stand up to such a test or not, the fact remains that some time ago Polish whisky producers found themselves under pressure from their British counterparts. The thing was that the label was in English. It did say "Old Polish Whisky" (who says 15 years isn't old?), but that wasn't good enough. Only the word "whisky" could be left in the original (it had to be—there is no Polish word for whisky any way) and all the rest had to be in Polish, evidently so that there would be no danger of the Polish product being mistaken for Scotch. Could it be that British distillers were afraid of competition? Anyway, the Polish industry obliged—but it was not caught unprepared. It had anticipated just such trouble and fearing even worse things to come, it had a trump card up its

The Philippines has a small whisky industry which blends imported malt with locally produced grain spirit.

169

sleeve—its own method of making whisky. This is the younger brand, the Zamkowa (Royal Castle) bourbon whisky, produced from a mixture of first-grade rye and barley spirits and made, blended and matured according to original technologies protected by Polish patents. So, the two whiskies are now on the market, and whatever happens, Polish whisky drinkers can be sure of uninterrupted supplies.

Many factors work to the disadvantage of Polish whisky. First of all, it's quite simply the lack of tradition of whisky drinking in the country. Secondly, it is not exactly the cheapest drink you can get. So, since original whiskies are imported too, people who entertain and decide to serve whisky are likely to go for the snob value of the real McCoy. And then, there is yet another thing. The spirits that go into whisky are not rectified. They are raw—so they have not a little of the flavour and the aroma of—yes, moonshine. Now, the spirit used in the production of vodka is painstakingly rectified (when analysed chemically, it shows no sign of admixture), precisely to remove that flavour and aroma which [are] anathema to a full blooded vodka drinker. So, when served whisky, he will sniff at his glass, and probably exclaim, "But this stinks of moonshine". And that may very well be the end of that. Which explains also why not every Pole likes cognac, slivivitz, or Calvados—all of them drinks based on raw spirits. Just how much whisky is produced in Poland is a trade secret. However, the producers were prepared to give me a clue: the total output of the two brands, they said, represents 0·00035 per cent of the production of vodka in the country. So now, all you have to do is to find out how much vodka is produced and whip out your calculator. Anyway, whisky in Poland is indeed, quite literally, a "rare taste". But it's there if you care to look for it.'

Soviet Union

The Soviet Union does not currently distil its own whisky although it has in the past. One type, called Pollynnaia, was at one time produced near Odessa and was flavoured with wormwood. It was reputedly 'very popular in the southern parts of Russia', although it is difficult to imagine what it actually tasted like. It is even more difficult to find any Russian who

has ever heard of it. A type of Russian whisky was distilled after the Second World War and in 1954 *The Observer* in London quoted a leaflet issued by Gastronom No 1 in Moscow which stated that 'the process of producing sovietsky visky is complex and long'. A Russian friend has sampled 'sovietsky visky' and described it as 'amazing'. He was not being flattering.

Although the Soviet Union does not produce its own whisky it imports a great deal, largely from Poland and Czechoslovakia but also a fair amount of Scotch. In the early 1970s they were importing Scotch to the value of £180,000 and this has since increased steadily.

Spain

Spain imports bulk Scotch malt whisky and produces a whisky under the label Dyck (*D* estilerias *y C* rianza del Whis *k* y).

Switzerland

Three companies in Switzerland produce whisky, among them the French Pernod Company.

Tanzania

Tanzania produces whisky in Dar Es Salaam and another distillery has recently opened on the Island of Zanzibar. Both distilleries operate under the aegis of Messrs Duncan, Gilbey and Matheson of London.

Thailand

The Thais produce some whisky, one brand being called Red Cock.

Uruguay

Four brands of whisky are bottled in Uruguay under the labels MacDougall, Old Times, Spey Royal, and Gregson. This leads me to believe that they are mixtures of Scotch malt whisky and locally distilled spirit.

Venezuela

Venezuela imports Scotch malt whisky in bulk to mix with its own locally distilled spirit, to produce its own Venezuelan whisky. Seagrams, the North American based whisky manufacturers, also distil a local whisky in Venezuela.

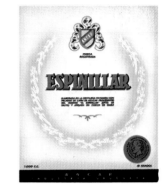

Two of the whisky brands made in Uruguay. The lower one readily admits that it is a blend of Scotch malt and a local spirit.

Wales

There was in the 19th century a small Welsh whisky distilling business but it was quickly killed by taxation. A couple of enterprising men have recently restarted the Welsh whisky trade using blended Scotch whisky flavoured with herbs. One must admire their enterprise even if one is a little dubious about their plans for building a new distillery 'comparable with any international distillery' on the banks of the River Tarrell in South Wales.

West Germany

West Germany produces its own whisky in some quantity and, indeed, both exports it to a number of countries and licenses it for production abroad (see Yugoslavia). At least one of its brands, Racke Rauchzart, uses a mixture of more than two dozen Scotch single malt whiskies.

Yugoslavia

Yugoslavia produces whisky under licence from West Germany under the Racke Rauchzart label. As the licensees write, 'Racke Rauchzart is one of the leading brands of whiskies in West Germany. It is well accepted in many countries all over the world and it becomes more and more popular'. Obviously this West German formulation hits the Yugoslav taste exactly because there is no reason why they should not produce their own blend as most other whisky-producing countries do. The word *rauchzart* (*rauch* is German for 'smoke', *zart* is 'gentle') describes the composition of this Yugoslav whisky. The *rauch* is the Scottish component, a mixture of more than two dozen single malts from the Highlands, the Lowlands and Islay; three, five, eight, ten and 12 years old. The *zart* is the local component, presumably spirit distilled from Yugoslav grains. It sounds a fair enough drink.

Zambia

Zambia has a similar arrangement to Tanzania with Messrs Duncan, Gilbey and Matheson.

The size of this bottle of Welsh whisky is indicative of the size of the Welsh whisky industry. The company who manufacture it claim that in the 4th century the legendary leader, Rhuallt Hir, perfected what was then known as the 'Spirit of Life'. The brew's main purpose was medicinal —its warming properties soothed the wounded and the infirm. After Rhuallt's death, the art of distillation was carried from father to son and it is said that Henry Tudor celebrated his victory at the battle of Bosworth with a keg of 'liquid paradise'. The Welsh whisky industry of the 19th century claimed that

'Welsh whisky is the most wonderful whisky that ever drove a skeleton from the feast, or painted landscapes in the brain of man. In it you will find the sunshine and the shadow that chased each other over the billowy fields, the breath of June ... the voices of men and maidens and the laughter of children ... your soul will burn with the Bardic fire of the Cymri.'

The whisky advertisements of modern distillers pall by comparison.

12 PROOF

'Proof' is confusing, even though everyone tells me how easy it really is. An official definition can be found enshrined in Clause 172(2) in the UK Customs and Excise Act of 1952: 'Spirits shall be deemed to be at proof if the volume of ethyl alcohol contained therein made up to the volume of the spirits with distilled water has a weight equal to that of twelve-thirteenths of a volume of distilled water equal to the volume of the spirits, the volume of each liquid being computed as at fifty-one degrees Fahrenheit.' Easy, isn't it?

Perhaps it would be well to go back to the beginning and find out what proof is all about. In the simplest terms, it tells you how strong an alcoholic drink is. In the earliest days of distillation, accuracy didn't matter all that much and they had correspondingly primitive ways of assessing alcoholic strength. As far back as the 15th century, they tested their spirit by pouring oil on its surface. If the oil sank to the bottom it was 'strong' spirit; if the oil floated, it was 'weak' spirit. Over the centuries, other methods have been evolved. The 'proof phial' was a glass into which the spirit to be tested was poured and then vigorously shaken. Bubbles or 'beads' would then form and the time they took to disappear noted. The longer the beads lasted, the stronger the spirit. Another method was to soak cloth in spirit and to see how readily it burned. Better known was the gunpowder method. The spirit was poured onto gunpowder which the tester then tried to ignite. If it would not light then it was under proof, if it burned with a steady blue flame it was exactly at proof, if it burnt violently or exploded it was over proof.

All these methods worked up to a point, but there was one thing they lacked. They were not, and never could be, accurate ways of actually measuring the strength of a spirit. The arrival of the excisemen and the growing interest of governments in the revenue that could be extracted from distilled spirits made the invention of an accurate, foolproof and practical measuring device imperative. The need was first met by a Londoner, John Clarke, in about 1725. He came up with a 'hydrometer and brandy prover' although he did not declare the idea publicly until 1746 when he published a book describing it. Although it had been demonstrated to the Royal

Society in 1730, and thus its bona fides proved, the government itself showed little interest and it was not until as late as 1787 that it was finally legalized by parliament to come into operation in 1788. Further acts of parliament refined its application. It was made permanent in 1801.

While all this was going on, serious doubts began to emerge as to the accuracy of Clarke's device. In 1802, a special committee was set up with a brief to

Glenfiddich is the most widely known of single malt Scottish whiskies. It is bottled at 70° British proof.

find a superior proof-testing method. In August 1802, the committee advertised for suitable inventions.

One of the first and most obvious contenders was a man called Bartholomew Sikes. He was an excise officer who was well known for his expertise in this field as his application made clear: 'If there is any part of knowledge in which I am more versed and fully grounded than any other', he wrote, 'it is the subject of

Seagram's Seven Crown is a blended American whiskey which is bottled at 86° proof, equivalent to 75° British proof.

Hydrometers for ascertaining the strength of spirits, and for reducing or raising them from one degree of strength to any other required strength by means of water or other spirits of different strengths.'

After selecting eight applications for testing, they chose Sikes' method in 1803. Unfortunately he died the same year and the £2000 award went to his widow. Sikes' hydrometer was finally adopted in the Hydrometer Act of 1818 and remains in universal use today. Put very simply, Sikes' hydrometer is a device which will float half in and half out of an equal mixture of water and pure alcohol.

So the excisemen finally got what they had always wanted—an extremely accurate measure of proof, the strength of spirit. Put as simply as possible, the official definition means that spirit at 100° proof weighs 12/13ths of the same volume of water at 51°F. This works out at about 57 percent alcohol and 43 percent water by volume. Similarly, 70° proof, the strength at which the Scots bottle all their whisky, is about 40 percent alcohol and 60 percent water by volume. This is quite strong enough for most of us.

Just to be difficult, the Americans calculate their proof differently. Their standard is based upon 50 percent of alcohol at 60°F. This makes a substantial difference, as can be gauged from the following table of equivalent proofs:

British	American
100	114·2
87·7	100
75	86
70	80

Most Scotch whiskies are exported to the United States at 86·8° American proof, or just over 75° British proof. So Americans in Britain who polish off a few glasses of 70° British proof whisky in the belief that it is a full 16° proof weaker than that which they drink at home could have a surprise when they stand up.

Now that Britain is a member of the European Community and has accepted metrication and decimalization, there is bound to be pressure to accept a Continental method of assessing proof strength, such as the Gay Lussac or Windisch. These are supposedly simpler than our own. After breaking my teeth on Sykes' system, I beg leave to doubt it.

13 GLASSES

Once I spent an evening of good conversation, drinking excellent whisky out of a jam jar and enjoying myself. I always call the occasion to mind when told from what sort of glass I ought to drink whisky.

While I do not recommend this as standard practice, the point needs strenuously to be made that the shape and size of the glass does not, in fact, make any difference whatsoever to the taste of the whisky. A good whisky is not spoiled by drinking it out of an ordinary tumbler, nor is an inferior one improved by drinking it out of the finest crystal.

Having said that, I will freely admit that if other senses are called into play, it is pleasanter to drink out of a good glass than a chipped and ugly one. I cannot conceive, for example, of really enjoying a good bourbon out of anything else but a hefty tumbler that sits in the hand comfortably and solidly and can be put down and picked up with confidence. Equally, a sinewy and elegant malt whisky like Macallan gives its best in a thin stemmed glass not too far removed from a champagne flute. Irish whiskey has always seemed to me destined to be drunk from the small tumblers, filled to the brim, that one finds in the bars of Dublin.

All these are matters of personal habit and taste. Even so, a few general points are worth making. First, the glass must be clean and polished; all good whiskies are crystalline and demand a receptacle which shows this off. Second, the glass should be clear and not tinted, coloured or crazed; all good whiskies have colour, whether it be the pale glow of the Canadian Club or the deep amber of a John Jameson. (The colourless Glen Grant malt whisky is the only exception I know and hardly invalidates the point.) Third, the glass should be of a fair size. Whiskies are generous drinks and do not go well with thimbles or liqueur glasses; pour them so that the recipient can see what he is getting. I buy whisky in bars as seldom as I can because a small whisky is a wet glass, a large whisky a wetter glass and even experienced barmen tend to look at me a little curiously if I order more than one double double. Don't drink whisky out of drinking horns, golden goblets, porcelain presentation cups, throwaway plastic beakers or any other exotic container—not if you can help it.

14 THE QUALITY OF WHISKY

If you add up all the various straight and blended whiskies available in the world, the total must run well into five figures: there are more than 5000 recorded blends of Scotch alone. To distinguish them all would be quite impossible. Yet each of them carries the signature of the cereals and the water from which it was made and of the climate in which it was matured. Vast differences are present. The contrast between an Irish Tullamore Dew and a Canadian Club is as marked as that between a Johnnie Walker Black Label and an Old Grandad Straight Bourbon. Yet all are excellent drinks in their own right.

Whiskies as different as these can be distinguished by the most insensitive palate. Much more difficult is to discern the differences between, say, two straight bourbons or two de luxe Scotch blends. You *can* taste a difference but it is a difference that is very hard to describe.

The main difficulty here is one of terminology. And it is in this area that whisky—and indeed all spirits—suffers in relation to wine. Over the centuries French viticulturists have invented and developed a complex vocabulary to describe their wines. They know precisely what is meant by 'dry', 'fruity', 'full', 'slaty', 'thin' and a whole vocabulary of other words that accurately pinpoint the most subtle and delicate differences between one wine and another. Such a language simply has not developed with whisky. Although people have been drinking whiskies for generations there is no corpus of received knowledge that is passed on from one generation to the next. Even the most judicious judge of whisky tends to a very few descriptive words like 'light', 'mellow' and 'smooth'. These are useful enough but patently inadequate to express the range and degree of differences between whiskies.

Moreover, there is a further difficulty quite unknown to the connoisseur of wine. Wine exists for the palate and the nose, first the bouquet and then the flavour. In fact, professional wine tasters go no further than this; they spit the wine out once they have tasted it. But whisky has an extra dimension—the throat. True, it appeals to the nose and the palate but after this it needs to be swallowed to let the aftertaste come through.

We must try to compare the various qualities, even if it serves only to provoke useful disagreement. So the terms I use in this section are not part of an attempt to systematize a vocabulary of whisky, nor, least of all, do they pretend to be comprehensive. All have, at one time or another, been used about whisky, although the usage has always been a personal one. Two further points: although I have, wherever possible, brought together two opposing qualities (sweet versus dry, light versus full), this does not necessarily mean that one is good and the other bad. A light whisky is no better or worse than a full one, or a luscious whisky more desirable than a clean whisky. A preference between whiskies is not a value judgment, merely the expression of a personal taste. Second, it seemed sensible to try to describe the qualities of whiskies under the headings of nose, palate and throat because these are the accepted three areas in which it works its magic. Obviously there is a great deal of overlapping; drinking whisky is one thing, not three separate processes. Nevertheless, the dictates of precision have to overcome what seems to most people to be commonsense.

One must assume that this Scot is comparing the colour and clarity of Tomatin with another whisky. Or perhaps he is so fond of his national drink that one glass is not enough for him.

Nose and palate

Nose

A professional whisky blender uses his nose and his nose only in judging whiskies. He almost never tastes or swallows them. Because he has to be coldly technical in his assessment and is not in it for the fun of it, this shows clearly just how much the sense of smell can tell about a whisky.

Sniffing a whisky—'nosing it'—before taking the first sip is almost instinctive. If you want to know more about whiskies, and thus enjoy them more, it is worth sniffing three or four times fairly deeply before you start to drink and, without making a great fuss about it, to continue to sniff between odd sips. The 'nose', or fragrance, of a good whisky comes from a subtle interplay of all the elements that have gone into it. In some Scotch whiskies, the flavour of smoke is very detectable; in some Irish whiskies a delicious oiliness comes across. In good bourbon you notice the sweet, clean smell of ripe grain; in Canadian a mild floweriness. All these qualities announce themselves to the membranes of the nose before the first sip is taken.

Pungent: All whiskies are pungent to the extent that all distilled spirits are pungent. To a degree this is an index of their proof strength. An incautiously strong sniff of whisky, warm from the still, would make the most seasoned drinker cough and splutter. The true pungency of whisky is a measure of its richness and its fullness. One would rightly expect the heavier Scotch malt and blended whiskies, and Irish whiskies, to have a necessary pungency, while the lighter malts and Scotch blends and—most definitely—American and Canadian whiskies will lack this. Indeed, what is a virtue in, say, Jamesons or Laphroaig would be a vice in, say, Canadian Club or Four Roses. Put another way, a pungent whisky gives a healthy assault on the nose, a non-pungent whisky caresses it. Put yet another way, a whisky could demonstrate one set of virtues on a raw Scottish morning which would be quite out of place in a Boston drawing room.

Flowery: In some ways floweriness is the opposite virtue to pungency. It does not announce itself immediately on the first sniff but emerges as a secondary and more evanescent fragrance. Floweriness is very much the property of the lighter whiskies. It would be totally masked and wasted in a peaty or pungent whisky. It is also much more noticeable in sweet and luscious whiskies rather than in dry and sharp whiskies.

Floweriness cannot be linked with any particular bloom, or type of flower. It has been rather attractively compared to the scent of a flower garden.

Palate

As with wine, it is the palate which makes the major distinctions between different whiskies and between the better and the worse. The warmth of the mouth makes volatile some of the alcohol, and the taste buds readily respond to this and the various congeners released with it. The taste buds on the tongue are astonishingly sensitive and have even detected whisky in a ratio of one drop in a pint of water. What is not so easy is to distinguish between the strong and sometimes conflicting flavours that can exist side by side in some whiskies.

As with the nose (nose and palate are, of course, closely connected), it is comparatively easy for the palate to sort out the strong and masculine whiskies from their milder and more elegant fellows. It is quite easy to detect differences between whiskies that should, in theory, be very similar, and it is always an instructive exercise to sample the Dufftown Scotch malt whiskies which are available, all using the same water, all using similar basic materials and all making their whisky at the same place, yet all recognizably different.

Sweet-dry: 'People like their wine dry on the label and sweet in the bottle' said one wise old wine salesman and there is much in what he says. It is somehow considered effete and even unmanly to prefer the sweet to the dry. There is a general tendency too, for light wines to be dry and heavy ones to be sweet.

Whisky, unfortunately, works in exactly the reverse way. Most people prefer the lighter and sweeter whiskies to the more robust and dry whiskies. Some of these latter, like the peaty Islay malts, are as dry as a bone and the most masculine drinks in the world, very much a minority taste. The lighter malt whiskies, like Glenmorangie, and lowland malts, like Rosebank, are very sweet by comparison.

In these whiskies, it seems to me, the sweetness of the malt comes through very clearly. But even these do not compare with the sweetness and lightness of American and Canadian whiskies. These whiskies do not lack masculinity. They sprang from those who broke the soil and shattered the forests of virgin North America, ploughmen and lumberjacks, Indian-fighters and backwoodsmen who demanded a strong, clean spirit to give them solace in their rare moments of relaxation in the struggle against a hostile world. Today the bourbon and rye whiskies that pour from the stills of America and Canada retain that strength and vigour but combine it with a refinement and elegance that emerge very clearly on the palate. Can you imagine a mint julep made with Scotch?

Light-full: I enter the lists of the 'light' controversy with some reluctance, but at least I will keep the battle short. In my view light has absolutely nothing to do with colour—it has to do with taste. Light whiskies are easy to drink, genial and undemanding. They tend to be sweet and flowery with a mild nose and aftertaste. Full whiskies deliver a solid assault on the senses. Sampled too young, they are harsh and fiery, cruel to the nose and numbing to the palate. Matured, they offer a symphony of balanced sensations. They are complex and rounded and develop on the palate, giving a substantial aftertaste.

The word 'light' sells whisky in the United States and Canada and it is no accident that among the most popular Scotch whiskies in North America are those which most closely approximate to North American native whiskies, the light coloured, mild, flowered, sweet and simple blends like Cutty Sark and J. & B. although even these do not outsell traditional Scotch.

Smooth/mellow-harsh: This is entirely a matter of maturing and is probably the simplest quality of all to detect. All mature whisky should be smooth and mellow (for practical purposes I take the words to be synonymous), and to be offered a really harsh whisky would indicate either that the distiller and exciseman had slipped up badly (a practical impossibility) or that you were drinking illicitly distilled liquor. Having said that, I must admit that I have drunk immature whiskies both in Great

Britain and North America. I have described them very unflatteringly. But while agreeing that they were not as mellow as they could and should have been given a few more years in the wood, they were in a different universe to some of the native whiskies I have tried. These were both brutal and bitter and gave me some idea of what the Americans must have suffered under prohibition.

Smoothness is immediately apparent to the palate; the whisky tastes pleasant and gently warms and stimulates the taste buds. Under-aged whisky has a rough and unfinished taste, burns the taste buds and irritates the membranes of the nose. Its pungency has not been softened by the passing of time, nor its fieriness cooled by evaporation, the breathing of the cask.

Luscious-clean: A luscious whisky is full and harmonious, as though every constituent is bringing out and emphasizing every other. It expands on the palate and, in a curious way, seems to have overtones of both sweetness and dryness. Some of the bigger straight rye whiskies have this quality, as do many of the Glenlivet malts and old Irish whiskies.

Corn husking in Kentucky during the early 19th century. The whiskey being drunk would be full and harsh probably with a definite woody aftertaste.

A clean whisky is not necessarily uninteresting but certainly uncomplicated, simple, straightforward and without pronounced pungency or floweriness. I always associate this with a slightly acid aftertaste. Some whisky drinkers I have discussed this with find that whiskies of this nature lack character and, certainly, there is little point in maturing them to a great age. Others find them pleasantly refreshing in contrast to heavier and more demanding whiskies.

Fruity-thin: These are by no means identical with the previous definition; I have taken them over from the vocabulary of wine and—I hope—with good reason. They describe very accurately the character of certain whiskies. A fruity whisky is rich and generous to the palate, pleasant to the nose and possesses a certain ripeness. Daiches mentions that one distiller he knew looked for the smell of pear drops and comments that this is 'reminiscent of the first aroma that comes of a fine Eastern malt'. I have occasionally detected a citrus or lemon flavour which I have much enjoyed and suspect that we may be talking of the same thing. A whisky of this kind will always deliver a substantial and satisfying aftertaste.

A thin-tasting whisky is immediately suspect as having been watered down. There is, of course, no objection to adding water to whisky but this should be at the dictates of the drinker, not the bottler. A thin whisky lacks body and pungency and has a noticeable lack of aftertaste. Cheaper bourbons and ryes are often thin while maintaining substantial proof strength. I suggest that this is because they are dangerously close to being, really, all neutral or silent spirit.

Throat

After the whisky has warmed the nose and stimulated the taste buds, it descends the throat and imparts a warm distinctive glow on its way. This has something in common with the sensation offered by brandy or rum but is totally different to the rasp given by vodka, gin or other neutral or redistilled grain spirit. I mention this to show that the 'throat' of whisky is not due merely to its alcoholic strength.

This pleasantly warm sensation is quickly followed by the aftertaste, a residual reminder of one of the whisky's main characteristics. This is to say that the aftertaste of a thin, harsh whisky will be thin and harsh and, conversely, the aftertaste of a full and fruity whisky will be full and fruity.

The *intensity* of the aftertaste depends almost entirely on the proof strength of the spirit—the stronger the whisky, the greater the aftertaste. I say *almost* entirely because one or two single malt Scotch whiskies have, at normal proof strength, an amazingly long aftertaste. I am thinking of Laphroaig, Ardbeg and the heavier Islay malts, Talisker, Clynelish and one or two others. Normally proof strength is the only determinant. Here the law of diminishing returns soon operates. As the spirit gets stronger the glow becomes a burn and finally a conflagration, and the experience becomes unpleasant. I have sampled whiskies at 105° British proof. Fire water!

Fiery-rounded: The kind of warm glow given by a really matured and rounded whisky can readily be imagined and is easily experienced but many whisky drinkers—including myself—occasionally like a little fire in their whisky. This may not always be detected easily on the palate but offers an interesting little kick in the throat and, for some, positively enhances the aftertaste. It is purely a matter of personal taste. Some whiskies manage to combine smoothness and fire to a remarkable degree. Some Irish whiskies have this quality. A rounded whisky gives a smooth, even aftertaste. A really fiery whisky would be a bad one. But when I have been cold, damp and miserable, a whisky with a bite to it has been very welcome. And I think that the habit some stillmen have of taking their dram in raw whisky straight from the still owes something to this characteristic.

Bland-crisp: Blandness means that the malt gives very little to the throat at all, rendering up all its goodness to the nose and palate. It slides down the throat 'without touching the sides', giving only the faintest suggestion of an aftertaste. A practical demonstration of what I mean is to drink a very mild and sweet whisky immediately after a very heavy dry one. It seems to have almost no taste or aftertaste.

A crisp whisky gives a clean, fast but short-lived aftertaste. I find all Canadian whiskies have this quality.

More whisky words

William Heath-Robinson's imaginative interpretation, commissioned by Johnnie Walker, of the blending room at Kilmarnock.

Opposite: The blending hall supervisor 'noses' a sample from each barrel to ensure that it is not sour or burnt or has any other defect. This is the final check before bottling.

Below: Johnnie Walker's testing room in the late 19th century. Today the room looks more like a chemical laboratory, but it is doubtful whether these blenders are any less skilful than their modern counterparts.

The "JOHNNIE WALKER" experts testing whisky samples with the patent testing dial in the sample room.

There are other words, for good or ill, that can be used about whisky but are more limited in their application. Some could only ever be used about certain types of whisky. Others have a more doubtful provenance but I record them because I have heard them used seriously.

Peaty: This could only be used about Scotch whiskies, and more especially Scotch malt whiskies, because only these use peat for drying their malt. Peaty whiskies show the pronounced and unmistakable presence of peat smoke the moment they are nosed and offer even more evidence to the taste buds. Some people like it very much, others dislike it.

Woody: This is a characteristic of whisky left too long in the cask. By some obscure chemical process the whisky dissolves out deleterious substances, possibly resins, produced in the ageing wood, and they impart an unpleasant flavour to the whisky which 'draws' the mouth. The taste is quite unmistakable but luckily it is extremely unlikely that the overwhelming majority of drinkers will ever experience it. Whisky that has gone woody cannot be saved and should be thrown away.

Oily: This is a characteristic of very heavy whiskies, or of whiskies at very high proof strength, or usually both. Such whiskies would generally have a very full taste and a very big aftertaste. This touch of 'oil' is much appreciated by some whisky drinkers and they attribute the much desired 'bead' (see page 172) to it.

Leathery/rubbery: I believe these two words mean the same thing and point to too many feints in the finished whisky. This would effect its 'cleanness' and give a heavy nose.

Smoky: This is akin to peaty but not necessarily the same. Irish whiskeys are smoky but not peaty to my taste.

Tarry: I used this word once to describe one characteristic of a dram I was sampling and the distiller was visibly upset; it was difficult to reassure him. But I liked the evanescent taste that I was trying to identify. It reminded me of the smell of country roads on hot summer days and a haze over the fields of stubble.

15 WHISKY DRINKS

Drinking one of the most famous and delicious of all cocktails—the Mint Julep.

Although whisky is an excellent drink in its own right, it has inevitably been mixed with other liquids to produce an enormous selection of drinks. These range from the unspeakable and undrinkable to the highly acceptable. At one end of the scale is whisky and lemonade (which, to their shame, is drunk by more Scots than you would believe) and at the other, are such drinks as Mint Julep.

In the cocktail age, whisky appeared in hundreds of disguises mixed with just about everything that was not actually poisonous. Since then, a number of classic combinations have survived the test of time and, indeed, demonstrated that whisky is a various as well as a single-minded drink. Some mixes—like a Manhattan—demand a special type of whisky. Others—like whisky and soda—cover the field.

The following selection of whisky, and whiskey, drinks is utterly subjective—some are well worth drinking, others are notable for their awfulness. The only thing they all have in common is that they use whisky as the base.

Whisky and water
If you don't like your whisky neat, this is the best way of drinking it. Some high proof whiskies demand a little water anyway. For experimental purposes, I have sampled whiskies at 105° proof (UK) and found them interesting, but not sustainable. I would normally add a little water to 80° proof (UK) whiskies and often just a drop or two to the normal 70° proof, although at that strength, I mostly prefer my whiskies neat. I know a number of people who do drink neat whiskies of a very high proof strength, but I cannot honestly recommend it. It seems to me that the nose and aftertaste are so aggressive that the drink is out of balance.

Use pure cold water with whisky. I have nearly always found tap water perfectly suitable, although over-chlorinated water is bad. In the United States I once drank bourbon with very heavily chlorinated water and it tasted vile. The very best diluent is, of course, the same water that went into the whisky itself—that is from the burn that went into the Scotch, 'from the well that went into the bourbon'—('bourbon and branch water') or from the spring that went into the Irish.

Whisky with ice
It is quite common to hear whisky purists point out that ice destroys the nose of a good whisky by chilling the congeners— those mysterious substances which gave whisky its unique character. I think they are misguided, although I understand their motives, and I believe the vast majority of whiskies are harmed very little, if at all, by being served with ice. The standard blends, the popular bourbons and almost all the Canadians are light in character and do not possess a great deal of nose. They mix with almost anything. Having said that, however, I think that icing a fine malt is a shame. Here the nose is an essential component of the enjoyment of the whisky and anything that lessens it is to be deplored. For the same reason, malts would do badly in mixes and cocktails; they are too assertive and idiosyncratic to marry with anything but water.

Whisky and soda—Highball
This—put harshly—is a fizzy drink that tastes of whatever whisky is in it, be it Scotch, Irish, bourbon, etc. There can be no exact recipe because there is an infinite number of variations, from nearly-all-whisky to nearly-all-soda. Half-and-half is probably most popular. Plain soda from a syphon or bottle is normal, but I understand that the proprietary sparkling spa waters, such as Vichy, Pellegrino or Perrier, are also acceptable.

Whisky and ginger ale
'Whisky and dry ginger'; 'Scotch and ginger'; this is a very popular combination using Scotch, but not so much using other whiskies. I have drunk Irish and bourbon with ginger, and have cared for neither. One of the problems here is that ginger ales can be very sweet and overpower the taste of the whisky itself. There are traps too; 'Canada Dry', for instance, is a trade name and not a description of the contents.

The proportions are according to your taste, but if you like ginger ale mixed with your (blended) whisky, you probably like it well enough to want to taste it. A good measure of whisky with the glass topped up with ginger ale and iced is normal. A famous variation is the *Horse's Neck* which has the addition of a long twist of lemon peel over the side of the glass.

Presbyterian
Crush two ice cubes and put them in a tall glass with 3 parts bourbon, 3 parts chilled soda water and 2 parts chilled ginger ale. Using a long-handled spoon, stir to combine the ingredients thoroughly. Squeeze a strip of lemon rind over the glass and drop it in. Serve at once.

Broken Leg
Pour 2 parts bourbon and 5 parts hot apple juice into a warmed glass. Add four raisins and a slice of lemon and stir with a cinnamon stick.

Toddy

Toddy is a mixture of whisky, sugar and hot water. I know no better recipe than the one that Sir Robert Bruce Lockhart joyously gave to the world in his splendid book *Scotch*:

'Toddy, excellent both as a cure for the cold and/or as elixir of life, requires careful preparation. The ingredients are sugar, boiling water and, preferably, a well matured Scotch whisky. First you heat the tumbler with warm water and, when the glass has reached a comfortable temperature, you pour out the water. Then into the empty glass you put two or three squares of loaf-sugar and add enough boiling water—a wine glass should suffice —to dissolve the sugar. Then add a wine glass of whisky and stir with a silver spoon; then another wine glass of boiling water, and finally to crown this liquid edifice, top it with another wine glass of whisky. Stir again and drink the contents with slow and loving care. As a cure for cold, take your Toddy to bed, put one bowler hat at the foot and drink until you can see two.'

I have only ever drunk Toddy made with Scotch whisky, although an Irish whiskey Toddy sounds good enough in principle. Japanese whisky likewise. And why not a Toddy with some of the fuller American straight ryes? Surely a drink to be nurtured.

American Whiskey Cocktails and Mixes

The Americans invented cocktails. The word was first recorded in 1809, although the *Oxford English Dictionary* says that it is 'a slang word of which the real origin appears to be lost'. The actual definition is 'a drink consisting of spirits mixed with a small quantity of bitters, some sugar etc. Chiefly U.S.'. This is accurate as far as it goes but leaves out the vast majority of those spine-chilling mixtures of sugary liqueurs with exotic names. There must have been many thousands of these produced by over-inventive or un-scrupulous barmen—cacophonies of yel-low, green and purple liquids that would wreck the digestion of a carthorse. A few classics, however, have survived the taste of time and among the very best of them are certainly those with a solid basis of bourbon or rye whiskey.

Manhattan

This is a classically simple drink, for which the basic ingredients are 1 part Italian vermouth to 2 parts rye whisky or bourbon, with a dash of Angostura bitters and ice.

There are literally hundreds of variations on this austere basis, but the drink itself remains to me perfect of its kind. It is undeniably a sweet drink and there are two obvious variations to make it slightly drier. The medium Manhattan substitutes a half-and-half mixture of French and Italian vermouth for the Italian vermouth, and the dry Manhattan is made using French vermouth only. This latter version is often accompanied by a twist of lemon.

As with the Old Fashioned there is a pretence that other whiskies can be sub-stituted and Scotch Manhattans, Irish Manhattans and the like are all listed. My advice would be to steer clear of these.

Mint Julep—An American Dream

For every one person who has actually tasted a Mint Julep, there must be a hundred who are familiar with the name. It is said with some justice that it is impossible to make outside the United States because you cannot have the proper feel for it if you are not an American. I will still, however, give my favourite julep recipe which comes from David A. Embury's book, *The Fine Art of Mixing Drinks*:

'Pre-chill the glasses. In the bottom of each, place a tablespoon of sugar syrup and, if desired, stir into it a few dashes of Angostura bitters.

'Distribute 3 or 4 small sprigs (not just the leaves) of mint over the bottom of the glass but do not bruise or crush. Pack the glass full with crushed ice and fill with bourbon to just below the top. Churn with a long spoon to settle the ice and start the frosting process. Refill with ice, add enough bourbon to bring to desired height, and insert straws.

'Place drinks in refrigerator for at least 5 or 10 minutes (a half hour is better); add garnish and serve.

'One of the greatly disputed points about Juleps is whether or not to float a spoonful of rum on top of each drink. To your true Kentucky colonel, this is rank heresy. It does however, add an exotic

The Old Fashioned
One of the truly great cocktails. The name in fact comes from the glass, and versions can be made using gin, rum and brandy. Whiskey is by far the most popular, however, and the recipe is given on page 185.

The Mint Julep

touch which many people like. I like Juleps either with or without the rum, but if you do use rum, use only a good Jamaica rum and at least 8 years old, and use not more than 1 teaspoonful.

'I will also make one single concession to my rule of "nothing but bonded bourbon" for a Julep. Southern Comfort, which of course has a bourbon base, makes an excellent Julep.

'If any of your teetotaller friends attend your Julep party, I fear you will have to serve them plain iced water. I know of no prohibition variety of the Julep.'

The Old Fashioned

Apart from the dry martini, the Old Fashioned is probably the greatest cocktail of them all. It is satisfyingly simple, as all great drinks necessarily are. To make it you need a short squat tumbler (in the United States there is a special glass called an Old Fashioned Glass, which is becoming readily available in the U.K.), a bottle of bourbon or rye whiskey, some sugar and Angostura bitters. Put a lump of sugar in the glass and soak it with the Angostura. Crush it with a spoon and add a little rye whiskey, stirring until all the sugar is dissolved. Add a few ice cubes, twist in a thin paring of lemon peel and add 2 oz (60 ml) of rye.

Bourbon or blended American whiskey can be used, but rye has always struck me as the best. Yet again, it is said that Scotch Old Fashioneds, Irish Old Fashioneds, and so on, exist. I have even seen them described in respectable books. But my own experience, nose and palate tell me that these are poor drinks.

Scotch Whisky Drinks and Cocktails

I personally do not like to see Scotch butchered in mixes and cocktails, but there is no reason why I should impose my own puritanical views on others. In the following section I have chosen what seem to be the least offensive.

Atholl Brose

This most ancient and famous—though now surely seldom made—Scotch whisky drink—must take pride of place. I have sampled it, and even made it once or twice, but I thought it no more than a curiosity. There are a number of recipes

with a great deal of variation. I will give that of the late Duke of Atholl who, after all, ought to know!

'To make a quart [approximately 1 litre] take 4 dessertspoons of runny honey and 4 sherry glasses of prepared oatmeal. Stir these well together and put into a quart [1 litre] bottle; fill up with whisky; shake well before serving.

'To prepare the oatmeal, put it into a basin and mix with cold water to the consistency of a thick paste. Leave for about half an hour, pass through a fine strainer, pressing with the back of a wooden spoon so as to leave the oatmeal as dry as possible. Discard the oatmeal and use the creamy liquor for the brose.'

Beadleston

Shake 2 parts Scotch, 1 part French vermouth and a dash of Angostura with ice. Strain and serve. This, in fact, is a dry Manhattan using Scotch instead of bourbon. If the vermouth is reduced down to a few dashes, the drink is sometimes known as *Blue Bell*. Then, if the Angostura is replaced by a dash of orange bitters and a dash of Cointreau, it is called a *Green Briar*. Substitute a dash of orange bitters, a dash of apricot and a dash of white crème de menthe for the Angostura in a Beadleston and the drink becomes a *Trinity*. A Beadleston with a dash of orange bitters and a dash of fresh lemon juice becomes a *Hole-in-One*, and with a dash of Cointreau and fresh lime a *Churchill*.

Flying Scotsman

Shake 2 oz (60 ml) Scotch, 1½ oz (45 ml) Italian vermouth and 1 tablespoon (15 ml) each sugar syrup and bitters with ice. Strain and serve. A variation, *Rob Roy*, without sugar but with lemon peel is, of course, a Scotch Manhattan.

Robbie Burns

Shake 1 part each Scotch and Italian vermouth with 3 dashes Benedictine and serve. This drink is called *Bobbie Burns* in the United States, but F. Marian McNeill, the expert and eminent cookery writer, insists that it is 'Robbie' not 'Bobbie'. One sensible American authority says it should be made with Drambuie rather than Benedictine as Drambuie has a Scotch whisky base.

The Continental
Shake 8 parts rye whiskey,
2 parts fresh lemon juice,
1 part sweetened single cream
and 3 dashes Jamaica rum
with ice. Strain and serve.

Bourbon Cooler
Fill a tall glass with cracked
ice. Pour in lime juice—it can
be fresh or cordial—to the
halfway mark. Add 1 oz
(30 ml) bourbon and top
up with pineapple juice.

Canadian whisky cocktails

Canadian whiskies are so light that they suffer from the reverse problem of Irish whiskies. They are so unassertive that their delicate flavour would be lost if mixed with more obtrusive liquors. And it would be disgraceful to mix a really superior Canadian whisky with anything, just as it would be to mix a Scottish pure malt with, say, ginger ale. (I have, alas, seen this done many times.)

Brooklyn

Shake 2 parts Canadian whisky, 3 parts French vermouth and a dash Amer Picon with ice. Strain and serve. Why Canadian whisky is used in a cocktail of this name is a mystery to me. There is, not surprisingly, an American whiskey version.

Canadian Cocktail

Dissolve 1 teaspoon sugar with 2 oz (60 ml) Canadian whisky and 2 dashes Angostura. Shake with ice, strain and serve. This is obviously a Canadian version of the Old Fashioned.

Imperial Fizz

Shake 1 part Canadian whisky, 1 part rum, the juice of ½ lemon and 1 teaspoon sugar with ice. Strain into a tall glass and top up with soda water.

Ink Street

Shake 2 parts Canadian whisky and 1 part each fresh lemon and orange juice. Strain and serve. This cocktail actually sounds a little more palatable than most.

Liberal

Shake 1 part each Canadian whisky and Italian vermouth, 3 dashes Amer Picon and 1 dash orange bitter with ice. Strain and serve.

Irish whiskey cocktails

Most of these are variations on general whisky cocktails, but I would recommend caution because of the particular flavour of Irish whiskey. In my view it mixes even less palatably than Scotch.

Chauncey Olcott

Shake 6 parts Irish whiskey and 1 part each Italian vermouth and dry sherry. Strain and serve.

Cold Irish Coffee

Mix 2 parts strong iced coffee, 1 part Irish whiskey, ½ part Cointreau and a scoop real vanilla ice-cream in a blender. Serve in a chilled glass.

Everybody's Irish

Shake 2 oz (60 ml) Irish whiskey, 5 dashes green chartreuse and 3 dashes crême de menthe with ice. Strain and serve with a green olive; wearing, I assume, green socks and a shamrock.

Iwo Jima

Shake 2 oz (60 ml) Irish whiskey, 2 dashes each curaçao and Pernod and 1 dash each Angostura and maraschino with ice. Strain and serve with a twist of lemon peel. This particular recipe was recorded with some indignation by Joe Rosenthal, the American war photographer, who took the famous photograph of the U.S. Marines raising the Stars and Stripes over the battle-shattered Pacific island. He pointed out they had no ice on Iwo Jima—to say nothing of curaçao, Pernod, Angostura, maraschino and Irish whiskey!

Whisky punches

The Oxford English Dictionary defines punch as 'a beverage now usually composed of wine or spirits mixed with hot water or milk and flavoured with sugar, lemons and some spice or cordial; usually qualified as brandy, gin, rum, tea, whisky etc.'. I would not quarrel with this description except to say that a gin punch sounds a bit off-putting and that cold punches are becoming increasingly popular as summer drinks. Whisky-based punches are among the best.

Artillery Punch

Mix together:

1 quart (1 litre) rye whiskey
2 bottles claret
1 quart (1 litre) strong black tea
1 bottle Jamaica rum
½ bottle gin
½ bottle brandy
2 oz (60 ml) Benedictine
1 pint (½ litre) fresh orange juice
½ pint (¼ litre) fresh lemon juice

This is a well named punch, but it tends to be a little dry.

Whiskey Squirt
Crush half a small peach into a glass. Shake 2 oz (60 ml) bourbon, 1 tablespoon sugar syrup and 1 tablespoon curaçao with ice and strain over the peach. Top up with soda water.

Ward Eight
Shake 2 parts rye whiskey, 1 part each lemon and orange juice and a teaspoon of grenadine with ice. Strain into a tumbler and top up with soda water. Garnish with a cherry and a slice of orange.

Cold Whisky Punch

Thinly peel three lemons and put with their juice into a large jug with ½ pound (225 grams) white sugar. Add 1 quart (1 litre) boiling water. Stir to dissolve and leave to cool. Strain into a bowl and stir in a bottle of Scotch. Chill before serving.

Gay Gordon's Punch

Mix together:
1 quart (1 litre) whisky
2 bottles brandy
2 bottles claret
1 quart (1 litre) fresh lemon juice
Sugar to taste
2 sliced bananas
2 sliced oranges
Chill well. Just before serving add 3 pints (1·8 litres) of dry champagne. This was a favourite drink of Ellaline Terriss, an English actress in the 1920s.

Hot Whisky Punch

Infuse 6 tablespoons tea in 1 quart (approximately 1 litre) boiling water. Strain this over 1 pound (500 grams) lump sugar and a thinly sliced lemon. Stir in a bottle of Scotch and serve immediately.

Quick Whisky Punch

Mix a can of frozen lemon concentrate and one of orange with 6 cans of cold water. Add 2 bottles rye whiskey and ¼ pint (120 ml) cherry cordial and mix together well. Shortly before serving, add several handfuls of ice cubes and 1 quart (1 litre) soda water (or more if you prefer).

Whisky Cup

2 quarts (2 litres) bourbon
1 bottle Jamaican rum
1½ pints (just under 1 litre) fresh orange juice
1 pint (½ litre) fresh orange juice
½ pint (290 ml) grenadine
¾ pound (375 grams) sugar
2 pounds (1 kg) strawberries
A cupful fresh, crushed pineapple
2 quarts (2 litres) soda water
Put the strawberries in a bowl with the crushed pineapple and sprinkle the sugar over them. Pour the rum over and cover. Leave to stand overnight. Add lemon juice, orange juice, bourbon and grenadine. Chill. Just before serving add ice and chilled soda water.

Whisky flips and nogs

Flips are basically spirits shaken up with sugar and whole eggs. Nogs are basically spirits shaken up with sugar, eggs, milk or cream. One basic recipe for each (as given first below) will cover the whole spectrum of whiskies. Thus there will be a bourbon flip, an Irish flip, and so on. An electric blender is a great help here.

Whisky Flip

Shake 2 oz (60 ml) whisky, 1 teaspoon sugar and 1 raw egg with ice. Strain and serve.

Whisky Nog

Shake 2 oz (60 ml) whisky, 8 oz (240 ml) milk, 1 raw egg and 1 teaspoon sugar with ice. Blend and serve with nutmeg on top.

Auld Man's Milk

This is a recipe of Meg Dods, a great friend of Sir Walter Scott, as given by F. Marian McNeill and is undoubtedly the progenitor of the modern egg nog.

Separate 6 eggs and beat the yolks with 1 quart (approximately 1 litre) milk or single cream and sugar to taste. Add about ½ pint (250 ml) whisky to this. Whip the whites and fold in, stirring all together in a china punch bowl. Flavour with nutmeg or lemon zest.

Egg Nog of the Commonwealth Club, Richmond, Virginia

This comes from Alice B. Tocklas' famous cookbook, and she says it has been used at the Club for more than a century. It is always served on Christmas mornings.

The ingredients are:
24 eggs
2 quarts (2 litres) single cream
1 quart (1 litre) whipping or double cream
1½ pounds (750 grams) sugar
4 oz (120 ml) rum
4 oz (120 ml) brandy
2 quarts (approximately 2 litres) bourbon
Separate eggs, and in a large bowl thoroughly beat the yolks. Add the sugar slowly and mix together well. Stir the mixture over a low heat. Stir in the bourbon, rum and brandy and then add the single cream slowly, mixing it thoroughly. Whip the egg whites until they are stiff and mix in. Lastly whip the cream lightly and fold this in.

De Rigeur
Shake 2 parts rye whiskey, 1 part fresh grapefruit juice and 1 part honey with ice. Strain and serve.

Millionaire
Shake 2 parts Curaçao, 1 part grenadine or raspberry syrup and 1 egg white (to each 2 drinks) with ice. Add 8 parts whiskey in small amounts shaking between times. Strain and serve. Add a few dashes of Pernod to this cocktail and it becomes a Millionaire Royal.

Whisky Sours

I believe that the only decent Whisky Sour is made with American bourbon or rye whiskey, but Scotch can also be used.

Shake 8 parts whisky, 2 parts fresh lemon juice and 1 part sugar with ice. Made with bourbon, I find this a most pleasing and evocative drink and a great pleasure to prepare. Some people add a couple of dashes of Angostura, but I think this is unnecessary. Without any sugar, this drink is occasionally called a *Palmer*. Add soda water to it and it becomes a *Whisky Collins*.

Whisky Coffees

These all derive from the original *Irish Coffee*, still almost universally recognized to be the best of them. Some magic in the flavours of coffee and Irish whiskey produces a taste quite different from either, but within which you can still distinguish the original elements. There are a number of slightly different ways of making Irish Coffee, but basically you put 1 teaspoon or so of sugar in the bottom of a goblet and add very hot, very strong, fresh coffee —'instant' just will not do. Stir these to make a sweet heavy mixture and gently pour in a good measure of Irish whiskey. Stir, or not, according to taste. Then gently float onto the surface of the drink a good measure of heavy cream, pouring it over the back of a spoon so that it floats on top of the hot liquid. Sip carefully so that the coffee-whiskey flavour comes through the cream.

As far as can be ascertained, Irish Coffee was first invented at Shannon Airport shortly after the war. It was imported into the United States thereafter by enthusiastic journalists and became very popular very quickly.

Whisky based liqueurs

It was inevitable that a drink with the qualities of whisky would produce liqueurs. Indeed, it has always rather surprised me that it has not produced more. All of them, by definition, are sweet, perfumed and powerful. I don't drink them myself, but millions of people do—with enormous enjoyment.

American Whiskey Liqueurs

Southern Comfort: Although the formula for this bourbon based liqueur is a secret, there is a distinct flavour of peaches to it. In spite of the fact that it has been a popular drink in the southern United States for many years, it is a comparatively new arrival north of the Mason-Dixon line and in more foreign parts. It is bottled at 100° American proof.

A cocktail containing 2 parts of Southern Comfort to 1 part of fresh lime juice is called a *Canasta*.

Irish Whiskey Liqueurs

Irish Mist: This is made from very old Irish whiskey, Irish heather, honey and herbs— exactly parallel ingredients to those of Drambuie, yet the drinks are totally different. It is difficult to describe the taste of these liqueurs, except to say that it relates to Irish whiskey in precisely the same way that Drambuie relates to Scotch. Irish Mist was first sold in Tullamore in 1829 and is bottled at 70° proof.

Irish Velvet: Jamesons call this liqueur 'Original Irish Coffee Liqueur' and it is specially blended for that purpose. It contains Jamesons 70 whiskey mixed with strong black coffee and sugar and I can see no other use for it than that stated on the bottle. The short cut process of making Irish Coffee by using this, takes some of the fun out of the operation. Irish Velvet is 40° proof.

Scotch Whisky Liqueurs

Drambuie: This is the grandfather of them all and is at least 200 years old. It is made from a mixture of Highland Malt whisky, heather, honey and herbs. Traditionally it was invented especially for Bonnie Prince Charlie while he was in exile in France and given by the Prince to Mackinnon of Strathaid in gratitude for his loyalty. More probably it was formulated in Skye and the Prince came across it by accident and liked it. This made it popular, in the first place on the island itself and later over the whole of Scotland. The process, however, was a slow one; it was only in 1892 that the name was registered as a trade mark and 1906 before it was made on any scale. It is 70° proof.

Glayva: This new whisky liqueur only appeared recently and is already quite popular. It is similar to, though sweeter than Drambuie.

Drambuie is one of the most popular whisky-based liqueurs. The recipe for it has been in the hands of the Mackinnon family for generations and is a closely guarded secret.

INDEX

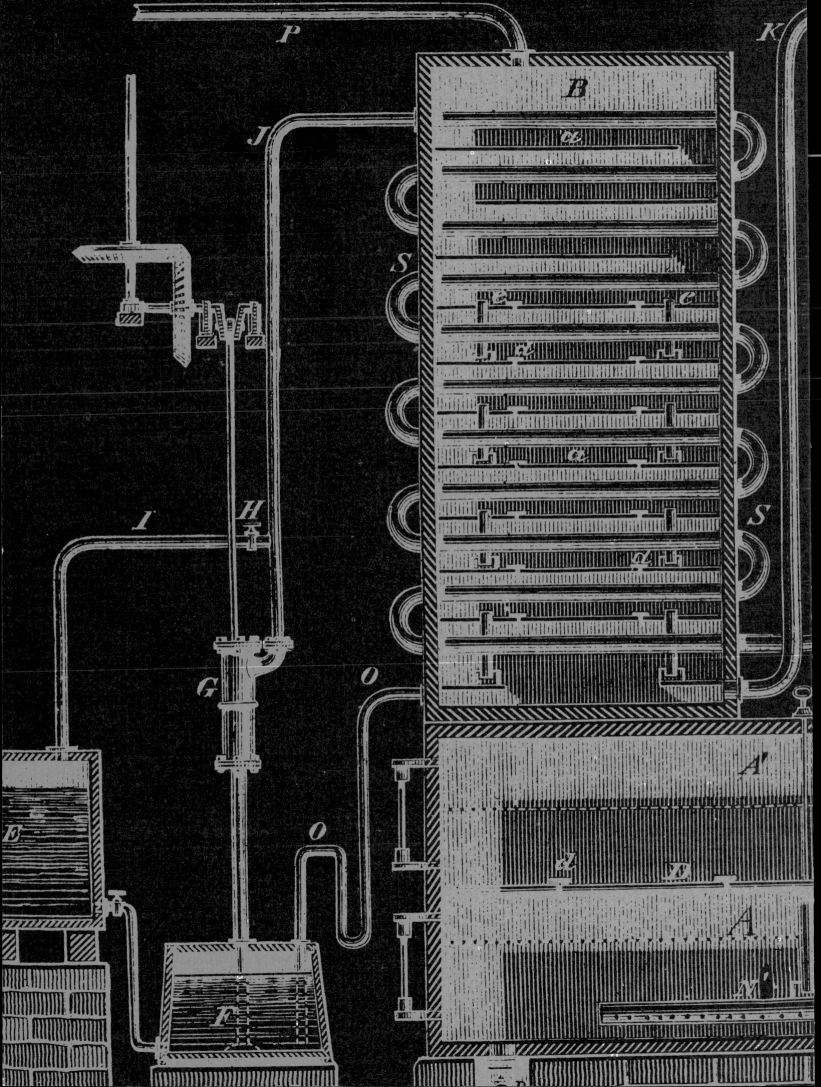